YOU TAKE OVER, GOD. I CAN'T HANDLE IT.

OTHER DEVOTIONS IN THE SERIES

I Can't, God Can.
Jane Cairo, Sheri Curry, Anne Christian
Buchanan, and Debra Klingsporn

MEDITATION™ SERIES **FOR TEENS**

YOU TAKE OVER, GOD. I CAN'T HANDLE IT.

(DAILY DEVOTIONS FOR GUYS)

Kevin J. Brown and Ray Mitsch

JANET THOMA BOOK

THOMAS NELSON PUBLISHERS
Nashville

15777—Take PATCH, km
YOU TAKE OVER GOD, I CAN'T HANDLE IT
ARCHIVE: NELSON DISK

ABCDEFGHIJKLMNO**ABCDEFGHIJKLMNO**✠☜★☆❖◄☜⑩◙⊗✳✳ (DENSITY CHECK)

Published in Nashville, Tennessee, by Thomas Nelson, Inc., and distributed in Canada by Lawson Falle, Ltd., Cambridge, Ontario.

Scripture quotations are from the NEW KING JAMES VERSION of the Bible. Copyright © 1979, 1980, 1982, Thomas Nelson, Inc., Publishers.

Scripture quotations noted CEV in the text are from the Contemporary English Version of the Bible. Copyright © 1991, Thomas Nelson, Inc., Publishers.

Library of Congress Cataloging-in-Publication Data

See back of book

Printed in the United States of America
1 2 3 4 5 6 — 97 96 95 94 93

Introduction

You've made a choice to pursue one of the greatest challenges there is—health and wholeness. You can make it in your recovery, one step at a time. But we hope you'll seek help along the way from supportive friends or family, from a counselor or therapist, from a recovery group. You'll travel some rugged terrain on the road to recovery and it will be much easier to make it through if you have someone you can talk with along the way.

We wrote these devotions to cheer you on in your victories and to give you support in the tough work ahead. You may be struggling with a drug or alcohol addiction. You may be recovering from sexual abuse or some other kind of physical abuse from one of your parents or relatives. You may be struggling with the painful effects of peer pressure. Whatever you're dealing with, wherever you are in life, we are here to offer you a hand and to give you a picture of how some other folks, just like yourself, have begun and continued on this journey.

Who are "we"? you may be asking. We are professional therapists, who work every day with people in their teens who have a vast range of life experiences. We've identified ourselves throughout the meditation by adding our initials, K.B. for Kevin Brown and R.M. for Ray Mitsch, after each devotion. We are hoping that the Scripture and meditations in this book will help you discover that life is an adventure and that you can have fun along the way. We also hope you will look to God as your greatest strength. Without Him, you don't have much chance of a successful journey.

Kevin Brown
Ray Mitsch

A NEW YEAR'S THEME

Test all things; hold fast what is good.
—1 THESS. 5:21

Welcome to a new year! Many things ahead will test your commitment to recover from addiction. It is important to develop a guiding purpose that will help you make decisions. Today's passage will do just that. It is simple and to the point. Throughout the year to come, you will need to be ready to "test" everything. Ask yourself what effect a situation or decision might have on your recovery. Sometimes, testing may mean trying a new behavior you have never tried before and risking success (or failure). It is important that you are willing to test the areas you are growing in. Always be ready to ask yourself, "Am I going in the direction I set out for myself at the beginning of the year?"

The last part of the passage is probably the hardest— "hold on to the good"—because it is a principle that encompasses every part of your life, from your relationship with your parents to relationships with teachers, friends, girlfriends, and anyone else you come into contact with. No doubt, today will present you with opportunities to hold on to the good and test everything. Begin the new year on a solid note of holding on to the good in all things!

■ *Father, help me to test everything and hold on to the good in the year to come.*

R.M.

Walking the Crooked Path

He who walks with integrity walks securely,
But he who perverts his ways will become
known.
                                        —PROV. 10:9

Daniel found it easy to lie. He discovered that being confident and keeping an innocent look on his face made others believe him. He had gotten pretty good at it, and it was a skill he had been using quite often, because he had many things to explain away. He was almost always on the verge of getting caught for some of the things he had done, and he hated consequences, so he lied.

In therapy, even Daniel didn't seem to know what was and wasn't true. He lied so well that it was almost easier than telling the truth. The bad thing was that those close to him had begun to see what he was up to. They stopped believing him, even when he *was* telling the truth. Because of this, Daniel had started getting nervous and began making mistakes.

When you tell the truth, you don't have to quickly make up stories to cover your tracks, and you can be sure that you have done right. Daniel might have avoided trouble in the short run, but eventually he risked his integrity, and people started believing him to be a liar. Therefore, Daniel had to watch his step constantly and remember all the stories and to whom he had told them, in order to keep from getting caught.

■   *God, I want to be a man of integrity, whom others respect and believe. Help me to change.*

                                                    K.B.

RUNNING WITH PURPOSE

Do you not know that those who run in a race all run, but one receives the prize? Run in such a way that you may obtain it.
—1 COR. 9:24

What does your recovery look like? Does it look like you are making decisions in terms of your recovery? If your friends are going out to have a good time and ask you to come along, you will have to decide between partying and staying consistent with your plan for recovery. How will you choose? Will you throw all caution to the wind just because you want to go out and not be so serious about the "recovery stuff"?

It gets pretty tiring working your program so much. Recovery is tiring business! There are times, though, that you will have to decide just how serious you are about recovering from your addiction. That is exactly what runners have to do in a race. They must decide at some point in the race whether they are going to quit or run for the prize. That isn't all that different from having to decide what to do when your friends ask you out. Running with a purpose often makes decisions like these a lot easier because you can ask yourself, "Is this good for my recovery or not?" If the answer is yes, go for it! If the answer is no, then watch out!

■ *Father, help me to run with a purpose that guides my decisions every day.*

R.M.

SETTING LOW GOALS

> *I run toward the goal, so that I can win the
> prize of being called to heaven.*
> —PHIL. 3:14 CEV

Because he didn't do much of anything when he was using, Buddy believed he wasn't capable of much. He was satisfied with C's and D's, and he told his parents to be happy that he wasn't failing anymore. His parents went along with him, allowing him to scrape by as long as he attended N.A. meetings and seemed to be working his recovery program.

But Buddy was selling himself short. He was capable of much more than he believed. When he was using he began to think of himself as a failure, a burnout. So when things got a little better, he was satisfied and didn't push himself to do more.

This way of thinking holds back recovery. You must push yourself and not be satisfied with little bits of progress. As soon as someone sits back and becomes lazy about his work in recovery, he begins falling back into old beliefs that he is a failure who will never amount to much. That is the very thing you are trying to change.

Don't be satisfied with small gains. The world is now open to you in ways that weren't possible when you were abusing substances. Each time you reach one goal, set another. Don't become lazy; that is a sign of a relapse about to happen.

■ *God, help me to continue pushing myself to reach for
bigger and better things.*

K.B.

DON'T DO IT ALONE!

If anyone thinks himself to be something,
when he is nothing, he deceives himself.
—GAL. 6:3

One of the biggest mistakes you can make is to think you can recover alone. A common myth most teens believe is that they are invincible. In other words, they believe that bad things only happen to other people. So they are immune from anything bad that happens.

Today's scripture passage suggests that if you overestimate your abilities or think you are more than you are, then you are nothing. That doesn't mean you don't count; it means you have put yourself in a position to sabotage your recovery. Therefore, if you think you are more than you are in terms of what you can accomplish, you are deceiving yourself and setting yourself up for sure disaster.

What does this all mean for your recovery? You must force yourself to get involved with others whether that is through a support group or by maintaining an ongoing relationship with someone who can hold you accountable. Don't expect yourself to accomplish something that cannot be accomplished alone. You may think you are strong, but remember the passage for today. If you think you are strong, beware of the disaster awaiting you. Ask someone to alert you to the obstacles ahead.

■   *Father, help me to be humble enough to accept that I*
cannot do my recovery alone.

R.M.

IT TAKES TWO TO TANGO

*When someone slaps your right cheek, turn
and let that person slap your other cheek.*
—MATT. 5:39 CEV

Like most addicts, you've probably been in a lot of
fights. Maybe you've fought with your parents about getting off your back, or with others who have confronted
your chemical abuse. I sometimes ask addicts what they
like about fighting. They look shocked and tell me they
hate it. So I ask, "If you hate it so much, why do you
fight back?"

Any fight, verbal or physical, takes at least two people. One feels wronged and decides to hurt the other in
return. The other person then feels attacked and fights
back. Next thing you know, each leaves the argument
feeling that he's right and the other is a jerk.

What would happen if one person didn't fight back?
It's really hard to have a fight with only one person.
Since you're working on changing things about yourself
that hurt other people, why not work on not fighting
back? After all, when did you ever have one of those
long arguments when you left feeling like things were
great? Instead, state clearly your side of the story, and if
the other person doesn't believe you or won't listen,
then leave it at that. You'll feel much better, and the
other person will see the change in you.

■ *God, help me not to fight back and just make things
worse in an argument.*

K.B.

WHAT DO YOU DO WITH GUILT?

"O LORD, take away the iniquity of Your servant, for I have done very foolishly."
—2 SAM. 24:10

Although many males do not admit it, guilt is a part of their everyday experience. Guilt presents a real dilemma for most guys. In order to handle guilt adequately, you need to have control over your pride. For most guys, pride is a real obstacle in recovery. If you have a big ego and a lot of pride in yourself, then guilt is going to be a problem.

When David was guilt-stricken over his actions, he surrendered his pride and admitted his guilt. This was not easy to do. You must practice continually surrendering pride, whether in relationships with others or in your relationship with God. The admission of guilt is part of this process. If you have enough humility to admit you have done a foolish thing, like David, you are in a position to effectively see whether your recovery is going in the direction you want. If you can't do this, your recovery will get sidetracked by your pride and ego.

How did David so easily surrender his pride to admit his guilt? It probably *wasn't* easy for him; after all, he was the king. But David knew he would receive forgiveness. God is faithful; He will forgive when we surrender to Him.

■ *Father, help me to surrender my pride to You.*

R.M.

EVEN GOOD MEN HURT SOMETIMES

"There is none like [Job] on the earth, a blameless and upright man, one who fears God and shuns evil."
—JOB 1:8

If people got what they deserved, then bad things would happen only to bad people. Unfortunately, this is not true, and bad things sometimes happen to even the best people. An example is Job. Even God considered him to be a solid, good man; yet many rotten things occurred in his life. His family was killed, his wealth was lost, and he suffered intense illness.

Job's closest friends tried to explain his troubles, saying that something must be wrong with Job; he must have done a terrible sin to deserve the bad things happening to him. These friends told him to simply admit that he was a horrible person, blame it on God, and die. But Job realized what very few persons ever understand: Sometimes bad things happen to good people.

Often when bad things happen to us, we look for someone else to blame—parents, friends, teachers, even God. In recovery, things are supposed to get better, so if things go wrong when you're doing the best you can, you might look for a convenient excuse. But don't fall into this trap! Becoming mature means dealing with the good *and* the bad. Blaming only helps you to avoid the responsibility of manhood. Remember, even good guys feel pain sometimes.

■ *God, when recovery is painful, help me to avoid convenient excuses or blaming others.*

K.B.

PASSING JUDGMENT

*In whatever you judge another you condemn
yourself; for you who judge practice the same
things.*
—ROM. 2:1

It is easier to find fault with others' behavior than with
your own. You can find plenty wrong with an opposing
team or a group of people you don't hang around with.

Finding fault with everyone else is an effective way to
avoid looking at your own behavior. You don't want to
look at yourself because of what you might find there.
You're afraid that if you actually looked at the things you
have done, you couldn't bear it. Therefore, you don't
look, and you dig yourself deeper into the hole of relapse. To keep your recovery on track, you need to evaluate your behavior realistically.

It is interesting that we often find fault with behavior
that we see as our own weakness. For example, the son
who criticizes his father for not listening doesn't listen
himself. Of course, if he can get his father on the defensive about his poor behavior, the son won't be held accountable for his own. Notice what the verse for today
says about this. Whatever you criticize others for is the
point on which you are condemning yourself. So the
next time you to criticize someone, check your own behavior. That's one thing you can change!

■ *Lord, help me to examine my own behavior rather
than finding fault with others.*

R.M.

TRAPPED BY YOUR MISTAKES

His own iniquities entrap the wicked man,
And he is caught in the cords of his sin.
—PROV. 5:22

Jim's eyes darted back and forth as he talked. His hands clenched into fists and then unclenched. He could barely sit still. His parents were confronting him on some of the things he had done since his last session, and Jim was trying to explain them in a way that he wouldn't get into trouble. It was easy to see that he was lying.

He had been out late on the weekend, and both parents had been waiting when he came home. His bloodshot eyes gave him away. But Jim apparently thought he could scam his way out of the situation. Each day before the session he had created more stories to prove his point, and every time he talked he got himself deeper into trouble.

Lies are like that. Once you start, you must tell more to make the pieces of the story fit. You get deeper and deeper until pretty soon even you get confused about what is true and what is not.

The only way out of this predicament is to tell the truth. Naturally you will experience some consequences of your actions, probably worse than if you had told the truth in the first place. But this pain will eventually result in regaining your parents' confidence. Being a man means being honest, no matter what the result.

■ *God, help me to stop covering my tracks by lying. Part of my recovery is to become honest.*

K.B.

KNOWLEDGE BY ACTIONS

"Why do you call Me 'Lord, Lord,' and do not do the things which I say?"
—LUKE 6:46

The proof is in the pudding." That is exactly what Jesus meant in the verse for today. It was easy for people to call Him Lord and yet not reflect that belief. The real proof of any change is your behavior. Any knowledge you have gained through the recovery process is confirmed by the way you act. If you don't act consistently with what you have learned, there is little evidence you have learned anything at all.

Many boys who come through our hospital program know more than anyone about treatment and the recovery process, but it doesn't show in their actions. They are filled with insight into others' recovery, but they can't direct their own. They haven't put into action what they have learned and talked about.

It takes no energy to talk a good game, but it takes a tremendous amount of energy to make good on what you say. That is the true proof of the transformation you seek. Can people see it? Will people be able to identify changes in you? Challenge yourself to "walk the talk" of recovery. Try not to say anything about others' recovery unless you have practiced it yourself.

■ *Father, help me to walk the talk of recovery!*

R.M.

YOU WILL GET BURNED PLAYING WITH FIRE

Can a man take fire to his bosom,
And his clothes not be burned?
—PROV. 6:27

John started abusing drugs when he was thirteen. Now, at seventeen, he had a lot of regrets. John had spent so much time devoted to drugs, that he didn't know how to do much more. There was the time spent worrying about where to get it, when to use and when not to, finding the money, not getting caught, avoiding being without, and so on. Never once had he really considered what all this was doing to him; he was too busy worrying about getting high.

It wasn't until he began to clean up his life that he could see the pain he had caused himself. No one trusted him. No one cared about him unless he had some good drugs to share. He had no really close friends. He had made a mess of his life, something he deeply wanted to clean up.

"If you play with fire, you will get burned." Most drug and alcohol abusers cannot understand this phrase; they can't feel the pain they are causing themselves. When you can't see or feel the fire, you don't realize that you are getting burned. Most see this only after the mess has gotten so big they can no longer deny it is there.

When will you be ready to admit that the fire you have been playing with is burning you up?

■   *God, help me to stop pretending that everything is okay and begin cleaning up the mess I've made.*

K.B.

PLAYING THE CROWD

"You shall not follow a crowd to do evil; nor shall you testify in a dispute so as to turn aside after many to pervert justice."
—EX. 23:2

People are always tempted to follow the crowd. What crowd do you play to? Guys who are athletes? The outcasts from your school whom you are trying to impress? It seems that no matter what type of crowd you are playing to, the process is always the same. At some point in time, you have to sacrifice something in order to get the response you desire. You often sacrifice your values.

A person who plays to the crowd has usually lost the ability to act independently because he is always adapting his actions to get the approval he desperately seeks.

That may happen to your recovery if you don't confront that tendency in yourself. If you are the type to play to the crowd, then your recovery is in jeopardy. The first time you are faced with a decision to choose recovery or the crowd, what will you choose? Of course, you say, "Oh, that will never happen to me!" Those are the famous last words of a person headed for relapse. Confront this tendency in yourself today by examining your motives for following the crowd. What do you seek from them? Approval? Attention? The choice between recovery and approval will set the course for continued recovery or relapse.

■ *Father, help me to choose recovery instead of the crowd.*

R.M.

IT'S OKAY TO *FEEL* ANGRY

Be angry, and do not sin.
Meditate within your heart on your
bed, and be still. —PS. 4:4

Ryan would fly into rages and do crazy things, like punching holes in walls or swearing at teachers. When he drank, he would totally lose control. Just before coming for treatment, Ryan went out with some friends, drank too much, and trashed another kid's front yard. The police recommended rehab instead of jail.

Ryan told me that when he felt angry, he didn't know what to do. It was as if a switch went off in his head, and he would become someone else. He believed that his anger made him irresponsible, as if another person were doing the bad actions.

What Ryan didn't realize was that anger is not behavior. Everyone *feels;* that is normal. Unless we do something about those feelings, however, they come out as actions. All feelings are expressed one way or another. Ryan needed to learn how to talk about his feelings, instead of acting them out. Talking is a much safer way to express anger than drinking, getting stoned, hurting people, or damaging property. Plus, you get into much less trouble.

Next time you feel yourself losing control, stop, breathe deeply, figure out why you feel so mad, and talk to someone you trust about the feeling.

■ *God, help me, when I am angry, to calm myself*
down and talk about what is bothering me.

K.B.

NEVER SAY NEVER

Peter answered and said to Him, "Even if all are made to stumble because of You, I will never be made to stumble."

—MATT. 26:33

The phrase "never say never" warns us against making a statement that we will inevitably reverse at some time and look like a fool. All too often we make such a rash statement and regret it.

One of the things I like about Peter is his humanness. We can learn much from his honest portrayal in the scriptures. In the passage for today, Peter was convinced that he had strength to withstand any attack and stand by Jesus. Needless to say, he overestimated his abilities and susceptibility to fear. He wasn't willing to admit his weakness to common human emotions, and he virtually set himself up to look like a fool as he ran from the Garden of Gethsemane.

Are you like Peter? Do you overestimate your ability to withstand temptation throughout your recovery? If you think you will never fall into the same trap as the others, you have set yourself up for a tremendous fall, just like Peter. You need to face up to your weaknesses. At first, that seems like an awful task, but it is crucial to keeping your recovery on track. If you don't, you are sure to be taken by surprise by something (or someone) that will trip you up, and you will find out all too soon about your weaknesses.

■ *Father, help me to be realistic about my weaknesses.*

R.M.

A REAL MAN

*He who is slow to anger is better
than the mighty,
And he who rules his spirit than
he who takes a city.*
—PROV. 16:32

Most of us wish to be successful. No one sets a goal for his life of being a janitor or a garbageman. In fact, most guys I work with would like to run a business or be the president of a company, someone in charge, whom others look up to and admire. Many guys also believe that to get ahead you have to be tough and not put up with a lot of crap. They tell me that you have to be aggressive and put others down in the process.

In fact, however, that is not the case. Some of the happiest men I have met are not rich and famous and don't get ahead by making others look bad. They are in control of their anger. When things get tough for them, they respond calmly to the situation and still make careful, well thought out decisions. Because they don't get worried and flipped-out when things go wrong, they usually make better choices.

In the long run, money and power will not really make you happy, because there is always someone richer and more powerful than you. But when you are calm in difficult situations you will really be more satisfied, even if you are a janitor and not president of the biggest corporation in the world.

■ *God, help me to be calm even when others are nervous and frantic.*

K.B.

HEARING FEEDBACK

Felix was afraid and answered, "Go away for now; when I have a convenient time I will call for you."
—ACTS 24:25

John, you don't want to change! You didn't even hear what we said to you." John, a member of an adolescent group I led, was being confronted about his defensiveness. "I did too," he said. "I heard what you said, but you were wrong. I'm not like what you think; you are just misjudging me. You have no right to tell me what is wrong with me!" Do these words sound familiar to you? Have you ever felt misjudged and condemned by what people said about you?

There are times throughout your recovery when someone will think your behavior is out of line with what you have said you are committed to accomplish. That person may love you enough to bring it to your attention, but your reflex is to deny it. You don't want to hear negative feedback. You almost instantly feel the pain of rejection.

Strive to listen to feedback from people you trust. They are risking their relationship with you in order to be honest with you. That isn't easy. Most people don't want others to be honest with them. But just how important is your recovery to you? Is it worth the pain of someone's pointing out your dysfunctional behavior? If it is worth it, you've made a big step toward recovery.

■ *It is important to accept the price of negative feedback to continue in your recovery.*

R.M.

TRUSTING YOURSELF TOO MUCH

There is a way which seems right to a man,
But its end is the way of death.
—PROV. 14:12

It was near the end of Robert's time in the rehab unit. He was about to return home and try to begin living a clean and sober life. He would have an extremely difficult few months until all the new things he learned began to kick in.

The group tried to tell him how tough things would be at first. He would be at his old school, where all his drinking buddies were. His family still did not trust him. His neighborhood was full of people waiting to party with him. Even Robert's old girlfriend would tempt him to get drunk with her. But Robert thought he could handle it, and he got upset when the group told him he wasn't looking at the problems he would face.

I saw Robert several months later when he was waiting to see his therapist. Sure enough, the group was right. He had relapsed, started drinking again, just a few days after leaving the hospital.

When you rely too much on your own thinking, the same way of looking at things that got you into trouble, you see only part of the picture. It is important to listen to others and know that until your recovery has been going well for at least six months, you will not be able to see things clearly enough to make it.

■ *Lord, help me to find friends who don't use who will get on my case if I mess up.*

K.B.

THE GREAT LETDOWN

He came to the disciples and found them asleep, and said to Peter, "What, could you not watch with Me one hour?"

—MATT. 26:40

You will have many letdowns in your recovery. Countless young men who have come through our program depended on their friends to carry them through recovery. They depended on these friends so much that when their friends relapsed so did they. They hadn't learned to make their recovery a thing that was theirs and theirs alone.

Imagine how Jesus felt when He asked His closest friends to support Him in prayer and they fell asleep! What an abandoned feeling to have your friends fall asleep on you.

There will be times during your recovery when it will seem your friends have "fallen asleep" on you. You feel they have abandoned you. When this happens you must remember that you are pursuing your recovery for yourself. Are you committed enough to your recovery to do it even if your friends don't support you? If so, you are prepared to take the good with the bad. You will enjoy the support while you have it, and when you don't have it you will realize that your friends are human and that you are recovering because you are convinced that it is necessary for you to be healthy.

■ *Father, help me to recover for myself and not for others.*

R.M.

Keeping Angry Feelings Inside

Don't get so angry that you sin. Don't go to bed angry. —EPH. 4:26 CEV

Many people use drugs and alcohol to cope with unhappiness. It is as if they are trying to play doctor and give themselves medicine to make the pain go away. Usually the problems only get worse and the depression becomes stronger.

What they don't realize is that their deep feelings of emptiness come from anger. You see, anger that is kept inside and not talked about with others begins to worsen. It's like saving money in a bank—every time you add to the account it grows, with interest. Pretty soon you have a lot of money stored up. Every time you go to bed angry, you add to the account, and you begin the next day angrier than the day before. And anger kept inside for too long becomes depression.

What this means is that in order to get over those bored, empty, miserable feelings, you must begin looking at what is making you so angry. Instead of trying to play doctor and medicating yourself, begin to think about what has made you angry. Then talk about it with someone. Don't keep it inside; that will make you miserable.

■ *Before I go to sleep at night, help me Lord to resolve the things that have made me angry.*

K.B.

BECOMING WORTHLESS

They followed . . . after the nations who were all around them, concerning whom the LORD had charged them that they should not do like them.
—2 KINGS 17:15

I'm sure you have heard one of your friends call someone "worthless." What that usually means is that the person doesn't amount to much to the speaker. In God's eyes, though, it takes time to become worthless.

When you embark on a lifestyle that is self-pleasing and following others, you begin a process of becoming worthless. You begin to erode your own sense of worth, and your worth to others as well. Over time, people begin to lose respect for a person who doesn't respect himself. They don't start thinking someone is worthless right from their first meeting. Instead, they follow the example presented by that person when he doesn't respect himself. Therefore, the process begins and ends with you. If you don't respect yourself enough to live a life that follows God and your values, why should anyone else respect you?

How do you maintain your worth? Essentially, follow what you know is right. In other words, follow God. Key in all of your decisions to your values. Ask yourself, "Is what I am thinking about doing consistent with what I say I believe is right?" Depending on your answer, you will know what to do and the actions you need to follow.

■ *Father, help me to follow what You want me to do.*
R.M.

PUTTING UP A FRONT

A wicked man hardens his face,
But as for the upright, he establishes his way.
—PROV. 21:29

Jack was a fake. He acted tough, bragged about things he had never done, and tried to impress everyone. The problem was that he couldn't back up his stories, and people started questioning him. Outside, Jack made himself out to be a hard guy who could hold his liquor better than anyone. Inside, he was insecure and didn't like himself very much, and that was why he made up stories about himself.

Jack wanted to be accepted so much that he started going to parties with some friends he knew his parents wouldn't like, and he got drunk most weekends with them. He convinced himself that he was having a great time; when he got drunk he felt tough, like the stories he had made up.

But when he sobered up, he still felt insecure and didn't like himself. The partying and booze just covered up the unhappy feelings for a while. Meanwhile he had rejected several good friends and made his parents suspicious of him. The new friends were lots of fun when there was a party, but the only thing that mattered to them was having a good time. Jack discovered a hard lesson about life: When you create a reputation for yourself, you have to live up to it.

■ *Be careful about the impression you give off; you will have to live up to it.*

K.B.

HOPE FOR A FOOL

Do you see a man wise in his own eyes?
There is more hope for a fool than for him.
—PROV. 26:12

I'm sure you have been around kids who think they have the "world by the tail." They're arrogant, proud, and conceited. The scripture passage for today makes it clear that there is more hope for a fool than for someone who thinks he is wise. Why is that? Because someone who thinks he is wise often is the last thing but wise. On top of that, he isn't much of a learner.

At various times in your recovery it is easy to get smug and feel like you know how recovery works, and you are more than willing to let everyone else know that as well. Too many guys during the recovery process act like experts on everyone's recovery but their own. It is pretty hard to keep the focus where it belongs, and it takes a strong confrontation to get them back on track. They often get defensive and even abusive because they don't like to hear the truth about themselves.

It is hard to keep the focus and "be wise" about your recovery. It is sometimes painful to confront the realities of your recovery. When you want to help everyone else, be sure to look at your own recovery first.

■ *Lord, help me to be wise about my own recovery, and not think I'm wiser than I am.*

R.M.

A LEGEND IN HIS OWN MIND

> *For there is not a just man on*
> *earth who does good*
> *And does not sin.*
> —ECC. 7:20

Seth thought he was a pretty great guy. The girls liked him, he was popular, he was good looking, he was captain of the football team, and he even made decent grades. However, he drank a lot and did a lot of drugs. And when he was high, drunk, or both, he could be pretty mean.

Because he thought so much of himself, he wanted to get his way even if it meant hurting others. One time he had sex with a girl he didn't even like, getting her drunk and taking advantage of her. He once loaded his car up with friends, got high, and drove around with a baseball bat, knocking the mirrors off the sides of cars. Sometimes he would drive into a gas station, fill up his car, and drive away without paying.

He considered himself to be a pretty good person; he even went every week to the youth group at church. While there were ways he was a good person, there was a lot of bad. But drinking and drugging have a way of closing your mind to the bad. You begin to make excuses for yourself, and you tell yourself that you're okay even when you're not. Until you are honest with yourself about how things *really* are, there is the danger that you will not see the whole truth.

■   *God, help me to stop thinking I am better than I am.*
   To recover, I need to see the truth.

                                                              K.B.

Woe to the Wise

Woe to those who are wise in their own eyes,
And prudent in their own sight!

—IS. 5:21

Do you know someone who is wise? Maybe it is someone helping you with your recovery. Maybe it is your dad or mom or a "hero" you look up to. Wise people have one thing in common: They realize the danger in becoming proud of what they know. They are humble enough not to realize they are wise.

John was arrogant and thought he knew everything. He listened to no one about his behavior or his harm to others. He cared only about himself. He tried to be everyone's therapist, but got no help for himself. When his time in the program came to an end, he had gained only more arrogance. His goals were unrealistic and self-serving.

I heard about John sometime later. He had relapsed and was in jail. Sometimes you pay severe consequences when you think you are wise and clever. You are sure to relapse when you think you have figured out the recovery process. You need someone to keep you centered on your goals for recovery. It is almost impossible to maintain the kind of perspective necessary to be successful. We all need someone we can trust to tell us the truth when we are drifting away from our goal.

■ *Father, help me to find someone I can trust to keep me on course in my recovery.*

R.M.

A CHIP ON HIS SHOULDER

If you are angry, you cannot do any of the good things that God wants done.
    —JAMES 1:20 CEV

Sean had a big chip on his shoulder. It was easy to see that something was wrong; he showed it every time he talked. He always got the last word. He made a smart-aleck comment when anyone said he was wrong. Sean would argue, even when it was clear that he had made a mistake.

Underneath his know-it-all attitude was intense anger. He had lost respect for his parents because they were constantly fighting. His father drank too much, and got mad when anyone pointed it out. His mother was always picking at his father's mistakes, and sometimes she would say things like, "I hope you don't turn out like your father." Sean was stuck in the middle, and he was sick of it.

Sometimes people try to control their feelings by acting tough. Sean did that. His arguing, getting the last word, disrespect for others, and not admitting to being wrong were ways of controlling others.

In reality, Sean's attitude didn't control anyone; it made others dislike him and not want to be around him. What Sean needed to learn was to listen more and speak less. When he got angry and acted demanding and defensive, he only made himself more isolated and unhappy.

■   *I know I need to watch my angry attitudes. Teach me, Lord, to listen more and react less.*

                                            K.B.

DON'T BE A SNOB!

Do not set your mind on high things, but associate with the humble. Do not be wise in your own opinion. —ROM. 12:16

I don't know a single teenager who goes out of his way to be arrogant and conceited. Most try to go in the opposite direction to be absolutely sure they are not perceived as snobs. But they really don't accomplish what they are after. Instead, they end up with a miserable sense of self-esteem. No one is really attracted to someone who is always "ripping" on himself.

One of the best ways to deal with the tendency to beat yourself up in order to not be a snob is to attempt to help someone else who is the underdog in your school. This might be someone who is straight and is always getting teased by your peers. It may be someone who is somewhat of a loner and needs a friend. It takes a great deal of inner strength to take a step like this and "lower" yourself to help someone else who doesn't have any friends. It also is a signal that you are willing to swallow your pride on behalf of someone else. The most effective way to overcome arrogance and pride is to help out someone who is less fortunate than yourself.

■ *Father, help me to help others and keep from being proud and arrogant.*

R.M.

QUICK TEMPERS

He who is quick-tempered acts foolishly,
And a man of wicked intentions is hated.
—PROV. 14:17

I first met James in the quiet room of the rehab unit where I was working at the time. The quiet room is a place where upset, angry, or out-of-control people could chill out and get their act together. He had gone there because he had started swearing and tried to punch a nurse. He was having a lot of trouble withdrawing from a severe crack addiction and was having difficulty keeping himself under control.

James got mad when I pointed out to him that he was acting crazy. He took a swing at me, and if I hadn't ducked just in time he probably would have knocked me out.

That behavior was what kept getting James into trouble. The crack made his thinking bizarre, especially when he wasn't high and felt sick. He would quickly lose his head and go off for little or no reason. Everyone he knew—family, friends, teachers, and so on—was afraid of him. When the high becomes more important than people you love and care about, you tend to make bad decisions.

Recovery is difficult at first. Like James, you may quickly lose your temper, because things inside feel pretty bad. Watch that temper; it will surprise you if you are not ready for it.

■ *God, I need to be careful not to act foolishly. Help me to watch out for my quick temper.*

K.B.

BEING DIFFERENT

Who makes you differ from another? And what do you have that you did not receive? . . . Why do you glory as if you had not received it?
—1 COR. 4:7

Some people take pride in being different. Matt was like that. He delighted in making sure everyone in the group knew he was different. Sometimes he was quiet, and everyone wondered what he was thinking. On other occasions, he was the group leader, and everyone admired him. He always found ways to stand out.

Matt is a "sitting duck" for relapse. The reason for this is that he is always determining his next move by everyone else. Instead of making up his mind according to what is best for his recovery, he determines what he does according to what will get the most attention. If his priority is being different, he has little freedom to do much else than something "different." So if his parents say, "You know, Matt, you really ought to go to your A.A. meeting," Matt might choose not to go just to be different.

Always remember who made you truly different by creating you with strengths and weaknesses. God didn't make a mistake when He created you. Whatever abilities and weaknesses you have, God has given them to you for a reason—for your good—and that allows you the opportunity to thank Him for helping you to grow.

■ *Father, help me to be different in choosing recovery over attention.*

R.M.

YOUR CLOTHES TELL A LOT ABOUT YOU

*You have turned for me my mourning
  into dancing;
You have put off my sackcloth and
  clothed me with gladness.*

—PS. 30:11

You can tell a lot about a person from what he wears. Businessmen wear suits. Priests wear clerical collars. At a funeral you are supposed to wear black. At a school formal you wear a tuxedo. But would you ever wear a potato sack?

In Old Testament days, when someone experienced grief or was in mourning, he wore sackcloth. That way everyone who saw him knew something was up. They might say, "David's wearing the sack again, he must be grieving."

Part of recovery is changing behaviors that tell others you are an addict. Often substance abusers wear things that identify them as such. Dressing in all black, wearing a cap or shirt that advertizes a brewery, or wearing coke spoons around the neck are just a few things that identify you as a stoner, burnout, or partier.

When you give off signals with your clothes, others believe you do the things your clothes say you do. You should be aware of the way you present yourself and the statement you make by what you wear. The next time you get dressed, think about what others will see in you. Make a decision to present an image that says, "I'm in recovery and don't use anymore!"

■ *God, help me to be aware of the messages I give off
   by the things I wear.*

K.B.

TAKING IT EASY

I will say to my soul, "Soul, you have many goods laid up for many years; take your ease; eat, drink, and be merry."

—LUKE 12:19

One of the worst mistakes you can make during recovery is to take the same attitude as the poor fellow in today's scripture passage. He had effectively deceived himself into thinking he had gotten all he needed to coast through life. What is the problem with resting on your laurels? Can't someone rest after struggling to gain so much?

The problem isn't rest; it is self-deception. He thought he deserved rest because he had done so well for himself. That is often what happens to someone who has struggled through treatment and is working his recovery. The "clock" in his head goes off, and he says, "I think I have done enough for now. I deserve a rest and can coast for a while." The myth here is that if you have worked hard at your recovery there will come a point where you can kick back and take it easy and let your momentum take you the rest of the way. If that is what you think, you couldn't be more wrong!

Recovery requires constant attention. This doesn't mean a compulsive, rigidly focused kind of attention. It means that you need to realize that recovery is a lifestyle rather than something you do. The more you can build recovery into your daily living, the more likely you will find it.

■ *Father, help me to make recovery part of my daily life.*

R.M.

CLEANING UP YOUR LIFE

"He reveals deep and secret things;
He knows what is in the darkness,
And light dwells with Him."
—DAN. 2:22

Your life is like a very large house, with lots of rooms. When someone is serious about recovery, he invites his higher power, God, into the house to help clean it up. Usually there is a feeling of excitement, as your life begins to get straightened out, like the feeling you get after cleaning your room, when suddenly you can find things you thought were lost.

After a while, you realize you need to clean other rooms, so you and God start working there. Eventually you've cleaned up much of your life and are feeling proud of the job you've done. Sometimes this is when people realize there is a dark, hidden closet, full of things from their past, and they're not sure they want to clean it out. So they try to hide a few things that hold them back from really doing a thorough job.

Beware! Recovery, like housecleaning, takes a lot of work. You cannot be satisfied with a halfway job. It is even dangerous to quit when you feel the chore is 99 percent complete. Those few things you hold on to from your past may be the very things that cause you to fail and relapse. When you make the commitment to get better and ask God for help, you need to finish the job.

■ *Recovery takes a long time. Will you quit before the job is done?*

K.B.

POWERLESSNESS

[They] turned their backs before their enemies. . . . Neither will I be with you anymore, unless you destroy the accursed from among you.
—JOSH. 7:12

A young man told me once he could manage recovery by himself. "I don't need to sit around and listen to people whine about their problems. I can do this on my own." He later was back in my office having been charged with his second arrest for driving while drunk. He had obviously not learned his lesson.

The most critical lesson to learn in recovery is the understanding and admission that you are indeed powerless over your addiction. Until you understand that, you will continue in your denial. You will deceive yourself into thinking you have the power to overcome addiction and, like the young man, do it by yourself. However, you have made yourself liable for disaster. You are not looking at your weakness for what it is. It is like going into battle with no armor on. The result will be just like Israel's—get up and run!

The bottom line is that without God you cannot overcome your addiction. He alone is able to change your habits and get rid of all the things that set you up to fail in your recovery. Are you ready to get rid of the things that continue your addiction? Are you ready to surrender to Him, and admit your powerlessness?

■ *Father, help me to be strong enough to admit my powerlessness to You.*

R.M.

It's Okay to Feel Weak

"My power is strongest when you are weak."
So if Christ keeps giving me his power, I will
gladly brag about how weak I am.
—2 COR. 12:9 CEV

Everyone has a difficult time with recovery. Some might tell you they just decided to stop drinking or using drugs and did fine, but they didn't really recover. They simply stopped one part of the problem. The hard part of recovery is admitting that you are weak. It's really tough for guys to admit they are weak, especially since everyone thinks guys should be so strong.

Think about some of the things guys think of as strength. Maybe it's the size of their muscles. Maybe it's the fact that people can't hurt them. Some guys believe strength is proven by the number of girls they have sex with. Others believe strength is measured by the amount of liquor they can hold before puking. Very few admit they are proud of the fact they are weak.

Usually we are not as strong as we make ourselves out to be. Having big muscles doesn't mean you can cope with life's problems. Being able to drink a lot probably means you are not strong enough to stop.

After admitting we are weak, we can turn to God for help. And each time we do, we grow closer to God, depending more on His strength.

■ *God, help me to feel good about being weak, because it makes me depend on You.*

K.B.

THE EASY WAY

"Strive to enter through the narrow gate, for many, I say to you, will seek to enter and will not be able." —LUKE 13:24

Why is this so hard?" Tim asked. He was experiencing some difficulties at this stage in overcoming addictive behaviors. "You've played basketball, Tim. What is the most satisfying game you can remember?" I asked. "We were playing the top-ranked team," he answered, "and we had prepared all season. Not that we didn't take the other teams seriously, but we knew that if we could beat this team, we had finally arrived as a respectable ball club. It was great! We actually beat them in the last minute of the game."

Is this story familiar? Aren't the things we have to work hardest for the ones that provide us with the most satisfaction and pride? What fun do you have when you beat the weakest team in your league? Not much. Yet many guys expect recovery to be easy, and they relapse very quickly.

When they do relapse they wonder what went wrong when it was going so well. What has happened is that they ease up in their desire to have a recovery worth the effort and get blind-sided by a friend offering them a drink. Don't be too quick to think something is wrong when the way gets tough. You're dealing with tough issues that will make your recovery that much stronger.

■ *Expect the way to be tough if your recovery is to be worth it.*

R.M.

FOLLOWING YOUR DESIRES

If we follow our desires, we cannot please God.
—ROM. 8:8 CEV

Addiction is simply following your desires, despite the pain it causes. You feel like drinking or getting high, and so you do. When this creates problems in your life, you cope by drinking more or getting higher. And the problems just keep getting worse.

Recovery means choosing to let God be in charge of your desires. Instead of using when you feel like it, ask God to handle those feelings, and choose to not use. By doing this, you can stop following your feelings and begin following God's desires.

Relapse, on the other hand, is when you stop following God's desires for you and begin following your own again. By doing this, you get farther away from what is best for you, and again are under the control of your own cravings for alcohol and drugs. Either you please God by doing what He wants and staying clean, or you chase your longings and lose control of your addiction. It is impossible to please God and still follow your desires.

■ *God, You want the best for me. Help me to follow You instead of seeking out my own pleasure.*

K.B.

KEEP YOUR FOCUS

*One thing I do, forgetting those things which
are behind and reaching forward to those
things which are ahead.* —PHIL. 3:13

If you shoot for nothing, you are sure to hit it!" It is
important to maintain a clear focus about what you want
to accomplish in your recovery from addictive behaviors. Keep your concentration on your goal. Put everything out of your mind except what you are striving for.
You also need to forget what has happened in the past.
The past can be the greatest burden during recovery.
When you get discouraged, or when things don't go as
well as you had hoped, you will drag out the old weight
of the past and say, "See, you really couldn't do it after
all. Just as I was afraid of."

There is another important element in the recovery
process—humility, the recognition that you still have a
long way to go. Paul was very aware that he didn't know
everything. With this in mind, he was able to keep his
focus because he knew problems would arise because
of his weaknesses. When these problems did crop up,
he saw them as opportunities to learn more rather than
beating up on himself for being such a failure. Do you
see the difference?

So forget the past, strain for your goal, and maintain
the understanding that you will make mistakes, but they
can be opportunities to learn.

■ *Remember to keep your focus—forget, strain for your
goal, and show humility.*

R.M.

IT'S NOT JUST DRUGS AND ALCOHOL

Tell the young men to have self-control in everything.   —TITUS 2:6 CEV

I've stopped drinking, so am I finished with recovery?" you may be asking yourself. Many people make the mistake of thinking their problem is the substances they are abusing. So when they stop getting drunk and high, they think the problem is gone.

Besides quitting drugs and alcohol, the addict must also look at himself and what he has become. He must admit the wrongs he has done to himself and to others, and begin making things right. He must look at his faults, admitting mistakes promptly, and continue to ask God to change attitudes and behaviors that create problems. He must continue to seek God's will in his life and tell others about the changes he is making.

Addiction is more than the substances people abuse. It is a way of life. Addictions are like trees whose roots go very deep. The substances are only the part of the tree you can see. To change the whole person, the hidden things must also be changed. Substance abuse only shows that the person has deeper problems that must be admitted and worked on. Recovery is not just sobriety; it also is changing your life so that the drugs and alcohol don't ever take over again.

■   *Don't quit before you have made the personality changes needed to keep your life in control.*

K.B.

ENTANGLEMENTS

*Since we are surrounded by so great a cloud
of witnesses, let us lay aside every weight,
and the sin which so easily [entangles] us.*
—HEB. 12:1

Are you willing to do what it takes to recover from addiction? Tom was a young man I worked with for some time in the hospital. He was the type of guy who loved to "have his cake and eat it too," as the old saying goes. In other words, he wanted to overcome his addiction—at least that's what he said—but he wasn't willing to do what it took to rid himself of things in his life that made it difficult for him to overcome his addiction. He didn't want to get rid of drug paraphernalia, which he cherished because of its value. He didn't want to change his friends because he thought he was strong enough to resist when they offered him drugs. However, Tom thought the only way to have fun was to include drugs and alcohol. Therefore, he didn't see a way to let go of these things if he was intent on having fun. Of course, the important question for Tom to answer was: Am I going to have fun or am I going to do what it takes to recover from my addiction?

There will be times when you will have to make such decisions. Sometimes you will have to let go of what you are sure is your last chance for fun, just to stay true to your recovery.

■ *Father, help me to throw off the things that keep me
from continuing in my recovery.*

R.M.

ON YOUR GUARD

Be on your guard and stay awake. Your
enemy, the devil, is like a roaring lion,
sneaking around to find someone to attack.
—1 PET. 5:8 CEV

Frank's recovery was going well. He was excited and proud of himself for coming so far. After admitting he had a problem—alcoholism—he started to make things right with his family and others he had hurt. For the first time in a long while, things seemed to go right. He felt strong and in control. That was a mistake.

Believing he was strong, he fooled himself into believing he could drink limited amounts. He thought he could have one beer, but no more. He went to a party where he drank only one beer and no more. Boy was he excited! He thought he was firmly in control of his drinking, so he let down his guard and stopped caring about whether he could handle his addiction. Three weeks later, he got completely wasted.

You can learn from Frank's story. First, don't get proud. Remember, you are not making the difference; God is. You're the one who got into trouble. Second, don't take back the control you once gave to God. When you're in control, you make a mess of things. Finally, don't let down your guard. You can't afford to think everything is okay, because it's not. In recovery, you need to remember that you're just one drink or one high away from where you began.

■ *God, help me to remember that the way back down is quicker than the way I've climbed thus far.*

K.B.

A FRIEND'S REBUKE

Do not reprove a scoffer, lest he hate you;
Rebuke a wise man, and he will love you.
—PROV. 9:8

Not all of your friends will accept readily the idea that you are recovering from your addiction. Many of them, no doubt, have come to rely on you as an excuse for their own addictive behavior. They probably will not want to hear all that you have learned about addiction, because they may have to change their own behavior. Therefore, it will be easier for them to reject you and your insight than to change themselves.

This will be exceedingly difficult to take. You will be tempted to give up your commitment to recovery because these people don't support your recovery. Unfortunately, you find just what your friendship was made of—addictions. Addiction is the glue that held your friendships together. Some of your friends will say the same thing Felix said to Paul, "Go away! I don't want to hear anymore!" They won't want to hear about your recovery because they, like Felix, are afraid of the truth.

So what will you do? You need to surround yourself with people who have proven that they will support your recovery. Don't go on word alone. Watch them and see if they walk the talk of their support for you. If so, stay close because you will need them for support.

■   *Father, help me to find people who will support me*
and my recovery when others don't.

R.M.

NARCS

"When . . . you warn the wicked, and he does not turn from his wickedness . . . he shall die in his iniquity; but you have delivered your soul." —EZEK. 3:18–19

In the drug peer group at school, there is a code of honor that if you tell on someone for using drugs, you are a narc. Teens who come to the hospital for treatment often feel as if others are narcing on them. That is because groups of peers confront each other twice a day for breaking rules of not following their treatment. The truth is their peers have learned how to really care about them and won't let them get away with the crazy behavior that got them into trouble.

The sad thing is that in order to be cool in the drug peer group, teens let each other totally destroy their lives. If friends would care enough to bring problems to the attention of someone who could help, people could be prevented from becoming addicts or alcoholics. Instead, problems are covered up and become worse.

If you care about someone, don't let him make a mess of his life while you stand by and watch. It would be like letting your good friend put a loaded gun to his head and pull the trigger. When you care about someone, you stop him when he tries to hurt himself. If being a narc means saving a friend's life, maybe it's not such a bad thing after all.

■ *Do you have friends who care enough to stop you from destroying yourself? You should find some.*

K.B.

WHO ARE YOU POINTING AT?

Who are you to judge another's servant? To his own master he stands or falls. Indeed, he will be made to stand, for God is able to make him stand.
—ROM. 14:4

We have an amazing capacity to overlook our own faults, yet easily see what everyone else is doing wrong. By doing this we stay away from feeling bad about ourselves and admitting our problems. Have you ever noticed that the bad things you point out in someone else are the same things you struggle with?

If you ever meet up with someone who just drives you crazy, slow down long enough to ask yourself: "What is there about this person that bugs me so much?" The answer will probably be very revealing—that is, you may see that what bugs you in that other person is a quality you also have that you need to change.

This approach in relating to "problem" people helps you keep your focus on what you can truly change— your own faults and shortcomings. Usually, you can't do much to change other people. But you can change yourself.

Paul, the writer of today's passage, made it clear that we will be held accountable for the actions and characteristics we judge in others. The key in staying humble and not becoming judgmental is focusing on ourselves and what we can change rather than always pointing out the faults of others.

■ *The appropriate focus for recovery is on you and the issues you need to change rather than others and their issues.*

R.M.

DON'T BLAME MOM AND DAD

The son shall not bear the guilt of the father,
nor the father bear the guilt of the son.
—EZEK. 18:20

My mom's always on my case, and my dad never believes me," complained sixteen-year-old Brian. "If they would only let up on me, things would be better, and I wouldn't get high."

Brian really believed this. He thought his parents were to blame because things were so bad. And he was waiting for them to make his life happier so he could start his recovery. Brian wanted his parents to do the real work of recovery for him.

Addicts often want someone else to rescue them, or do their work for them. People who have used alcohol or drugs to cope with life's problems are used to instant relief, so they expect recovery to be instant too. They want instant relief from the pain and the rotten consequences they are suffering because of their dependency. When relief does not come instantly, they blame others or look for others to do the work for them.

Brian's addiction was not his parents' fault. Brian had become addicted because of choices *he* had made. Recovery, even though it would be long and difficult, would also be his choice and responsibility. As long as he blamed his mom and dad, however, he would be stuck, waiting for them to do the work he needed to do.

■ *Are you waiting for someone to do your work for you? Be responsible for yourself.*

K.B.

FOOLING OURSELVES

If we say that we have no sin, we deceive ourselves, and the truth is not in us.
—1 JOHN 1:8

Have you ever been around someone who truly believed there was nothing wrong with him? You know from watching him that something is desperately wrong, but you can't put your finger on it. The tendency to deceive ourselves runs strong in all of us. Do you ever wonder why?

The reason why we deceive ourselves is to preserve what little dignity we feel we have. That may have been your case before you sought treatment. It is incredibly difficult to finally come to the place where you admit something is wrong and overcome the innate tendency to cover up weaknesses and limitations. We believe quite falsely that if we were to admit that something is wrong we will feel so awful about ourselves that we might as well die. Besides that, we also believe that everyone will abandon us anyway when they find out the problems we are dealing with. So we hang on to our self-deception in spite of the harm it is causing us.

Cultivate an ability to listen to what people say about your behavior; it could keep you from shooting yourself in the foot and furthering dysfunctional behavior. Cultivate the truth within you, and you will live it on the outside.

■ *Father, help me to not deceive myself that nothing is wrong when others tell me otherwise.*

R.M.

DENYING IS LYING

*Keep your tongue from evil,
And your lips from speaking guile.*
—PS. 34:13

I don't have a drinking problem; I just like to have a good time once in a while." Sound familiar? When first confronted, people with substance abuse problems try to claim that they have things under control. Some really believe it; others know they have a problem but want people to get off their back. Some people even have tried to quit, found out they couldn't, and still deny they have a problem.

There is a word for this: *denial.* Denial is really lying. Because addicts are afraid to admit they are out of control, they try to convince everyone that they still have it together.

Even after addicts admit they have a problem, there is all sorts of lying going on, like, "It doesn't hurt anyone but me," or "Can't you see it's not my fault?" or even "I know I need to stop someday, but I'm still young and want to experience the wild life for a while." These statements are all lies, keeping addicts from taking responsibility for the problems their drinking and drugging create, not only in their lives, but in the lives of others around them.

■ *Do you lie to cover up your responsibility? Lies will stop your recovery completely.*

K.B.

PREPARE FOR RELAPSE

Therefore let him who thinks he stands take heed lest he fall. —1 COR. 10:12

Picture in your mind a little boy who is showing off for his mom on his favorite piece of playground equipment—the monkey bars. A section of the monkey bars is a single piece of wood or metal, that is not very high, on which he has learned to walk across without falling. As his mother looks on, he proclaims, "Look, Ma, no hands!" The moment he takes his eyes off the bar to make sure his mom is looking at him, he loses his footing and falls. The fall injures his pride more than anything else.

The best way to prepare for relapse (because it will happen if you don't) is to determine when you are most likely to take your concentration off your recovery. This is most likely to happen when you are with your friends. It is easy to take your eyes off the "bar" and fall flat on your face and wonder what blind-sided you. It is important to expect obstacles; when they arise you are much less likely to get discouraged and instead deal with them in an effective way. It is even more important to understand that even your friends may become obstacles to your recovery. This usually isn't because they are trying to, but because they aren't as concerned with your recovery as you are.

■ *Father, help me to prepare for relapse by expecting obstacles and dealing with them.*

R.M.

BEING GREEDY

Have you found honey?
Eat only as much as you need,
Lest you be filled with it and vomit.
—PROV. 25:16

He kneeled over the camp's toilet. Eric and a friend had together polished off a bottle of 151 proof rum. They dared each other to drink straight shots, drinking so fast, they didn't realize how drunk they were. With the room spinning and feeling terribly sick to his stomach, Eric didn't seem quite as cool as he thought he was.

Trying to prove how macho he was, Eric had made himself look like an idiot. Now he was embarrassed and would be going home from camp as soon as his parents arrived. And the sad thing was that he probably wouldn't learn from his mistake.

People do incredibly stupid things because of alcohol and drugs. Yet they continue ignoring their problems, pretending to enjoy life and thinking everything is okay. Greedily they rush into dangerous situations, only to find they've created another problem and cannot find the high they were looking for, that would make it all worthwhile.

Until they can stop and look at what they are doing, like Eric, they will constantly search, running in circles, like a dog chasing its tail. Has your greedy appetite for more fun, more thrills, more booze and drugs, made you happy, or has it made you sick?

■ *Help me to be satisfied with the good things You give me, instead of what makes me miserable.*

K.B.

NEVER FORGETTING

I acknowledge my transgressions,
And my sin is ever before me.
—PS. 51:3

There are times throughout your recovery that you are haunted by your many problems and things you have done badly. It seems we always forget the things we have done well. David, the writer of Psalm 51, mourned his sin of adultery. He wasn't able to forget his sins; they always haunted him, day and night. He just never seemed to forget his downfalls. Does this sound familiar to you?

It is important to the success of any program of recovery to give yourself permission to forget the things you have done badly and press on toward the future. This doesn't mean an intentional forgetting of things in order not to feel bad about yourself. It means letting go of the ammunition you use to shoot yourself in the foot every time you fail. That is far from helpful.

Never forget how well you have done in the past and just how faithful God has been throughout your recovery. Never forget that you may have failed in some period of your life, but this doesn't have to write the script for your future. Also remember that God forgets your sins as you confess them; you are the one who haunts yourself with your failures.

■ *Father, help me to forgive myself just as You forgive me and free me to move on in recovery.*

R.M.

GOD MUST REALLY HATE ME!

Behold, God is mighty, but despises no one;
He is mighty in strength of understanding.
—JOB 36:5

Seventeen-year-old Joseph started to sob. He talked through his tears about his regret over things he had done when high, people he had hurt, nasty things he had said, stupid mistakes he had made. Then he said something he really feared, "God must really hate me!"

He talked about how hard recovery was, and how nothing seemed to be going right for him. He felt as if God were out to get him back for the negative behaviors stemming from his addiction. With God against him, he figured that true recovery was almost impossible.

Joseph was relieved to hear that depression is a natural part of recovery. For a long time, he had covered up those feelings with drugs or alcohol, and now that he was straight, those feelings started to come out. God has no desire to punish him or rip him apart inside. In fact, He is incredibly understanding.

Don't let your feelings affect the way you look at God. If you do, you will turn away from His help, rely on your own strength, and be right back where you started. Instead, accept your feelings, good and bad, and talk to God and to someone you trust about them.

■ *I don't blame You, God, for my miserable feelings. I trust You to help me cope with them.*

K.B.

CONTROLLING THE "RIGHT" THINGS

*He who is slow to anger is better
than the mighty,
And he who rules his spirit than
he who takes a city.*
—PROV. 16:32

Sometimes we get confused about our priorities. We want to control things that we have the least ability to have any effect on, and we don't control the things we have the most power to change. It is a paradox of life that we get our eyes on others rather than on ourselves, because it is easier to criticize others than it is to look closely at our own behavior and realize that we might be out of control. Such a realization really hurts, and our self-esteem drops.

It is truly an asset to be able to harness the energy you usually express through anger and impulsiveness. In fact, you indicate strength by holding back your temper rather than by blowing everyone out of your path. As the scripture passage for today makes clear, someone who understands his limits and focuses on constructive things is much more "valuable" than someone who can overcome an entire city! In addition to that, the ability to be patient and control your temper shows strength, and that same strength can be used to direct and keep a program of recovery on track. To control your temper is to control yourself, and that is the only thing over which you truly have complete control.

■   *Father, help me to control my temper and focus on my recovery.*

R.M.

A CITY WITHOUT WALLS

Whoever has no rule over his own spirit
Is like a city broken down, without walls.
—PROV. 25:28

In the old days, cities had strong walls built around them. That was to be sure that enemies couldn't just march in and take over the town. A city without walls to protect it was a sitting duck for anyone who wanted to destroy it.

Addiction is like a city without walls. Anytime you felt like getting high or drunk, you would just go and do it. Before recovery you didn't give much thought to protecting yourself from the consequences of your chemical abuse.

Now you have begun to build protective walls around your life. God is giving you the bricks and is even helping you to complete the project. From this point on, if you keep building, your life will be safer from the things that kept you from being healthy, that kept you addicted to harmful substances and made you miserable enough to want to destroy your life. With God's protective wall around you, your future will be much more secure.

■ *Help me to build walls around my life. With Your help, I can decide who and what to keep out.*

K.B.

A SOLID FOUNDATION

> *"Everyone who hears these sayings of Mine, and does not do them, will be like a foolish man who built his house on the sand."*
> —MATT. 7:26

For people who live on the shores of a lake, today's passage conjures up images that we have often seen tragically depicted in the news. The story is often the same. A huge storm strikes and lashes its waves on the shores of the lake. The unfortunate home owners pay dearly for living so close to the water's edge. Modern technology has allowed us to get around the usual limits of building on sandy soil, but in the days of Jesus no one was dumb enough to build on sand. Sooner or later it was sure to cave in, and the owner would lose everything.

Recovery isn't much different. I have counseled countless guys who would like to get the quick fix for their recovery. The quick fix, though, is like building on sand. It is sure to give way to the first storm that hits. Are you willing to put in time and effort to build a solid foundation for your recovery? That means persevering through the hard work of taking feedback from others, getting someone to hold you accountable for daily living and the decisions you make, and being willing to admit your weaknesses when they get the best of you. That is much easier said than done.

■ *Father, help me to build a solid foundation throughout my recovery.*

R.M.

FIRST THINGS FIRST

"Put God's work first. . . . Don't worry about tomorrow. It will take care of itself. You have enough to worry about today."
—MATT. 6:33–34 CEV

Many teens come to us for help in sorting out a tremendous mess of confusion inside. This is especially true for those who have been abusing alcohol and/or drugs for some time. Feelings, thoughts, fears, and desires get messed up because these teens have not been taking care of themselves physically and emotionally. Everything is one big blob inside.

When you start sorting all this out, often you don't know where to begin. You look at the whole mess and can't figure out what is the most important thing to work on. The problem is that everything seems to need fixing so badly, that it's hard to point to one thing to begin with.

That is why the A.A. group came up with the 12 Steps of recovery. They help you to look at the whole chaotic jumble and work through the problems one step at a time. The Bible has a suggestion too. It suggests that there is one thing that is most important in all of life: You need to put God in charge of your life. If you do that, and if you take one day at a time, all the other stuff will not only make more sense, but will start to fall into place.

■ *The first step on your journey through recovery is to put God in charge of each next step.*

K.B.

HARD DECISIONS

All things are lawful for me, but I will not be brought under the power of any.
—1 COR. 6:12

I can do anything I want!" A young man was discussing his options relating to his substance abuse. He seemed bent on demonstrating his independence in spite of the fact that he had been in trouble numerous times over his abusive behaviors. "Nobody is going to tell me what to do!" he went on. "That is absolutely true," I replied. "No one can make you do anything you don't want to do, but what do you want for yourself?" He was determined to prove that everything was permissible for him, but he was showing just how out of control and dependent he truly was. He had surrendered the right to choose what he wanted in order to prove his independence.

Many guys think being different is proof of their independence. It is actually proof of how dependent they are. If their parents tell them not to do something, these guys do it anyway. If their parents tell them to do something, they won't do it. Doesn't sound very independent, does it? Sometimes the toughest decision you will make is the one that looks like what other people want you to do. The difference is that you are making the decision to further your recovery rather than please them.

■ *Father, help me not to worry about others' opinions of what I am choosing to do.*

R.M.

WHO'S IN CONTROL?

Do not be like the horse or like the mule,
Which have no understanding.

—PS. 32:9

Ed thought rules were stupid. Every time someone in authority set limits and rules for him to follow, he would get angry and break them on purpose. The last straw was when the police picked him up for being stoned and for breaking rearview mirrors off cars with a baseball bat.

Ed had an important, but difficult, lesson to learn. He needed to learn to follow life's rules. If he didn't learn to control himself, he would end up in jail and be controlled by others.

Some people never get that message. They go through life angry and rebellious, choosing to let their desires control them rather than their common sense. Instead of finding the freedom for which they are looking, they find themselves in situations where they have no freedom at all.

The only way Ed could learn to become a free, mature adult was by understanding that rules, laws, and limits are necessary. By choosing to follow them, he would be given more freedom because he could be trusted to exercise it wisely. On the other hand, the less control he showed over the freedom he had, the more control others would have to take over his life.

■ *Will anger and fighting the rules result in more or less independence for you?*

K.B.

TAKING RESPONSIBILITY

David said to God, "Was it not I who commanded the people to be numbered? I am the one who has sinned and done evil."
—1 CHRON. 21:17

Why is it so hard to take responsibility for something we have done poorly? Often the reason is that we don't like to feel bad about ourselves. We go to such lengths to avoid responsibility that we become addicted to drugs and alcohol. We have such an all-encompassing feeling of worthlessness and "yuck" about ourselves that we hurt emotionally and sometimes even physically. Added to this, we feel that if we can find a way to make it go away, it will no longer be a problem—it will be "out of sight, out of mind." That is why alcohol and drugs are so alluring.

The truth is that taking responsibility for your actions is what truly builds your self-worth and self-respect. It is funny how what looks like it will tear us down is actually what builds you up. Taking responsibility for what you have done is a recognition that you make mistakes and are willing to look at this reality honestly. That takes courage, and it will help you feel good about yourself. You will build your self-respect as well because you will begin to establish the reputation of a person who has the guts to say that he has done something wrong and can take looking at it and growing from it.

■ *Father, help me to accept responsibility for my actions rather than run from it.*

R.M.

MOVE YOUR BODY PARTS

"If your hand or foot causes you to sin, chop it off and throw it away! . . . If your eye causes you to sin, poke it out."
—MATT. 18:8–9 CEV

Those two verses sound pretty grim! No one really needs to start chopping off body parts to make it. But you may have to watch those body parts when they start leading you back to old patterns that you know will get you into trouble.

Your hands are used to handling beers, joints, or other things that cause problems. Your feet walk into trouble, to friends who are getting high or to parties where drinking is going on. Your eyes watch things and notice where the action is.

Likewise, your hands can be used to doing things that keep you from danger, like gesturing no. Your feet can walk you out of situations where you might be tempted to go back to the old life. Your eyes can be alert for problems ahead and warn the rest of your body to move in another direction.

One psychiatrist who works with us says, "Move your body parts." What he means is that recovery involves using your body to do the right thing. Your body can either help you relapse or keep you clean. Don't let your senses or body parts be in control of your recovery. Make your body do what you want it to—stay clean, one day at a time.

■ *How can you move your body parts to help in recovery today?*

K.B.

LISTENING AND DOING

Be doers of the word, and not hearers only,
deceiving yourselves.   **—JAMES 1:22**

A teacher once told me, "I don't know what you know until you show me." It is interesting to watch how people handle their knowledge of recovery. Knowing a lot about recovery is quite a different matter from putting it into practice. The writer of today's passage makes it quite clear that it is easy to deceive yourself into thinking that knowing something is all there is to it. The problem is that listening isn't enough to prove that you really know something. Anyone can tell me how to play basketball, but showing me how to play is the crucial issue.

Being able to show what you have learned is critical because it shows just how convinced you are of its worth to you. If you use it and fail, you can at least say so and help someone else avoid your mistakes. On the other hand, you maintain a safe distance if you never put into practice what you preach.

The last important truth about doing what you have learned is that it gives you an opportunity to learn it better, and it becomes a part of who you are. The more you practice your recovery, the more you will build a lifestyle that secures a healthy, abstinent future.

■   *Father, help me to not only listen but also do what I have learned.*

                                                        R.M.

TAKING THE STRAIGHT PATH

Teach me Your way, O LORD,
And lead me in a smooth path.
—PS. 27:11

The shortest distance between two points is a straight line. That may be the only thing I remember from high school geometry. In life, when you want to go somewhere there are usually many ways to go, but only one path leads straight there. Recovery is a straight path, too, but there are lots of side tracks and paths leading away from the one you know you should be on.

The straight path, of course, is working the 12 Steps of N.A. and A.A. and following God's directions. Every time you relapse or start doing the things you know in your heart are not right, you take a side path. When you follow too many of these side paths, you find yourself completely lost or back where you started. At that point you pick up where you are and begin walking the straight recovery trail again.

Often, friends will try to lead you onto one of these other paths. Sometimes it may seem easier, or like a shortcut. Beware, there is no easy road to recovery, only a straight path from where you are now to your goal of a substance-free life. When you feel tempted to take another route, stop and ask God's directions.

■ *Think of some of the side roads to recovery. What happened when you left the straight path?*

K.B.

DOING WHAT IT TAKES

> *"I will guard my ways,*
> *Lest I sin with my tongue;*
> *I will restrain my mouth with a muzzle."*
> —PS. 39:1

Few temptations are more trying than the tremendous pull to join in your friends' fun. You feel left out, and worse yet you may be thought of as a "party-pooper" and may not be invited to anything else that would be fun. You will always have to be vigilant, on the lookout about situations that will put your recovery to the test. It is tiring, but necessary business.

The writer of the passage for today draws a pretty ridiculous word picture for us, but he makes an important point to those who are serious about recovery. If you are serious about watching yourself and following your recovery you may have to "muzzle" yourself in order to accomplish your goals. His goal was to keep his tongue under control. He also realized his weakness around "wicked" people, and feared he might slip. He was so serious about keeping from falling that he was willing to muzzle himself in order to keep from getting into trouble! Now that is a serious commitment. What kind of commitment do you have to your recovery? Are you willing to do what it takes to assure success? That may mean some difficult situations with your friends, who may not understand your seriousness.

■ *Father, help me to do what it takes to follow through on my recovery.*

R.M.

HANGING TOUGH

*But Daniel purposed in his heart that he
would not defile himself with . . . the king's
delicacies, nor with the wine which he
drank.*
—DAN. 1:8

Daniel was a young man who avoided the pressure to
conform. After being taken into slavery by the Babylonians, he was picked out of all the captives as one of the
brightest and best of the slaves. Then he was offered the
best of everything, including the richest food and the
best wine.

But Daniel wanted something different. He politely
asked if he could be a part of an experiment. Instead of
rich food and wine, he asked that for ten days he be
given vegetables and water. At the end, if he was not
healthier than those on the other diet, he would conform.

You can learn two things from Daniel. First, and most
obvious, watching what you put into your body makes a
difference in how you do in the long run. Some substances hurt your body and mind, and they should be
avoided. Second, it's okay to suggest that those in authority try it your way for a short time. If that doesn't
work, agree to do it their way.

Daniel's plan worked so well that he went on to become a strong and trusted leader of the slaves taken by
Babylon. Be like Daniel; watch what you put into your
body, and be wise about the way you ask for things you
want.

■ *Next time you disagree with your parents, try Daniel's way.*

K.B.

STUMBLING

We all stumble in many things. If anyone does not stumble in word, he is a perfect man, able also to bridle the whole body.
—JAMES 3:2

We all stumble in many ways. We expect to make mistakes. But when we actually make them, we really beat ourselves up badly. It's almost as if we are willing to make mistakes right up to the moment we make them, and then switch our expectations and beat ourselves up as if we weren't supposed to make a mistake!

It is important to put mistakes in their proper perspective to bring about a successful recovery program. Expect mistakes not only before you make them, but also after you make them. Many people think that once they are on a smooth roll in recovery it will last, and they will have no more problems. That couldn't be further from the truth. Even worse, it is a set-up for disaster. What will happen when there are problems? Does it mean you have failed and might as well give up? If it means you have failed then you might as well quit now, because you are human and will make mistakes.

On the other hand, if you accept the fact that you will blow it once in a while and give yourself a break without wallowing in self-pity, you will succeed in your recovery.

■　*Father, help me to accept my mistakes as part of the growth process toward recovery.*

R.M.

RELAPSE

A man who wanders from the way of understanding
Will rest in the congregation of the dead.
—PROV. 21:16

The word *relapse* means "to go back to old behaviors and habits." Most drug and alcohol addicts relapse at least once, usually many times. They promise themselves they'll never do it again—this time their recovery is real. A few days or weeks later, they're back at it.

Some people go into rehab and learn all the things they need to make life without substances possible. Some even go to Alcoholics, Narcotics, or Cocaine Anonymous after rehab. They mean to quit. They are miserable from the drugs and alcohol. But their commitment just doesn't last; most people start using again. Why?

People relapse because they begin to believe they can handle it. They can have one drink, one joint, one speeder, one tab of acid, one snort, and not be addicted again. Then, the old habit creeps up on them and takes over, and they relapse. If you stray from the straight path of recovery, even just one little step, you are addicted and headed for death.

■ *Don't try to fool yourself. No addict or alcoholic can handle "one little" anything.*

K.B.

A CONDEMNING HEART

*We know that we are of the truth. . . . For if
our heart condemns us, God is greater than
our heart, and knows all things.*
—1 JOHN 3:19–20

There are times in your recovery when you struggle
with self-condemnation. You are drawn to the many
things you have done in the past to hurt others and to
hurt yourself, and the opportunities in your future that
may be lost because of poor decisions. This is most
likely to happen when you face adversity in present circumstances. When you may not do as well as you had
hoped, you come face to face all over again with the
cruel reality of your limitations.

The passage for today speaks to the pain of self-
condemnation. We need to remember that we can find
rest in the midst of such accusations from our past when
we realize that God is bigger than any accusations our
hearts and minds can throw at us. There is nothing He
can't deal with. The reason Jesus came was so that we
might not be harassed by our past, and to give us an
even more peaceful future with Him.

How can you make this practical? You must confront
the accusation for what it is—a false accusation. The
past is behind, and you are moving ahead. You need to
tell your accuser (yourself) that those things no longer
have a hold over you, and you are going to live according to the future.

■   *Father, help me to answer the accusations from the
past with living for the future.*

R.M.

CHOOSING TO FEEL WORTHLESS

Will you turn my glory to shame?
How long will you love worthlessness
and seek falsehood? —PS. 4:2

Some people choose to stay unhappy. There are a lot of depressed addicts running around, feeling totally worthless inside, but they're doing nothing about it. Richard was one of those people.

Richard came into rehab because he felt empty and miserable. Yet, when others tried to show him that his own choices made him feel that way, he would get angry. Richard was stubborn. And stubborn people have a difficult time making changes, even when they know they are unhappy. Richard was more interested in doing his own thing than in changing, so he chose to stay stuck in his own self-pity and unhappiness.

Facing up to the truth about yourself can be hard, especially when others know the truth about you before you do. Unfortunately, it usually *is* others who first see things that need changing in our lives. The next time someone points out something he or she thinks you could do differently, don't get mad or depressed. Listen to what they have to say, and you may discover an area for growth and health.

■ *God, help me to listen to those who care and use their ideas to make my life better.*

K.B.

Painful Memories

*Then the chief butler spoke to Pharaoh,
saying: "I remember my faults this day."*
—GEN. 41:9

At times in your recovery you will be reminded of painful decisions you have made. Sometimes you may think, "Isn't it enough to have a substance abuse problem? Do I have to be reminded of my mistakes over and over again?" This situation may bring forth relapse, because you once medicated your pain by drinking or using drugs. When you feel this pain all over again, you will be tempted to fall back into old, abusive behaviors.

When you are high you can make believe there is no pain, no problems to deal with in your life. When you decide to give up such behavior, you will have to come up with some alternative to deal with the pain that you face on an almost daily basis.

One thing you can do is to remind yourself that not all pain is bad. Sometimes pain indicates growth and maturity. If you look at the situation more closely you may realize that the reason you are feeling the pain is because you have made a healthy decision, and it feels awkward. You needn't run away from this kind of pain. It represents growth and progress in your recovery process.

■ *Father, help me to remember that not all pain is bad, but a sign of growth.*

R.M.

CAN GOD FORGIVE WHAT I'VE DONE?

*If we tell God about our sins, he can always
be trusted to forgive us and take our sins
away.* —1 JOHN 1:9 CEV

Jack had made a breakthrough. For a long time he
had a terrible attitude. He figured it was a tough world
out there, so he had to win at all costs. That meant he
didn't feel bad about walking on others—it was better to
hurt someone else than get hurt yourself. Recently,
however, he discovered something about himself: He
was a jerk.

By thinking only about himself, he had pushed away
those who could help him recover. And now he was left
with only himself to depend on. Through his recovery
he discovered that he was the worst person to depend
on but that the people who were good for him didn't like
him very much because he was such a jerk.

Jack thought that if people he could trust didn't like
him very much, God must certainly hate him. Since he
wanted to make things right, he knew he needed God's
forgiveness, but he was afraid God could never forgive
him for what he had done.

Jack was relieved to hear that God can and will forgive us, no matter what we've done. If we just talk to
God about what we regret doing, God promises to forgive us and totally forget our sins. We ask, and God
forgives; it's as simple as that.

■   *God, I've done rotten things. I humbly ask You to
forgive me and give me a new start in life.*

K.B.

WEIGHED DOWN

Anxiety in the heart of man causes depression,
But a good word makes it glad.
—PROV. 12:25

What is weighing you down today? Maybe it is a relationship or your grades or an activity you're going to participate in. As the passage for today makes clear, anxiety weighs us down. It is something that plagues us if we don't find ways to release it. Imagine someone wearing a backpack. With each new worry, another weight is added to the backpack. Before long, the person is crawling from the weight of the pack. Is that how life feels to you? Does it feel like you are hemmed in on all sides and can't get away?

How do you free yourself from the tremendous weight of anxiety and worry? The best way to begin to get the "monkey" of anxiety off your back is to make your need known to someone who you know is safe and willing to help you. This person will give you the kind and cheerful word to carry you on your path to recovery. This "word" may be verbal encouragement or a physical expression of support, helping you to let go of some of your anxiety. Take the responsibility to get the help you need to continue on your way to health.

■ *It is important to make your need known to others to get the support you need.*

R.M.

DAN'S NEW LIFE

*I beg you to offer your bodies to [God] as a
living sacrifice, pure and pleasing.*
—ROM. 12:1 CEV

During our last two sessions together, Dan was struggling to give up control of his alcohol abuse to God. He wanted me to show him some kind of ritual he could go through to do it. And though I kept telling him there wasn't one, he couldn't believe that all he had to do was ask God to take control. That seemed too simple.

But that's all there is to it. You don't have to walk on hot coals, take a cold shower, or sleep on a bed of nails to give control of your life and recovery to God. You simply have to believe that God is good, knows a lot more than you, and is stronger than you; then, ask Him to take control of your addiction and begin to change the way you deal with life.

Dan finally made up his mind that he really did need something different. He had tried everything he could think of and nothing had worked. So together, we prayed and asked God to lead Dan away from dangerous choices and toward health and sobriety. Dan's decision to give God control of his recovery and his body was the beginning of his new life.

■ *Lord, help me to stop trying to look for some intense
experience. I need You to be in charge.*

K.B.

STRAIGHT PRIORITIES

Let the lowly brother glory in his exaltation.
—JAMES 1:9

It's pretty easy to get your priorities all messed up when you keep your eyes on external things. One of the reasons for this is that the people around you follow their own patterns and rules. They know nothing about what you want for your life and where you are heading. The problem comes when you compare yourself to these people. The situation worsens when you assume that they know where they are going and that they are worth imitating. When this happens you begin to put others in charge of your life and values.

The importance of well-defined goals for your recovery cannot be overemphasized. When you have goals and values for your recovery you can go back and look at them when you feel yourself getting pulled into others' values. Many times your values will seem reversed from those around you. It's hard to keep your priorities straight. The best way to do this is to continue to evaluate what you do so that it is consistent with what you want for your recovery.

■ *Father, help me to keep my priorities straight.*

R.M.

A LOOK INSIDE

Let us search out and examine our ways,
And turn back to the LORD.

—LAM. 3:40

Something was bothering Jake. For two months he had been doing well in recovery. He had given up trying to be in charge of his sobriety, and he understood that God had made the real difference in his life. But he felt that something was holding him back.

Jake couldn't quite put his finger on it. He felt as if his life were in slow motion—even on instant replay, where he was doing the same things over and over. He couldn't understand why he wasn't moving forward in his recovery.

Jake needed to start working on his moral inventory. He was full of regrets and mistakes about his past that he needed to look at honestly. And until he started looking back and dealing with those things, he would have difficulty moving on.

Your experiences may be different from Jake's, but you also must look at your past. Don't be afraid of past mistakes. By confronting your guilt and regret, you will be able to move forward to a new life.

■ *God, with Your help I can confront my past. Help me to consider both the good and the bad.*

K.B.

BELIEVING LIES

*"God knows that in the day you eat of it your
eyes will be opened, and you will be like
God, knowing good and evil."*

—GEN. 3:5

If I didn't know better, I'd think God delights in making me miserable!" A guy vented his frustration over the hassles he faced after leaving our program. He had grasped the importance of admitting his powerlessness over addiction and his responsibility to keep himself healthy. He was sure everything was looking up for him.

When we face adversity, the first thing we do is look for someone to blame it on. Sometimes we believe exactly what Satan told Eve—God is only in the business of protecting Himself; He doesn't really have our best interests in mind. The minute we let that lie seep into our conscious minds, we are in trouble. If God doesn't help us, then who will? The only logical conclusion is no one but ourselves. This leads to choosing behaviors that are geared toward accomplishing goals in the short term. We quit thinking about our recovery in terms of a life-long commitment.

No one ever said recovery was easy. If it was, it wouldn't be worth striving for. And no one ever said God would make everything easy for you. He wouldn't be much help if He did. You need to struggle with life and its hassles in order to grow and be able to handle hassles in the future.

■ *Father, help me to face adversity without blaming You.*

R.M.

HEAVENLY FATHER, EARTHLY DAD

God is not a man that He should lie,
Nor a son of man, that He should repent.
—NUM. 23:19a

There comes a time in recovery when you recognize that you can't stop messing up. No matter how hard you try, things just keep getting worse, and the addiction is totally out of control. You need something or someone to take control and help you out of the mess you have made. Since letting the drugs or alcohol be in control hasn't worked, and others can't do it for you there is only one place to turn: to God.

Most people don't understand God very well. Usually they see Him as being just like their dad. When you are angry at, scared of, or just can't relate to your earthly dad, this can be quite hard. Many people even quit trying in recovery because turning to God is so frightening.

But God is not like your earthly dad! God doesn't make mistakes. He cares for and loves you a lot, and He wants you to recover. Because of this, God is someone who can be trusted 100 percent of the time. And since He created the entire universe in only six days, one person's addiction is pretty easy for him to handle.

So next time you don't know where to turn, and things feel completely out of control, look to your heavenly Father for help. He's waiting.

■ *Heavenly Father, take control of my life and my addiction, and guide my recovery program.*

K.B.

WHOM ARE YOU SERVING?

Therefore do not let sin reign in your mortal body, that you should obey it in its lusts.
—ROM. 6:12

I'm sure you have probably heard the old saying, "Actions speak louder than words." In spite of all the "smoke and mirrors" many guys prove just how into their recovery they are by what they do. They may say they are really working hard, and may even fool people into believing them. The one sure proof of how committed they are to their recovery program is what they do. Their actions show exactly whom they are allowing to "reign" in their bodies. If you serve or allow to reign in your body a commitment to God and recovery, the results will be obvious. On the flip side, if you do not allow your commitment to recovery to reign over your decisions, that will show quite clearly as well.

I often ask a client what I would see if I followed him around with a videotape camera and taped everything he did in a day. Would I see him doing things that would suggest he was making decisions consistent with his commitment to overcome addiction? Or would I see situations and behaviors that would be confusing and contradictory from what he says? Think about it. Do you behave like you talk?

■ *Father, help me to act in such a way that people can see my recovery in process.*

R.M.

CHOOSING TO BE A SLAVE

You can be slaves of sin and die, or you can be obedient slaves of God and be acceptable to him. —ROM. 6:16 CEV

First, the bad news: You are a slave.

Now, the good news: You can choose whom You will serve.

We all have to serve a master. Once, you allowed yourself to be a slave to your addiction, which got you into trouble and made you feel pretty bad. But there is someone you can choose to serve who will set you free: God.

You can allow yourself to follow your desires, pretending you are free, or you can willingly choose to put God at the head of your life and follow Him to sanity and full recovery.

When you were drinking and drugging you thought you had some kind of independence, usually from feelings of boredom, unhappiness, or emptiness. But this freedom had a high price. Drugs and alcohol controlled your way of looking at things. They were your master.

Now you can choose to follow God, who wants to help you through your recovery. When you turn your addiction over to Him, He frees you from the misery of and chains of slavery to your addiction and gives you strength to cope.

■ *God, help me to see that following You offers more freedom than following my own desires.*

K.B.

DODGING RESPONSIBILITY

Then the man said, "The woman whom You gave to be with me, she gave me [fruit] of the tree, and I ate."
—GEN. 3:12

I don't think I could have been as blunt and blaming as Adam was in the Garden! He had the nerve to actually blame God for his sinfulness. He didn't stop there! If that wasn't enough, he went on to blame his wife for his problems as well. Adam's response is typical of all of us when we are caught doing something we know we shouldn't do. We begin to blame and do whatever we can to dodge responsibility. That way we look better in our own eyes, and we hope, to others' as well.

Gary was that kind of person. As soon as he was confronted by anyone, his mind would set to coming up with some kind of excuse to get off the hook. He would try blaming the person confronting him: "If you hadn't made such a big deal of this, it wouldn't be a problem!" He would try to plead ignorance: "I didn't know that it was such a problem." If all else failed, he would turn to the classic defeated, devastated look of rejection and say, "I was just trying to (and insert some behavior, like "express my feelings")."

Does this sound familiar? Are you good at dodging responsibility? If so, you are on a course for relapse if you don't find somebody courageous enough to give you honest, direct feedback.

■ *Father, help me find someone who is honest when I dodge responsibility for inappropriate behavior.*

R.M.

WHAT WILL I SAY?

So the LORD said to him, "Who has made man's mouth? . . . Now therefore, go, and I will . . . teach you what you shall say."
—EX. 4:11–12

Fourteen-year-old Jack took a big risk in one session, when he promised his parents that things would be better from then on. In our next session alone, he shared some fears he was afraid to tell his parents.

"Look," Jack said. "I meant what I said last week, but when I got back to school the next day, I didn't know what to tell my friends. If they see me changing, they won't hang with me anymore. So what do I say?"

You should be ready to face your friends' resistance to your recovery. But you can't trust your own strength to do it. You need to rely on God.

God will give you the right words to say for every confrontation. You don't have to plan the right words for every occasion, because you don't know what you will encounter. But God does know what you will encounter before it happens. And He knows the words you will need to speak and will give them to you when you need them. You only need to be certain that you really want to recover, even if it means giving up friends.

■ *God, You know my fears. Give me Your words when I talk to old friends about my recovery.*

K.B.

WHOM ARE YOU LOOKING TO?

And my God shall supply all your need according to His riches in glory by Christ Jesus.
—PHIL. 4:19

It is easy to base your recovery on others and their belief in you. However, when those persons are gone or become less involved in your life, your motivation for recovery goes down the tubes.

Basing your recovery on someone else reveals a belief that you really can't do it alone, that you must have someone to help you. No matter how hard you try you will probably fail because the recovery process is placed in someone else's hands; and that person might not even know he plays such a critical role in your healing process. Therefore, he won't be as careful as you would be in doing the things necessary for a successful and healthy recovery. He simply can't meet this need because he doesn't know what you are seeking from him.

What will provide a firm foundation for your recovery? It is the fact that God will meet all your needs. He desires your growth and health, and will do whatever is necessary to help that come about. That will mean bringing people into your life who will support and encourage you and who also will confront and push you to stretch in your recovery. Look for them, for they are a gift from God, who will meet all your needs.

■ *Trust God to meet all your needs during your recovery.*

R.M.

MOM'S APRON STRINGS

Jesus looked at them and said, "There are some things that people cannot do, but God can do anything." —MARK 10:27 CEV

Don had a problem. His recovery was going well, but his mother wasn't comfortable with some of the changes he was making. She felt she had to look out for him and take care of him; he could do nothing without her help.

Addiction usually involves more people than the addict. Others kept him addicted by making excuses for him, by treating him like a child, by trying to take care of everything so he won't get mad and use. Don's mom was very wrapped up in his life, and he was starting to get frustrated with it. He knew it was time for a change.

Yet a part of Don liked being treated like a child. It felt comfortable. He didn't want to hurt her feelings, and he knew that talking to her about it would do just that. So he was stuck, thinking the situation was impossible to change.

Don had forgotten that nothing is impossible for God. After talking about this for a while, he made a decision to confront the problem and not worry about the outcome; God would take care of that. This turned out to be a big step for him. His mother took it hard at first, but she saw that Don was really growing and began to treat him with more respect, which gave a boost to his recovery.

■ *Lord, some people in my life mean well but are holding me back. Help me to deal with them.*

K.B.

KNOWING EVERYTHING

If anyone thinks that he knows anything, he knows nothing yet as he ought to know.
— 1 COR. 8:2

Do you ever wonder why people we call "know-it-alls" are so annoying? Isn't it because we feel inadequate around them? It seems they have something to say about every subject. Often, though, the real reason why someone is a "know-it-all" is that he doesn't want to be found out as a fraud. He doesn't want people to think he is dumb, so he makes it a point to say something about everything. This way of interacting with people often exposes a deeply held fear of inadequacy.

It is interesting, as the verse for today suggests, that it is better to not act as if you know everything, because it shows humility and an understanding of just how little we really know. When you say "I don't know," you are willing to look at your inadequacies, and not be everything to everyone. It's healthy to admit how much you really don't know. It is also a way to keep in perspective your powerlessness over your addiction. The minute pride works its way in, you will find yourself trying to know everything about everything for everyone. That will be the time for relapse, and you need to pull back and get some feedback.

■ *It is important to not know everything so that your pride can be kept in its place.*

R.M.

ADULTS CAN'T BE TRUSTED

My son, keep your father's command,
And do not forsake the law of your mother.
—PROV. 6:20

In the world of teenage drinking and drugging there are two kinds of people: the cool and the narcs. Most adults are the second kind; if they know what is going on, they bust you. It's a sort of rule that teen addicts can't trust adults.

As you get older, you grow wiser and know more about life. You're not the same person you were at six years old. The world appears to be a much different place as you grow and mature, and you learn lessons as an adolescent that you would never have understood as a little kid.

Adults have progressed past adolescence, and they have learned a lot about life during that time. They know things that could help you if only you would ask. But thinking that adults can't be trusted keeps teen addicts from going to the people with knowledge and wisdom.

Recovery is about finding answers to your problems with drugs and alcohol. Instead of seeing adults as narcs, start looking to them as people who care enough to stop you from making dangerous mistakes. Instead of being afraid of being busted, start seeing confrontation as helpful and designed to help you grow. Stop avoiding the people who can help your recovery the most.

■ *God, I have difficulty trusting adults. Teach me to ask for help instead of running from the truth.*

K.B.

A FAITHFUL FRIEND

A friend loves at all times,
And a brother is born for adversity.
—PROV. 17:17

It is really easy to take our friends for granted. After a while we expect people to abandon us in hard times. As a matter of fact, some guys think there is something wrong with people if they don't take a hike when things start to go bad. So when you are in a pinch and find someone who doesn't abandon you, what do you do? Do you say, "Get lost. You'll leave before long too, so you might as well do it sooner than later"? Or are you one of those who says, "Go away. I don't want your help"? The first of these statements represents an attempt to not get hurt because someone leaves. The other statement is the old pride that gets in the way. Either way, you lose the support and friendship you need to face trials.

Never take faithful friends for granted. They are very precious because of what they stand for. They are there because they believe in you and what you are attempting to do. They want to encourage you and support you through whatever you face. Don't assume that they will leave too. Swallow your pride and accept the gift of friendship from your faithful friend. Today make sure to tell your faithful friend how much you appreciate his support of you.

■ *Father, help me to not take my faithful friends for granted.*

R.M.

OLD FRIENDS

The drunkard and the glutton will come to
*   poverty,*
And drowsiness will clothe a man with rags.
                                        —PROV. 23:21

Mark worked hard in family sessions at rehab. He had begun to rebuild some of the trust he had lost by sneaking out and getting high most nights. He had compromised on areas his parents thought he needed to change, and even helped design a contract that specified rules and consequences if he started messing up again. But there was one thing he refused to work on.

Mark would not stop hanging around his drug buddies. When his parents confronted him about this, Mark began yelling and swearing at them. He thought he could handle his friends because he was stronger now and he wanted to work at his recovery. In fact, he thought he could get his friends to change if he just tried hard enough.

Soon Mark relapsed. It just sneaked up on him after a friend offered him a hit off his joint. Mark didn't even think about what he had done until later that night. When you've been hanging around certain people, some things are just so much a part of your friendship that you don't think much about them. Your drinking or drugging buddies naturally want to drink or get high. Don't kid yourself; you are not as strong as you would like to believe. A solid recovery may require giving up some old friends.

■   *God, help me to break relationships that drag me*
    down and give me new ones to replace them.

                                                    K.B.

DYING TO RECOVER

*Put to death your members which are on the
earth: fornication, uncleanness, passion, evil
desire, and covetousness, which is idolatry.*
—COL. 3:5

Many guys fail to recover from substance abuse because they want to live in two separate worlds. They
want to keep one foot in drug-abuse and the other in a
drug-free world. Soon they drift wholly onto the drug-
abuse side because they're not willing to do what it
takes to be drug-free.

I ask guys, "What are you willing to do to recover
from your addiction?" Without thinking, most answer,
"Absolutely anything." Of course, this is in the safety of
the hospital or after they have gotten in trouble over
their substance abuse. "Are you willing to give up all
your friends who use drugs?" They begin to waffle on
their commitment, "what do my friends have to do with
it? Can't I recover without giving up my friends?" The
minute someone starts waffling, I know he isn't serious
about recovery. Evidently, it really hasn't gotten bad
enough.

A sort of "death" is necessary for you to stay on the
path to recovery. You must be willing to sacrifice anything in order to recover, including those who will be
your worst enemies even though they seem to be your
best friends. Recovery isn't without its costs. You sometimes experience loss when you decide to do what it
takes to recover.

■   *Father, be with me when I "put to death" the things
that are obstacles to my recovery.*

R.M.

IS THE MONEY WORTH IT?

How much better it is to get wisdom than gold!
And to get understanding is to be chosen
rather than silver.
                                                    —PROV. 16:16

Sean thought he had a great plan. Because drugs are expensive and most teens cannot afford a habit, he decided to save up, buy a bunch of drugs, sell enough to make a profit, and use the rest. There were two problems with his plan. First, he could not resist dipping in to what he had planned to sell. Second, he never figured on getting caught.

Because Sean was getting high every day, his thinking was clouded by the drugs. He really believed that pot helped him to think more clearly. Eventually, he started to make stupid mistakes, like selling in school. It wasn't long until people started talking, and Sean got caught. The judge gave him a choice of rehab and probation or spending some time in juvenile jail. Sean chose rehab and started his recovery.

Selling illegal drugs can bring you big money. But it doesn't prepare anyone for real life, unless you are preparing for a life in jail.

While the risks you are taking may not be as bad as Sean's, ask yourself if they are worth the danger you are putting yourself and others into. Not everything that seems good on the surface is really in your, or others', best interests.

■ *Reveal to me, heavenly Father, the lousy decisions I*
have made since I started using.

                                                    K.B.

HIDING YOUR RECOVERY

Therefore show to them, and before the churches, the proof of your love and of our boasting on your behalf. —2 COR. 8:24

I once heard a popular Christian singing artist sing the song, "I'd Rather See a Sermon Than Hear One Any Day!" That truth applies to the Christian life as well as to your recovery. It is pretty easy to get hooked into saying all the "right" things of recovery, and yet not really be serious about your recovery. In other words, you are doing a bang-up job of hiding your recovery. No one knows how well you are recovering unless you show it. It is the doing of our beliefs that gives them form, and they live for others as well as ourselves. They can see that you are indeed serious about what you talk about.

If you are working to "show the proof" of your commitment to recovery, you are communicating something to yourself as well. You are telling yourself by your actions, "Yes, this is important stuff, and I will risk doing it to recover from my addiction." It is an important message to give yourself. We often overlook how powerfully we communicate things to ourselves by what we do. Our behavior can often set the stage for more change in the future. It shows our commitment and our willingness to make our recovery stick.

■ *Father, help me to show proof of my recovery by what I do.*

R.M.

SEEING THE LIGHT

Jesus had said, "Before a rooster crows, you will say three times that you don't know me." Then Peter went out and cried hard.
—MATT. 26:75 CEV

Peter was in pretty intense denial for a while. First, he swore to his good friend Jesus that he would *never* lie about their friendship. And he was serious—so serious that he said he would rather die than deny he loved his friend. But later in the same day, Jesus was arrested. And when people asked Peter if he knew Jesus and accused him of being Jesus' friend, sure enough, Peter got scared and lied.

Now, Peter was no wimp. In fact, his nickname was "The Rock." You might say he was a pretty solid guy. But the fact is, no matter how strong you sometimes think you are, when you get confronted with something frightening, you have a strong urge to try to scam your way out of it. That's what denial is.

After you lie you have a choice. You can admit you lied and start your recovery again, or you can keep covering up and act like an addict. Peter realized he had gone back on his word. He felt so bad, he cried about it. But Jesus forgave him, and Peter eventually became one of the strongest leaders of the early church. What might have happened to the church if Peter hadn't admitted to himself that he had screwed up?

■ *I sometimes deny the truth, God, and get stuck in my own lies. Help me to be honest.*

K.B.

WHAT ABOUT HIM?

Peter, seeing him, said to Jesus, "But Lord, what about this man?" —JOHN 21:21

Oh, yeah? What about you? You aren't doing much either!" I had just walked in on an argument between two group members. One had confronted the other about not doing anything in his recovery in spite of acting like he had done a lot. He didn't like being called to account for his behavior. Very few of us like to be reminded that we aren't following through on what we say we are doing.

One of the easiest ways to divert attention from ourselves is to call attention to someone else's behavior. If we can get others to pay attention to how poorly someone else is doing, then the focus is off us and our irresponsibility. That makes us feel a little better about ourselves because we aren't being reminded of our limitations. That's exactly what Peter did. He tried as hard as he could to get Jesus to tell him about someone else's business. He no doubt felt uncomfortable about what Jesus had just told him about his need to follow Jesus. So Peter may have been trying to get the focus off himself.

It is important to face your limitations as squarely as you can. It may hurt, but in the long run it will bring you to a healthier outlook and a more solid recovery.

■ *Father, help me to face my limitations with courage.*
R.M.

HE'S GOT A REAL ATTITUDE

Wine is a mocker,
Intoxicating drink arouses brawling,
And whoever is led astray by it is not wise.
—PROV. 20:1

He used to be such a great kid. Now he's sarcastic with everyone, and he's always angry. What went wrong?" The parents had worried expressions on their faces. Their son sat across the room, looking out the window. His actions said he thought his parents were jerks and he didn't need to be there.

Perhaps you recall a scene like this from the beginning of your recovery. You didn't think you had a problem other than everyone's being on your back. But the alcohol and drugs were clouding your head so you couldn't see the problems.

You keep getting high or drunk because you tell yourself things are fine; if they weren't, you would have to admit your problem and quit. Meanwhile, you don't take care of problems, and your life falls apart. People who care confront you about it. But because of the lies you tell yourself, you just get angry and wish they would leave you alone.

People keep pushing you to be the best you can be because they care. Addicts must choose to stick with substances or to listen to those who care. As long as you love booze and drugs more than the truth, you will stay angry at those who love you most.

■ *Lord, help me to stop denying that I have done wrong and talk to the people I have hurt.*

K.B.

THE DECEPTION OF PRIDE

The pride of your heart has deceived you . . .
You who say in your heart,
"Who will bring me down to the ground?"
—OBAD. 1:3

There once was a great knight who had won many battles for the glory of his king, who awarded him many medals and commendations for his valor and leadership. The knight had one problem: he was very proud. One day, on his way to a most glorious battle, the knight passed a little boy who had come out to cheer him on. The boy called out, "Sir, do you know you have a hole in the back of your armor?" The knight stopped and addressed the boy: "Boy you know nothing of what you are talking about. I have the greatest armorsmiths in the country. They don't make mistakes like that. Even if I had such a hole, I would never be caught off-guard long enough to be hurt!" And off he rode to battle, where he was mortally wounded because he was too proud to check out what the boy said. He didn't protect the hole, and therefore was hurt.

This story is a good example of what happens when you receive feedback from others and decide not to believe them. If you take an approach like that to your recovery, you will set yourself up for sure disaster. There will never be a point in your recovery where you will not benefit from being reminded of the basics. So pay attention to feedback that directs you away from your pride.

■ *Father, help me to pay attention to the basics of my recovery and not be too proud to listen.*

R.M.

LOOKS CAN BE DECEIVING

Do not look on the wine when it is red. . . .
At the last it bites like a serpent,
And stings like a viper.

—PROV. 23:31–32

There are many reasons people start using alcohol and drugs. The one we hear most is that people want to fit in, to be cool.

It's hard to tell what others are like on the inside, but when they look really happy on the outside, you think maybe they are. You know yourself on the inside, and sometimes you don't feel great. So when you see people having fun drinking and drugging, it's natural to want to join in.

You see beer ads with really hip surfer dudes and great-looking women in small bikinis, and it all looks fun. Or you go to a party, and all the popular people are drinking and having what looks like a great time. But many of those beautiful people who seem to be handling life so well are bored and miserable inside. They just don't want to admit it. They may realize that alcohol doesn't make you feel as great as the commercials say. But they're still trying to get that high they see advertised.

Most people, like yourself, are looking for the thing that will make them content both inside and out. But when you watch people seeming to have so much fun, remember that not everything that looks great really is.

■ *Did substances bring you the happiness you longed for, or did they leave you still searching?*

K.B.

CHECK YOURSELF

*Let each one examine his own [actions], and
then he will have rejoicing in himself alone,
and not in another.* —GAL. 6:4

What is a test? Usually it is a means for cruel teachers
to torment their hapless and helpless students! Of
course, that is an overstatement. A test is a way to find
out what someone knows about a particular subject. It
is also a demonstration of that knowledge under a specific set of circumstances in one sitting. You learned it
over a period of time, maybe in many different places
(classroom, your room, the library), and certainly on
many different days. The teacher assumes that if you
can gather all the material together to communicate it
under those circumstances, then you can do it at any
time.

Throughout your recovery, you will need to frequently "test" your actions and progress in recovery.
You need to look at how committed you are to attending
meetings or calling the person who is holding you accountable for your behavior. Don't compare yourself to
someone else. That is a sure way to get discouraged.
Recovery is a process that is very individualized. It happens differently for different people in spite of the fact
that they all arrive at the same place—an ongoing recovery from their addiction.

■ *It is important to "test" your recovery process on an
ongoing basis.*

R.M.

WATCH OUT!

"Don't spend all of your time thinking about eating or drinking or worrying. . . . If you do, the final day will suddenly catch you."
—LUKE 21:34 CEV

I don't know why I do it. I don't want to do drugs, but before I even think about it, I'm high," Frank said. He kept on getting high even after he had said many times that he really wanted to quit. It's as if some people are so down on themselves that they choose harmful ways of coping with problems.

When your life is difficult and you've made many problems for yourself, there isn't much sense in trying to make it better. It's like having a big pack on your back: If it feels too heavy to carry anyway, what does adding one more thing matter? Addictions are like that weight. They are impossible weights, and after a while, you just stop caring. Eventually, you start living from one party to the next, from one drunk or high to the next. The future doesn't matter, just the pleasure of now.

The future someday will be today, however, so it is important to begin looking out, to begin emptying the pack. You may feel extremely burdened today, but if you improve a little bit each day, one day at a time, you will be able to spring to your feet to meet the future when it arrives.

■ *Watch out! Don't add more to an already overburdened pack of troubles.*

K.B.

GETTING AHEAD OF YOURSELF

"Do not worry about tomorrow, for tomorrow will worry about its own things. Sufficient for the day is its own trouble."

—MATT. 6:34

Fear is an awful feeling. All at once it caves in on us, and we feel helpless to protect ourselves and out of control. It is probably the feeling of being out of control that we hate most, because someone or something else has to be in control. However, fear is a stream that is constantly trickling through our minds. We can't completely escape it. We can try through addictions to medicate it, to make ourselves believe it isn't there.

It is important to remember that worry is a part of our everyday experience. Attempting to get rid of it is misdirecting our efforts and expending our energies in a way that leads to exhaustion and further problems. In addition to that, as Jesus makes it clear, tomorrow has enough trouble of its own. We don't have to make ourselves miserable by adding that to today!

You need to realize that you can do nothing about tomorrow, and you can't change history either. The problem is that you may not live that way. You may worry about tomorrow and use the past as an excuse to do nothing today. Concentrate on today—that is your challenge. It will be more than enough to keep you busy until tomorrow comes.

■ *Father, help me to concentrate on what I can change, and that is today.*

R.M.

ONE LAST FLING

Jesus answered, "Anyone who starts plowing and keeps looking back isn't worth a thing in God's kingdom!" —LUKE 9:62 CEV

Most addicts plan to clean up their act and get around to recovery eventually. They know they can't continue living the way they've been living. But they procrastinate, putting off recovery, trying to squeeze one more day of fun out of life.

Ask people what they plan to do in life and they'll give you some goal they have for the future. Some will say they want to be lawyers; others will say engineers or mechanics or architects. My guess is that very few would say addicts. So why are so many people addicted to alcohol and drugs?

These people thought they could put off recovery until they were older and had to get serious about life. They kept putting it off until they one day discovered they *were* older and hadn't done anything about it. Because of their addiction, they never really grew up.

What's really important to you? There are millions of excuses you can make to put off doing what is right. But none of these is important enough to keep you from allowing God to clean up your life and lead you down His path to recovery. Don't wait until tomorrow; when it gets here it will be today, and you'll still be waiting until tomorrow.

■ *God, nothing is as important as You. Guide my recovery, because I know I can't put it off until tomorrow.*

K.B.

PLAYING WITH FIRE

Then He struck the men of Beth Shemesh,
because they had looked into the ark of the
LORD.   —1 SAM. 6:19

Some people try to convince themselves that they can do what they have been told countless times they shouldn't do. That's what happened to the poor fellows who decided to look into the Ark of the Lord even though they knew the rule against doing so. That rule was there for their own good, but they thought they were different from everyone else. Unfortunately for them and their families, they were wrong. It's easy to look at this situation, and say, "I wouldn't have been that dumb!" But there are or will be many times through the course of your recovery where you might find yourself "playing with fire" the way these men did. If you play with fire long enough, you are sure to get burned!

Watch your pride and the belief that you are somehow different from everybody else. If you think you are invincible, you are sure to get careless and set yourself up to fail in some situation you should have avoided. There is nothing wrong with avoiding situations where you know you will fail. Why put yourself through such difficulties in which you inevitably will fail? You need to admit your weaknesses and do what you must to protect your progress in recovery.

■ *Father, help me to be realistic about what I can handle and avoid flirting with evil.*

R.M.

THE SHOW-OFF

"If you put yourself above others, you will be put down. But if you humble yourself, you will be honored." —LUKE 18:14b CEV

Darryl was too confident about his recovery. At first he found it easy to quit drinking; he just told himself he would stop, and he did. It was all a matter of willpower, and he told people that if they were as strong as he was, they could quit just as easily. In fact, he considered people who went to A.A. meetings to be weak.

What he didn't realize was that most addicts quit for short periods of time. They go for a week, two weeks, even a month or more without drinking or getting high and then start up again because they have convinced themselves they are in control. Of course they're not, or they wouldn't start again.

A couple of weeks later, Darryl acted like a total jerk at a friend's party, first puking on the carpet and then passing out in the bathroom. The great willpower about which he had been boasting became a joke at school.

A person who is powerless is a person who is humble. If you've really admitted to yourself that you need help to keep from using, you certainly have no reason to be proud. Anyone who really is working at recovery knows that he is just another addict trying to stay clean and sober one more day.

■ *I still have much work to do, and Your power, Lord, is making the difference in my life.*

K.B.

Resting on Your Laurels

"Do not . . . say to yourselves, 'We have Abraham as our father.' . . . God is able to raise up children to Abraham from these stones."
—MATT 3:9

Laurels were given to the winner of a contest in ancient Greece. They were a tangible symbol of what the person had accomplished. He could wear these laurels on his head for everyone to know what he had done.

The problem with accomplishing a lot is that you may tend to rest on your laurels. However, you can't rest on your past accomplishments. You must always strive to do and be better. That is what prompted Jesus' response in our passage for today. The Jews thought they could rest on their position as children of Abraham (their ancestral father) to carry them through rather than striving to be better. They claimed someone else's accomplishments to keep them safe.

You can never rest on your past accomplishments in recovery. If you do you will stagnate, and before long relapse. You must keep pushing to be better. The Olympic athlete doesn't take his gold medals back to the Olympics again and say, "I can get more because I got these!" No, he still has to compete and be better than everyone else in order to get another gold medal. Keep striving and don't rest on your laurels in recovery.

■ *Father, help me to not rest on my laurels and keep pressing for my recovery.*

R.M.

HUMILITY

Jesus got up, removed his outer garment, and wrapped a towel around his waist. . . . Then he began washing his disciples' feet.
—JOHN 13:4–5 CEV

One of the most important things to remember about your recovery is that you have to stay humble. Once you start to become proud of yourself and the things you have done, you begin to move backward and will take credit for things God has done. Pride ruins recovery.

In Jesus' day there was a custom that a servant washed the feet of the master's guests. That was because people wore sandals and got dusty feet when they walked around. One day Jesus acted like a servant and washed the feet of his disciples. Imagine that! God's Son, the King of the universe on His knees washing others' feet.

That's the attitude you need to have. Instead of being proud of yourself and thinking you are better than others, you need to be willing to act like a servant. The best way to do this is to start thinking of ways to be helpful to others and then doing things for them. That will be hard, because addiction has taught you to use others to meet your selfish needs, not to serve them. But with God's help, you can learn how to let getting what you want take second place to being a servant.

■ *Teach me to be like Jesus. I want to learn how to serve others and not myself and my own desires.*

K.B.

NEVER TOO HIGH TO FALL

"Your fierceness has deceived you. . . .
Though you make your nest as high as the eagle,
I will bring you down from there."

—JER. 49:16

What are you proud of? Is it how far you have come in your recovery program? Is it how long you have been clean of drugs? Is it that people look to you for advice and support in their recovery? There is nothing wrong with pride as long as it is properly handled. Pride improperly handled is toxic, and it sets you up to be deceived and to place confidence in things that will surely let you down. It is important that you find ways to keep your pride in the proper place.

The people to whom God was talking in today's passage had handled their pride improperly. They had allowed their accomplishments and other external things to be the focus of their pride and had lost perspective in the fact that God had allowed them such things in the first place. They had rejected the notion of their own helplessness and powerlessness to bring about such positive accomplishments and had made them as their own.

Pride handled in its correct perspective focuses on what God has accomplished in your life and on how He enables you to be abstinent for so long, or has been gracious enough to give you success and respect from others. Pride handled this way allows you to learn from others.

■ *Father, help me to place my pride in what You are doing in my life.*

R.M.

HURTING YOURSELF

Christ never sinned! But God treated him as a sinner, so that Christ could make us acceptable to God. —2 COR. 5:21 CEV

I guess I feel like I've got to pay for my sins, like I've got to hurt myself to make up for hurting others," said Rob.

Rob seemed determined to make a mess of his life, and we were trying to figure out why. He was a pretty good guy; he just made some stupid decisions. And the result was that he almost always felt bad about himself.

Rob had always figured he was a burnout and that was the way things were. So he was surprised when I told him he had a choice about the way he would be, but he was even more bewildered when I asked him why he made the choices he did.

Rob's response to my question made sense. I knew he hurt inside. He had just never admitted it to himself or anyone else. He kept messing up, thinking that it was the price for his mistakes.

With God, you don't have to hurt yourself to make up for your sins. Christ paid for our sins when He died for us. He paid the price so we wouldn't have to. Now we are free to get on with the work of recovery.

As long as you continue hurting yourself, you cannot make progress. Instead, you will be stuck trying to do God's work for Him.

■ *God, I accept your Son's death as payment for my mistakes.*

K.B.

PROPER HUMILITY

I am the least of the apostles, who am not worthy to be called an apostle, because I persecuted the church of God.

—1 COR. 15:9

It is truly a slam to call someone a snob. Most teens try to make sure they are not perceived as a snob. They really "rip" on themselves or cut themselves down. They believe this is the best way to make sure others will not see them as arrogant.

The goal you have chosen is indeed a worthy one—humility. We all appreciate someone who has great talent and at the same time is humble. But tearing yourself down is not the way to be humble.

Tearing yourself down, whether you do it out loud in front of others or simply to yourself, is a good way to feel rotten about yourself. You make it harder to accomplish anything—after all, how can anyone who is so bad accomplish anything?

Paul wasn't tearing himself down in our passage today. He was stating a reality that kept his pride in the proper perspective, and also reminded him of just how good God had been to him. The best way to be humble is to understand that anything you accomplish is not because of you solely, but because God has been faithful to enable you to do it.

■ *Father, help me to not tear myself down in order to be humble.*

R.M.

GOD DOESN'T MAKE JUNK

You have covered me in my mother's womb.
I will praise You, for I am fearfully and
wonderfully made. —PS. 139:13–14

Dan was working on seeing himself for what he really was. At first it was frightening, because he had denied for so long that anything was wrong. He had admitted for a while that he might have a problem, but now was seeing that he was worse off than he thought. He finally began to wonder why God had let him become this way; he thought God had made a mistake in making him.

If you're like Dan, you're wondering if God made a mistake in making you. Not at all! God never makes mistakes, and you're no exception. Even if you have screwed things up pretty bad, God still sees inside you to the person you really are, and He loves you.

When you were still in your mother's womb, God saw you and knew what you would become. He watched you grow, cell by cell, and cared deeply about you. And when you were born, and as you have grown into the person you are today, God has known every step you have taken. And He still loves you.

God sees what you have been and what you still can be. He made you—and He doesn't make mistakes—and that makes you a wonderful person.

■ *Thanks, God, for loving me in spite of the mess I've made of my life.*

K.B.

HEALTHY WEAKNESSES

The Spirit also helps in our weaknesses. For we do not know what we should pray for as we ought, but the Spirit Himself makes intercession for us.
—ROM. 8:26

It seems odd that there could be such a thing as a healthy weakness. But there is. A "healthy" weakness is a need we recognize we have.

Weaknesses serve the very important function of reminding us of our humanity. Sometimes we lose sight of the fact that we are, indeed, human and can make mistakes. If we try to convince ourselves that we shouldn't have weaknesses, we set ourselves up to be dissatisfied with our efforts in everything we do or attempt to do. When we, instead, recognize our weaknesses, we are reminded that we are human and we can give ourselves a break and be a little more forgiving when we make a mistake. Doing that makes us more able to cope with the usual hassles and mess-ups of a typical day, and it preserves our commitment to recovery.

Weaknesses also help us to understand where our true strength comes from. We need to work at our recovery, but it is God who truly blesses our effort and makes it successful. It is pretty hard to depend on God for our recovery when we think we are strong and free from weaknesses. We need to be reminded just how weak we are to realize that we can depend on God for the strength we need.

■ *Father, thank You for my weakness so that I can learn to depend on You for success in my recovery.*

R.M.

SUPERMAN

For by You I can run against a troop,
And by my God I can leap over a wall.
—PS. 18:29

Faster than a speeding bullet. Stronger than a locomotive. Able to leap tall buildings with a single bound." Each episode of "Superman" begins with those words. One of my favorite games as a child was to pin a beach towel around my neck and pretend I was the Man of Steel. Running around the house, I would conquer the world and believe nothing could hurt me.

Too often males try to be like that. It's one thing to play Superman when you're a little kid; it's completely different to live as if nothing really can hurt you.

The truth is that life can be difficult, and we all feel pain. Even those who seem to cope with every situation, no matter how hard, feel deep pain. There is no way to avoid it. Those who do try to escape pain by drinking or drugging are in denial.

Simply hiding your hurts makes you fake and hinders your recovery process. Instead of running away, turn to God and ask for help to cope with these feelings. He won't take them away or help you escape. But He will give you the strength and courage to face hurtful things.

■ *God, instead of my using substances for moral support, give me Your strength.*

K.B.

A BROKEN DOWN CITY

Whoever has no rule over his own spirit
Is like a city broken down, without walls.
—PROV. 25:28

The idea of a city with walls is foreign to us today. In Old Testament times, though, walls were common. There had to be some way to protect people from invading armies and other villains, and walls were the perfect solution. Walls were a way to protect people who defended the city as well as a means of keeping people out of the city. It is an interesting image the writer of today's scripture draws upon in terms of self-control.

Many guys think the best way to show their masculinity is to act it out aggressively or sexually, through abusive behavior toward others, or through the abuse of substances. This seems to be a common way to show just how "tough" they are.

The writer of Proverbs takes a different view of showing how "tough" you are. He states that the more someone is out of control the more vulnerable he becomes. We see that when guys on our hospital unit explode, making them more open to attack and hurt than when they learn to control their feelings. The one thing to remember is that you have to bring your walls down to explode. Maybe it would be better to learn how to control and express your feelings appropriately rather than exposing yourself because of your lack of control.

■ *It is better to learn self-control than to blow up at people, hurting them and yourself.*

R.M.

FIGHTING WORDS

A soft answer turns away wrath,
But a harsh word stirs up anger.
—PROV. 15:1

Peter didn't know when to back down. He got suspended from school for cursing at the principal. He lost his job because he got mad at the boss and refused to do what he was asked to do. His girlfriend broke up with him because of their constant arguing. His parents were always mad at him. And he was always getting into fights.

Whenever someone got mad at him, Peter would say something mean back, and a fight would break out. He couldn't see that he was making his life a mess.

When you get high or drunk, you can't see things clearly; your mind is in a fog. For Peter, this meant that he was always saying something obnoxious, which made the situation worse. The result was that Peter always came across as a hard-guy who was looking for a fight. He usually found what he was looking for.

Before you respond to someone who is angry with you, remember that keeping your head and answering calmly will prevent fights. When you feel angry, think carefully about the way you wish to respond and use a cool answer; you'll find that it usually makes the situation better.

■ *Help me to remember to chill out when I am angry*
instead of aggravating the situation.

K.B.

CONTINUE TO DO GOOD

Let those who suffer according to the will of God commit their souls to Him in doing good.
—1 PET. 4:19

It is extremely difficult to continue working your recovery if people disapprove of your choice to change the direction of your life. Suddenly, the whole journey of recovery doesn't seem worth it. This attitude, though, shows what your motivation is in recovery: to have approval from others. When they withdraw their approval, you lose your steam for recovery.

What few realize as they work through recovery is that more people than you can imagine are stuck in their own patterns of abuse and dysfunction. They will give you the hardest time and will be the most disapproving and discouraging in your recovery. It will seem as if they want you to succeed, only to burst your bubble.

Disapproval from others is probably the most baffling thing about recovery. You might assume that everyone will be delighted with your progress. However, your recovery will remind them of their lack of courage to confront their own addiction. Instead of confronting their addiction, they turn on you and make you the problem. So be ready. Don't be discouraged just because some people are not delighted with your recovery. You are on the right track, and their disapproval is proof of it!

■ *Father, help me to stick with my recovery work when people are disapproving.*

R.M.

YOU GET WHAT YOU PAY FOR

You cannot fool God, so don't make a fool of yourself! You will harvest what you plant.
—GAL. 6:7 CEV

The day our baby was born, my wife and I took many pictures. We planned to send them to friends and relatives so they could share our excitement. When the pictures came back, we were disappointed to discover that many were ruined because we had used a cheap camera. When you buy something cheap, "you get what you pay for."

Life is like that, too. You get back only what you put in. In other words, if you study ten minutes the night before a test, you shouldn't expect an *A*. If you scam people all the time, you shouldn't expect them to trust you. If you don't work hard at your job, don't expect your boss to give you a raise. If you get high or drunk to avoid life's problems, don't expect them to be gone when you sober up.

Recovery is hard work. When you attend A.A. or N.A. and work the steps as hard as you can, the rewards will be worth it. You will get back what you put into your program. The more hard work you do, the better able you will be to deal with life without substances clouding your brain. But if you expect recovery to be simple and quick, and put out only a tiny bit of effort, you'll get bad results, as we did with our cheap camera.

■ *God, since I get only what I work hard for in recovery, give me the strength to do my best.*

K.B.

WATCH YOUR INVESTMENTS!

*"Do not lay up for yourselves treasures on
earth, where moth and rust destroy and
where thieves break in and steal."*
—MATT. 6:19

You can always tell just how serious someone is about
recovery by the way he manages his time and energy.
Are you developing the habit of being accountable to
someone else who is further down the path of recovery?
If not, you need to re-examine your priorities. Time is a
limited resource, and you have to make some decision
about how you will use it. If you spend more time on
socializing and other things, your life is sure to show the
effects of such investments. On the other hand, if you
spend the time necessary to cultivate a solid program of
recovery by attending support meetings, keeping up to
date with a sponsor, or supporting others in their recovery, you will find success and growth.

Emotional energy is much the same. Where you invest it will show in your life. If you invest your energies
into obtaining things, in relationships, or in athletics,
your level of maturity in those areas is bound to show. If
you invest the necessary energy into thinking on and
investing in your recovery, it will show. When you make
such investments they will bring forth fruit in the same
measure and intensity with which you have worked at it.

■ *Father, help me to invest my time and energy according to my priorities.*

R.M.

THE TELEPHONE LINEMAN

*"The kingdom of heaven is like what
happens when someone finds treasure hidden
in a field and buries it again."*
—MATT. 13:44 CEV

Once a telephone lineman was digging a path for new telephone cables in a field. The trench digger he was using suddenly struck something hard and stopped. He dug a little deeper and discovered it was a chest full of gold coins and jewels, enough to make him rich for the rest of his life.

But he was an honest man. He felt that just taking the chest would be wrong. He wanted to do the right thing, so after work, he set about selling all his belongings. Now others thought he was crazy. Why would someone sell all the things he owned? Eventually, he raised enough money to buy the house and land he had been working on just a few days earlier. For such a great treasure, he had been willing to risk anything, including losing all his belongings and having others think he was nuts.

Recovery is like that buried treasure chest. Sometimes it means giving up lots of stuff. Friends who used to party with you might think you've gone insane. You might have to change your whole life to make it work. In the end, though, you have the treasure that will make you happy, while others are still living the same old, miserable lifestyle.

■ *Keep your eyes on the treasure. If you give up things you used to love, it will be worth it.*

K.B.

NO ROOM?

The wicked in his proud countenance
does not seek God;
God is in none of his thoughts.
—PS. 10:4

Sometimes we act as if time is infinite. We keep loading activities into our days and don't understand that sooner or later we will run out of time. Something has to give to make room for new things.

Do your parents ever remark that they don't know how you could possibly put one more thing into your room? One more poster or one more piece of stereo equipment would just about leave no room for you!

That is pretty much like life. You might find yourself doing more and more and, before long, you have no time to concentrate on your recovery. You will have to make a decision about what must go—an excruciating decision. It seems that each activity or person you have allowed to bid for your time has been extremely important. How could you possibly begin to scale back the time allotted to them?

What is most important to you? Recovery or time with a person or activity? Remember that to continue to grow into health you need to give recovery the time it needs. As long as you remain unfinished in the business of recovery, you really can't give friends and activities all of you.

■ *Father, help me to keep enough room to concentrate on my recovery.*

R.M.

BE QUIET!

Be still, and know that I am God;
I will be exalted among the nations,
I will be exalted in the earth!
                                        —PS. 46:10

You rush in the morning to get ready for school. You rush to class. You rush to lunch. You rush home and then to your job or studying. It's a big race to fit everything into the day.

With all this rushing around, when do you have time to think? It is important to have a time each day to be quiet and reflect on what God is doing in your life. How can you ever hear what God is saying if you're constantly in a hurry?

The best time to reflect on what God is doing in your life is in the morning. Later in the day you'll probably feel totally exhausted. But in the morning, things are usually quiet and more relaxed, so morning is an ideal time to talk to God and to listen as He gently brings to mind things you need to prepare for the day ahead.

Wake up fifteen to thirty minutes earlier than usual. Keep a notebook in your room and write down what God brings to your mind. Perhaps you might use this devotional each morning to give you ideas about things to talk to God about. Pick one thing and think about it throughout the day. A little quiet time each day will help you think more clearly about recovery.

■   *God, help me to remember to set aside a few minutes*
    each day to spend alone with You.

                                                        K.B.

WHAT ARE YOU PLANTING?

You have plowed wickedness;
You have reaped iniquity.
You have eaten the fruit of lies.
        —HOS. 10:13

What are you planting in your recovery program? Are you sowing the foundation for a good, solid recovery or are you allowing weeds to creep in? It is important to understand that the best way to sow the seeds of a good recovery is to keep firmly in your mind that you are indeed powerless over your addiction. God does the work of change in your life. Humility and a firm sense of who you are and the limitations you have to live with are important parts of staying on track and building for the future.

The best way to sow weeds in your recovery is to get the idea that you are doing pretty good. You may begin to think that you're a pretty strong person for doing as well as you are with your recovery. Read again today's scripture. What is the reason for reaping evil and eating the fruit of deception? It is the notion that you are sufficient all by yourself and that you can do it alone. The minute you begin to think that way you become a sitting duck for relapse. It is self-deception to leave God out of the picture in your recovery. When you do, you also leave out the power necessary for continued success.

■   *It is important to remember that you can't do your recovery without God.*

                                          R.M.

LOAVES AND FISHES

*[Jesus] broke the bread and . . . divided the
two fish. . . . [His] disciples picked up twelve
large baskets of leftover bread and fish.*
—MARK 6:41–42 CEV

I don't know if I can make it this way. I mean, there's
so much to learn, and I'm not sure I can remember it
all," Mike moaned. He was right; he did have a lot to
learn. And learning didn't come easy for Mike. He had
a learning disability that made it hard for him to understand new things. But even that doesn't make recovery
impossible.

Once Jesus fed five thousand people with two fish
and five loaves of bread. The disciples were like Mike;
they didn't believe they had enough to do the job. It
would have cost almost a year's pay to feed all those
people. But Jesus saw something the disciples didn't.
He knew that God could take something that seemed
too small and make it much bigger. That little bit of food
ended up feeding all five thousand people, with twelve
large baskets left over.

Like Mike, you may not think you have enough going
for you to make it in recovery. And you may be right.
But God can take the little you *do* have and make it into
something much bigger. If you start worrying, you're
not looking at what God can do. Don't give up because
recovery seems too hard. God will take your strengths
and multiply them, just as He did with the loaves and
fishes.

■   *God, take the things I have going for me and make
them bigger.*

K.B.

DIFFERENT RATES

Having then gifts differing according to the grace that is given to us, let us use them . . . in proportion to our faith. —ROM. 12:6

Just as God has given us different gifts to help His church, so also he has given us different abilities to deal with recovery. People work on recovery very differently and yet end up at the same place with equally good results. Certainly some important elements are found in almost all successful recovery programs, but at the same time there are a lot of differences that make those recovery programs very different.

You'll discover this if you compare your recovery program with someone else's. Many people make such comparisons, and they always think theirs is an inferior path to recovery. The problem is the eyes they are using to view others' programs. Our beliefs very much influence how we see things. If we don't feel good about ourselves, we are likely to view anything we do as inferior and anything anyone else does as vastly superior.

Comparisons are only as good as the perspective they are built on. If you are getting good feedback from others about how you are doing, you can look at someone else's path to recovery and remind yourself that it is okay to be different. It is one thing to be different and quite another to be better.

■ *Remember that just because your recovery is different it's not of poor quality.*

R.M.

GET READY

*When Jesus saw the man and realized that
he had been crippled for a long time, he
asked him, "Do you want to be healed?"*
—JOHN 5:6 CEV

When a person has been a certain way for a long time, he gets used to it. There are lots of people who don't change. They think it's easier to stay the way they are than to try to be different. Sometimes in therapy even little changes can take a long time when the person refuses to see that he needs to act differently.

Even when you know that you can't go on the way you are, you may not be entirely certain that you want to try new things. So before change can finally take place, you have to make your heart ready for it. Unless you do this, you will fight becoming the new person God is willing to create.

By entering recovery, you admitted to yourself that things were not good in your life. Now it is time to be absolutely certain that you want to be a totally new person. God is waiting for you to make that decision. Before you jump in too quickly and then later fight off what God is trying to do, take some time and get your heart ready for what He is about to do. Ask God to work in you to prepare you to become the new person He wants you to be.

■   *God, work in my heart to make me ready to accept
    the new person You want to make me.*

K.B.

RECOVERY PARADOXES

"Whoever of you desires to be first shall be slave of all."
                                        —MARK 10:44

A paradox is a statement that seems contrary to common sense and yet is true. In a way it is a statement that reverses something you thought was another way. Jesus used a paradox in the scripture for today. There are many paradoxes throughout treatment and recovery.

For example, think about the truth in admitting your powerlessness over your addiction. You have no doubt heard that this is the first step to recovery. The problem has been that you were unwilling to accept the fact that in order to overcome your addiction you must admit your helplessness to overcome it. Something about this just doesn't seem to make sense. It would seem to the average person that in order to overcome anything you must be strong. From this strength, then, you can begin to deal with your addiction. The problem with this thinking is that there is no recognition of the need for God in your life to make the kind of change you are seeking.

Don't get bogged down with paradoxes. Focus on the truth that as you are willing to admit your weakness you will also find new strength from God to carry out your recovery.

■ *In order to continue your recovery you have to be willing to admit weakness.*

                                                    R.M.

LETTING GO

*Let the Spirit change your way of thinking
and make you into a new person. You were
created to be like God.*
—EPH. 4:23–24 CEV

I don't know what God wants me to do next, but I'm ready to get on with my recovery." Sam had come a long way. By age seventeen he had been in rehab twice. Each time he said just the right things to make everyone think he was serious, but as soon as he got out he started getting high.

This time something was different. Even Sam wasn't totally sure what had made the difference, but he knew that if he didn't get it together soon, he would mess up what was left of his life. On the other hand, he knew himself very well and understood that it wouldn't take much for him to fail. He worried that nothing could change him, that maybe he was stuck in addiction forever.

It was encouraging for Sam to hear that he could be a new person. Even when you believe that it is impossible to change, when you've failed many times before, God still is able to make you different. Like Sam, you may know that things need to change, but feel hopeless because of all the times you've tried and failed. This time, stop depending on yourself and allow God to work in you. Where you've failed in the past, God can be successful if you'll just depend on Him.

■ *God, I place my recovery in Your hands and depend on You to remove whatever keeps me addicted.*

K.B.

WEAKNESS TURNED TO STRENGTH

The foolishness of God is wiser than men,
and the weakness of God is stronger than
men.
                                              —1 COR. 1:25

Recovery often requires the unexpected. In fact, some aspects of recovery will seem just the opposite of what you expect. Your peers have more than likely set a standard for strength that you buy into. It is to be strong and not let anyone see your weakness. If people see your weakness, they will take advantage of it and use it against you. Therefore, look out for number one and guard yourself from hurt or pain by not showing feelings that could be taken as weak. Sound familiar?

This attitude will hinder your recovery rather than help you. It will stand in the way of your learning how to express emotions appropriately and assertively without having to store them up. In today's scripture there is a reversal, or so it would seem, in that God's foolishness is wiser than any of our wisdom. That means if you follow what God says you may be branded weak and foolish. Ask yourself whether you would rather be foolish in other people's eyes and follow God, or whether you prefer to be wise in others' eyes and foolish about recovery. People will tell you that the healthy thing to do is to be a "fool." Then, you might as well be a healthy fool who overcomes his addiction than a sick wise man who stays addicted!

■   *Father, help me to follow Your wisdom rather than*
    the wisdom of others.

                                                      R.M.

PRUNING THE TREE

"He trims clean every branch that does produce fruit, so that it will produce even more fruit." —JOHN 15:2 CEV

Last summer a friend told me about the apple trees in his backyard. He said that if he left them alone, they would produce small, bitter-tasting apples. On the other hand, if he cut away some of the branches, the remaining apples would grow bigger and would taste much better.

Recovery is like taking care of apple trees. Many things in your life need to be removed to make it better. God the gardener slowly cuts away at the weeds that keep the good from growing. Patiently He watches over your life, seeing the negative attitudes and behaviors. With a snip here and a chop there, He prunes the branches, making certain what is left will be strong and healthy.

This pruning can sometimes be painful. It is not easy to let go of parts of yourself that are comfortable. But God sees the whole tree, and He knows enough to take away the things that keep you stuck in your addiction. If you really want to be healthy, you must trust that God's gardening skills are far better than your own. When His pruning gets painful, remember that in the long run the result will be a much better life.

■ *Lord, prune away what keeps me from being all I can be. Help me to be solid and strong.*

K.B.

THE DOOR TO TRUE STRENGTH

*It is sown in dishonor, it is raised in glory. It
is sown in weakness, it is raised in power.*
—1 COR. 15:43

The door to true strength is through your weaknesses.
Our culture has been quite good at making it absolutely
clear that it is bad to be weak, and good to be strong. In
movies, the hero is strong, unfeeling, and unflinching to
pain. He always wins and always gets the girl. What a
picture to live up to!

What movies often leave out is that the key to strength
is understanding weakness. If you don't know where
you are weak in your quest for recovery, then you are a
sitting duck for problems. How can you possibly defend
against something you don't know exists? It would be
like assuming you are not wounded when your body is
screaming for attention. Sooner or later it will shut down
and you won't be able to do anything. So it is to your
advantage to understand where you are weak. Once you
understand that you can begin to devise strategies for
protecting that weakness until you can grow strong in
that area.

Are you weak in dealing with friends who are still
using drugs or alcohol? Try to understand why you are
weak in this area. Talk to someone who can help you
figure it out. In the meantime, be careful of hanging
around these friends.

■ *Father, help me to accept my weaknesses and use
them to grow strong in my recovery.*

R.M.

DOES GOD KNOW WHEN I NEED HIM?

"The eyes of the LORD run to and fro . . . to show Himself strong on behalf of those whose heart is loyal to Him."

—2 CHRON. 16:9a

When you were a little kid, the world seemed small to you. You didn't know much outside of family, church, and school. As you got older you discovered a big world out there, with lots of people, places, and things. A child can easily believe that God is watching out for him, but a teen begins to wonder how God can have time to be with everyone in so many places.

Now that you've chosen to place God in charge of your recovery program, you need a lot of strength, a lot of God's attention. You've probably asked yourself, "What if God doesn't notice me when I need Him the most?" If you have, you're not alone. Most people ask that question at some point during their recovery.

It is important not to see God as another being among so many on earth. That makes Him too small. He is constantly looking throughout the entire world, checking out who needs His power and when. Your job is to trust Him; His job is to be there for you when you need Him most. Real recovery requires real faith. Even though you may not understand God, be certain He understands you and will be there when you are weak.

■ *Thanks, God, for knowing when I need Your help the most.*

K.B.

BOAST IN THE RIGHT STUFF

If I must boast, I will boast in the things which concern my infirmity.
—2 COR. 11:30

You may remember the movie *The Right Stuff,* about the earliest astronauts, who defied the odds to launch our country into manned space flight. They became heroes because of their courage and vision in such a daring program. They were cocky and self-confident about their talent, strength, and ability to carry them through almost any situation. Their self-confidence contributed heavily to our country's progress in the space race. The problem with such confidence is that it is based on things that are temporary and eventually fail. Sooner or later, these abilities and strengths give out, and then what are you left with? Do you depend on your intelligence and stamina to get you through recovery?

Paul came to understand that through his weakness God's grace and power to change could be seen. Therefore, Paul was even more intent on boasting about his weakness because it was proof of God's power to overcome any obstacle. It can be the same for you and your recovery. Don't fear your weakness. Hand it over to God and see what He can do. Through weakness, not strength, will you see how God can overcome the most significant obstacles to your recovery.

■ *Father, help me to let go of my weaknesses and give them to You to help me overcome them.*

R.M.

WALKING THROUGH THE FIRE

. . . You are going through testing that is like walking through fire. Be glad for the chance to suffer as Christ suffered.
—1 PET. 4:12–13 CEV

Jewelry stores have rows of gold earrings, chains, bracelets, and so on. Gold sparkles and looks rich, but it didn't begin that way. In fact, when it came from the mine, it was full of impurities and looked like a rock. In order to get out the garbage, it had to be placed over intense heat until the solid gold melted out.

Recovery is like that melting process. The addict starts out like gold ore, full of all sorts of flaws. He's unable to concentrate enough for school, has tons of problems, feels bad about himself, and can't get by without alcohol and drugs.

But God sees the gold inside. He knows that with some fire the imperfections can be melted away, and the solid man inside can begin to shine. So He allows difficulties and challenges to dissolve away the impurities. Meanwhile, the addict grows stronger as he handles harder problems.

Sometimes the addict resents the purification process, and thinks recovery is not worth the trouble. But you can be different! Instead of feeling angry about the fiery difficulties you must walk through, you can be happy that God cares enough to melt you and shape you into something rich and strong.

■ *God, thank You for helping me get rid of the garbage that keeps me from being my best.*

K.B.

Appearing weak

I was with you in weakness, in fear, and in much trembling. —1 COR. 2:3

Have you ever heard the sayings, "All that glitters is not gold" and "You can't judge a book by its cover"? Both of these sayings make it clear that the way things look may not always be how they actually are. Take the ant, for example. The ant doesn't look like much until you begin to understand just how strong it is. If you tried to carry on your back the equivalent of what an ant carries, you would be astounded by the tremendous amount of weight these tiny creatures manage on a regular basis.

Do you strive to look strong in your recovery? That may not be the best approach to having the best recovery from your addiction. Now, I'm not saying that you should go around looking and acting weak. On the contrary, your focus shouldn't be on how you look, but how you are. In other words, you need to concentrate on the character qualities that are needed for a lifestyle of recovery. Paul, the writer of today's scripture, wasn't concerned with looking weak and fearful. He kept his mind and life-focus on God and His power in his life. That is what you need to do. Keep your focus on God and His power to enable you to overcome your addiction.

■ *Father, help me to focus on character qualities that will keep me on the path to recovery.*

R.M.

How could God let this happen?

Don't blame God when you are tempted! . . .
Our desires make us sin, and when sin is
finished with us, it leaves us dead.
—JAMES 1:13–15 CEV

Every time Bill turned around, he was faced with another temptation to get high. He thought he had really turned his addiction over to God. He couldn't understand why God would allow so many temptations in his life. He asked, "If God really loves and cares about me, why doesn't He take away all my cravings, or make everyone leave me alone until I am stronger?"

Bill asked a question many addicts in recovery eventually consider. They start to accept that God is strong and can do anything. Then they wonder why God won't make their lives easier. Still looking for instant relief, they are angry that God lets them feel longings for the old days when they could just drink or get high to feel better. They blame God for their own desires.

For a long time, you allowed your cravings to control you. Now you are trying to change these yearnings. If God makes them dissappear like magic, you will never develop the strength to avoid drugs and alcohol, and someday they will again take over. It is easy to blame God for your problems, but be careful! Your desires are not God's. He will give you strength to handle them.

■ *Sometimes I blame You for my desires, God. Yet You didn't create my cravings; rather, You help me resist them.*

K.B.

DECIDE!

*"How long will you falter between t
opinions? If the LORD is God, follow
if Baal, then follow him."*

—1 KINGS 18:21

Boys have a tremendous capacity to dawdle. Once when I was fishing with my dad, I did a great job of dawdling. I wasn't fishing, and I wasn't helping either. I was just a waterbound version of a "couch potato." My father, in frustration over the bait I was wasting with my antics, said, "Either fish or cut bait!" In other words, decide what you are going to do, just don't sit there and do nothing. It was extremely frustrating for the serious fisherman.

That is what Elijah said to the Israelites—"Fish or cut bait!" Choose either Baal or God, whichever you believe deserves your trust. Are you on a plateau in your path to recovery? Sometimes plateaus are caused by indecision on your part, by your inability to make a choice. It may be because you don't want to make the wrong decision, or because you don't want to disappoint someone. Whatever the reason, remaining in limbo will slow your recovery. No matter what you choose, you will learn from it. If you're trying to always do the "right" thing, your efforts are misplaced; you will never please everyone. Concentrate on doing the right thing for your recovery, and you will be heading down the path to health.

■ *Father, help me to make necessary decisions in my pursuit of growth and healthy behavior.*

R.M.

GOD IS NOT YOUR FAIRY GODMOTHER

"Shall we indeed accept good from God, and shall we not accept adversity?"

—JOB 2:10

Many have a belief about God that makes trusting him in recovery hard. I call it the "Fairy Godmother Belief." You remember the story of Cinderella, who was so unhappy that she couldn't go to the ball with her stepsisters. Her fairy godmother appeared, waved her magic wand, and made everything wonderful.

Sometimes addicts think of God as a fairy godmother. They start recovery by admitting that drugs control them, and then turn things over to God. They expect God to do all sorts of magical things, while they sit around and do nothing. When the first problems appear, they wonder where their fairy godmother went; they get discouraged and sometimes quit because of the difficulties they encounter.

It doesn't work like that. Recovery requires much effort on your part; it's not magic. You must accept the bad things that happen as well as the good. Only in fairy tales are magic wands waved and people live happily ever after. In the real world there are hard times and struggles, and it takes work to become an adult who can cope with life after the drugs and alcohol are gone. Stop waiting for God to do all the work. He will help, but He will not work alone.

■ *Lord, help me accept the hard times as well as the easy ones.*

K.B.

WALK THE TALK

If anyone among you thinks he is religious, and does not bridle his tongue but deceives his own heart, this one's religion is useless.
—JAMES 1:26

Terry was a likable guy. Most of the group members looked up to him. He seemed to have a good grip on the treatment program and was willing to help others with his insight into their behavior and motivations, knowing just what to say at the right time. He also was willing to confront people who were "scamming" with their abusive behavior.

Terry had one problem: He was good for everyone else, but not for himself. By focusing on everyone else's issues, he avoided avoid dealing with his own. He knew all the right things to say about treatment and recovery, but he wasn't able to put it into action. In other words, he didn't "walk the talk." It probably would have been better if Terry had said nothing at all than to give advice and be totally incapable of using it for himself. It makes you wonder just how good his advice actually was.

It is important to check yourself every once in a while. Ask a friend for feedback about whether you're "walking the talk." Your words have little power if they don't apply to yourself. You must be consistent with your words in order to deserve being listened to by others.

■ *Father, help me to be consistent with what I tell others and what I actually do about my recovery.*

R.M.

VICTIM THINKING

You observe trouble and grief,
To repay it by Your hand.
The helpless commits himself to You.
—PS. 10:14

Gary took the principle of being powerless a little too far. He saw himself as a victim of circumstance. Since he was powerless, he reasoned that he didn't have to try very hard, that he would let God take care of everything for him. Because of this attitude, every time something went wrong, Gary just blamed it on his powerlessness.

This attitude is called "victim thinking." Many addicts believe that they can't control anything, including their own behavior. They blame events and other people for the way they act. Since it's not really their fault, they don't have to take responsibility for the things they say and do. Victim thinking can damage recovery because the thinker fails to act on the things he knows are right.

In reality, we do choose our own actions. No one can *make* you do anything you know to be wrong. When you chose to start on the path to recovery, you began to take responsibility for the things you did as a result of your addiction, and you chose not to be a victim anymore. Now you need to start thinking of ways you fall back into that victim thinking, and stop blaming other people or events for the choices you make.

■   *God, help me to stop being a victim and start taking responsibility for my decisions.*

K.B.

OF GROWTH AND PAIN

No [discipline] seems to be joyful . . .
afterward it yields the peaceable fruit of
righteousness to those who have been trained
by it.
—HEB. 12:11

Pain has an incredibly disorganizing effect. It seems the minute we sense it, we launch into well-worn behaviors to get rid of it. Some people get so desperate for relief that they turn to drugs and alcohol. What makes these substances so powerful is their ability to absolutely remove any hint of pain the person feels.

You have taken on the job of changing this pattern of coping. To do so, though, you must find a way to reinterpret pain. Not all of the emotional pain you experience is bad. Some of it may be healthy rather than a sign that something is wrong.

To reinterpret pain, you must grasp the idea that with growth comes pain. After they finish treatment, many guys go back to dysfunctional families. When they begin to have more healthy behavior, they find that their families are hanging on to dysfunctional behaviors and are uncooperative.

With growth there is some pain, and it's this kind of healthy pain that you should look for as a sign of growth rather than trouble.

■ *Father, help me to see the healthy pain in my life*
and not run from it.

R.M.

THE BATTLE INSIDE

*In every part of me I discover something
fighting against my mind. . . . What a
miserable person I am. . . . Thank God!
Jesus Christ will rescue me.*
                    —ROM. 7:23–25 CEV

You were right! It's a lot tougher than I thought. I feel
like every day I have to fight a war to make it without
using." When fifteen-year-old Mark first sobered up, he
felt great. Without the chemicals he had been using, he
could think clearly for the first time in quite a while. He
felt so good that he believed he had his addiction
beaten.

I knew that wouldn't last long, so I confronted him
with the fact that the old feelings and desires would return. Mark responded that all I ever talked about was
the gloomy and depressing stuff. He wanted to forget
the past and get on with his new life. So when the old
cravings returned and things got tougher, he was surprised.

Staying clean is a battle. It's a fight to stick with the
decisions you've made and not change your mind.
Every day you will have new hurdles, and you must
keep on fighting. Those who think things are all better
will be shocked when the battle begins again. While it's
okay to be excited when things are going well, don't get
so confident that you become blind to the upcoming
problems. And never start thinking that you can do it
without your Higher Power.

■ *God, You are my weapon in the battle to stay clean
and sober. Be with me as I fight to recover.*

                                        K.B.

UNDERESTIMATING CONSEQUENC

They have lied about the LORD,
And said, "It is not He.
Neither will evil come upon us."
—JER. 5:12

How could I have been so stupid! How did I miss that?" Fred had been working well in treatment when he realized he had underestimated the consequences of not following through on his commitment to choose new friends. He thought he would be different from everyone else and be able to live in two worlds—that of substance abuse and that of being drug-free. He had listened to his friends when they said, "Oh, don't worry. Nothing is going to happen just this once. Besides, aren't you man enough to not listen to those wimps who can't live their own lives?" It is hard to look at actions and their consequences realistically when someone whispers in your ear that whatever you choose won't have any consequences either way. It is usually in the presence of another person whom we want to impress that we forget all we have learned about looking at the consequences of our behavior realistically.

Remember that your choices will always have consequences whether you see them or not. If our decisions had immediate consequences we could avoid a lot of the pain in our lives. But that isn't how we learn. Sometimes it takes some pretty drastic consequences to get our attention.

■ *Father, help me to avoid underestimating the consequences of my decisions.*

R.M.

PERSONAL MORAL VALUES

You must stop doing anything immoral or evil. Instead be humble and accept the message that is planted in you to save you.
—JAMES 1:21 CEV

Personal moral values are beliefs or rules about what is right and wrong. Addicts lose their values because they stop listening to their conscience when it tries to tell them their behavior is wrong. Eventually they do anything to get high or drunk, even hurting those they love.

Now that you're in recovery, you can't just go around doing whatever you feel. That would mess up all the work you've put into your recovery thus far. Instead, start thinking about what is right and what is wrong. Since you're trusting God, His values should be your values.

Writing down your beliefs about right and wrong can be helpful. When you see in black and white your personal values, you remember them better. Start with the obvious things, like: "I don't believe getting high or drunk is right"; "Lying is wrong"; "Stealing is wrong."

As you progress in your recovery, you will begin to recognize more complex rights and wrongs. That is a sign that you are maturing and being more responsible. Remember, without a solid system of personal moral values you will do anything, even if it hurts yourself and others.

■ *God, teach me right from wrong, and help me live by these beliefs instead of doing what I feel.*

K.B.

HANG TIGHT!

Yet the righteous will hold to his way,
And he who has clean hands will be
stronger and stronger.

—JOB 17:9

Hang tight!" is a phrase used to remind someone to stay true to his values and principles. That's not an easy thing to do by any means. Some people won't be delighted with the changes you are making. They may even accuse you of being sicker than you were before treatment. The reason for this is that, before treatment, you made it comfortable for them to stay in their dysfunctional behavior. So your change demands some kind of change from them, and they may not want to undertake such a painful endeavor.

A positive aspect of learning to stand firm by your values and commitment to grow healthier is that you will grow strong. "Holding to your ways" helps you to grow. In response to criticism, you must formulate arguments against people's dysfunctional ways of thinking. When you do this, you will build a case against relapse and "old" behavior. When you break a bone, a physician will reset it and then put a cast on it to hold it in place. What results is often a stronger bone because the pressure of the cast has helped it to resist and grow stronger. There are innumerable ways resistance helps us to grow strong. So hang tight to your values for growth and recovery.

■ *Father, help me to "hold to my ways" of growth and recovery.*

R.M.

DIRTY JOKES

Stop all your dirty talk. Say the right thing at the right time and help others by what you say.
—EPH. 4:29 CEV

Your mouth can hurt you more than you think. The things you say often give others their best impressions of the person you are. That means you need to be careful about what you say.

When guys get together, often one will tell a dirty joke. Because you are working on improving your morals, you have to make a decision. Will you laugh? Will you tell a better one? All of the other guys are watching you, waiting to see your response, especially if they know you have been making some changes in your life.

If you are serious about the moral part of recovery, there is only one choice for you: You need to make a stand and let others know that this is something you don't feel comfortable participating in. If you don't, you give others the impression that nothing has really changed and that you are still part of the old crowd. If you do, you will create an impression that you are different. Who knows? You may even help someone else in the process.

■ *Lord, help me today to watch my mouth. May the things I say show how serious I am about changing.*
K.B.

PREPARE FOR ACTION!

Therefore gird up the loins of your mind, be sober, and rest your hope fully upon the grace . . . of Jesus Christ. —1 PET. 1:13

Peter could have just as easily been addressing people who were trying to overcome addictions because the instructions would be the same. He said for them to prepare their minds for action! It is easy for irrational, destructive thoughts to creep into your mind. Thoughts like "I should be done with this recovery thing by now, what's taking so long!" have to be confronted and dealt with before they take root and overcome you.

The next ingredient of a solid recovery is self-control. This takes a lot of practice; self-control is not won overnight. It is a character quality that is built. Sometimes even failure is necessary to realize its importance and finally make it work for you. It is also vitally important for your focus to be on what you can control throughout your recovery. The only thing you can control is yourself, so be self-controlled!

Finally, you must have a goal on which to focus. I once heard someone say, "If you shoot for nothing, you are sure to hit it!" That is true in recovery. You must have your goal firmly in mind in order to make good decisions that will guide you down the path to health. Without this goal, you will not take the action necessary to succeed.

■ *Father, help me to be self-controlled and focused on my goals.*

R.M.

IT'S THE THOUGHT THAT COUNTS

"I tell you that if you look at another woman and want her, you are already unfaithful in your thoughts."
—MATT. 5:28 CEV

It's frightening how guys' morals disappear as they spend more time involved in drinking and taking drugs. Stealing, scamming, lying, being violent, all sorts of other behaviors that they didn't do before the addiction became part of their lives. They stop caring about what is right, and care only about getting high. The behavior that causes the most problems is sex.

Jesus said that when you think about sex in your heart, it's as good as done. In other words, your sexual thoughts are just as bad as the act itself. As your morals decline, your thoughts are the first to decay.

Your thinking is an important part of recovery. How you think about things determines how you will behave. When you have sexual thoughts, as all guys do, you have to decide whether or not you want to keep thinking them. If you do, sex becomes a fantasy, and fantasies are just a short step away from actions. You can choose to stop dwelling on sexual thoughts and replace them with others. As you begin to develop better morals through recovery, start watching your thoughts. Remember, your thoughts determine what kind of man you will be.

■   *God, give me strength to guard against thoughts that hurt my developing morals.*

K.B.

THE LOVE OF AMUSEMENT

> *"The streets of the city*
> *Shall be full of boys and girls*
> *Playing in its streets."*
> —ZECH. 8:5

Some guys play around and never show growth in their recovery. They are forever waiting for something exciting to happen to move them on. Jim was like that. He was fun-loving, and everyone loved to be around him. But he was getting little done in his recovery. Despite remaining drug-free for quite a long time, he seemed to be stagnant. His favorite phrase was "When _____ happens, I can really get moving in my recovery." The blank was filled in by a variety of events that he was always looking forward to. He depended on external things to direct and move his recovery. These were no ordinary events either. They were things like a big youth conference he was going to or a motivational speaker of some sort. In short, he was hooked on having fun and being amused, and this was an effective means to avoid dealing with the nitty-gritty of recovery.

It is easy to tire of the hard work it takes to overcome addiction. That doesn't mean you must always be serious and never have fun. You have to be able to figure out when to be serious and when to have fun. If you use fun as a means of avoiding uncomfortable things, you will likely never get beyond the "childhood" stage of recovery.

■ *Learn to know when to be serious about your recovery and when to allow yourself to have fun.*

R.M.

SEX

Don't be immoral in matters of sex. That is a sin against your own body in a way that no other sin is. —1 COR. 6:18 CEV

Sam discovered sex one night at a party. He and the girl, whom he barely knew, had been drinking and smoking pot. The next day, Sam felt guilty, and when he saw her at school, he couldn't even look her in the eye.

His friends called him Studly. He pretended everything was cool and tried to make it sound great, but still felt pretty bad about it. At the next party, his buddies dared him to get another girl drunk and sleep with her. Rather than look like a wimp, he did. Again, when he sobered up he felt like a jerk.

Sam realized that he was doing something that should be special, but had become ruined because of what he did under the influence of chemicals. One of the biggest regrets guys have in recovery is the sexual choices they made when using. As you slide deeper into dependency on drugs and alcohol, your morals and values sink too.

Part of recovery is cleaning up your morals, making decisions about right and wrong. And one of the most important areas is sex. God cares about your morals, and He will forgive mistakes and help you to make better sexual decisions in the future. You must choose to clean up this area of your life.

■ *God, clean up my thinking and forgive my past mistakes. Help me to make better choices.*

K.B.

REFUSING CORRECTION

They have refused to receive correction.
They have made their faces harder than rock;
They have refused to return. —JER. 5:3

Burn me once, your fault. Burn me twice, my fault." If someone "burns" you the first time, it is because he caught you unawares. If it happens again, it is your fault for not watching. There will be many times throughout your recovery that you will need to learn from your mistakes, or they will come back to "burn" you again.

A common obstacle stands in the way of our learning from our mistakes. It is perfectionism—a belief that you must do everything perfectly. If you can't do something perfectly, you will probably not try. It is an absolute disaster when you try and fail because you have done the unthinkable—made a mistake. When mistakes are raised to such a high level of importance, you will probably not learn from them. Instead, you will close up shop and quit trying. After all, you think, a "failure" will never recover.

In order to be successful in your recovery you must expect mistakes (they will happen) and learn from them. That is something the Israelites refused to do. They would not learn from their error because they wanted to continue on their path to destruction. Avoid their mistake. Take direction from God and learn from Him.

■ *Father, help me to not be afraid of making mistakes so that I can learn from them.*

R.M.

SCAMMING GIRLS

*Woe to him who gives drink to his
   neighbor . . .
That you may look on his nakedness!*
   —HAB. 2:15

One of Carl's big regrets was the way he had scammed girls into having sex with him. He didn't care about whether it was right or not; he just wanted satisfaction even if he hurt them.

He would get girls drunk and then take advantage of them. While he was drinking and using drugs, he never really thought if he was hurting them. Now he realized that some of the girls might not have been willing partners, and that is considered date rape. He always bragged about it, and ruined the girls' reputations.

Now he was having to live with the damage he caused, and this was hard, considering he wasn't using booze or drugs to cover up his feelings of guilt. Carl also knew he would have to find a way to apologize to those girls. He was taking responsibility for the wrongs and hurts he had caused others. Carl understood that he was becoming free of his addictive past, because his feelings of guilt were returning after a long absence.

■   *God, help me to listen to my conscience and take
   responsibility for damage I have caused others.*

K.B.

SEEKING FORGIVENESS

Peter called to mind the word that Jesus had said to him, "Before the rooster crows twice, you will deny Me three times."

—MARK 14:72

After doing something we regret it is easy to avoid seeking forgiveness. By asking for forgiveness, we admit we have done wrong. We often deceive ourselves into thinking that if nothing is said, it will be forgotten, as if it never happened. Yet, just like Peter, we won't forget it. The next time we see the person we hurt we will immediately be reminded that we have unfinished business with that person.

Imagine what might have happened if Peter had said, "It's no big deal. Jesus knew I couldn't keep that promise. He'll forget about it." Because Peter didn't say that he had a restored relationship with Jesus. In addition, he showed us the importance of making amends to someone we have hurt or let down. It is important not only for the relationship but also for you as a person to make sure that your accounts with people are clean. It is important for your recovery to seek forgiveness when you have hurt someone. It is another important building block in developing integrity and honesty in your relationships. It also teaches you that people will forgive you, and you can experience the relief of having a restored relationship with others.

■ *Seek forgiveness from those you have hurt in order to keep your slate clean with others.*

R.M.

A BROKEN HEART

The sacrifices of God are a broken spirit,
A broken and a contrite heart—
These, O God, You will not despise.
—PS. 51:17

When you experience something that makes you feel terrible inside, it is said that you have a broken heart. Usually that means you have lost a loved one, like when you break up with a girlfriend. In recovery you are asked to look inside yourself to see things you have done wrong, that have hurt yourself and those you love. This also can result in a broken heart.

In recovery, especially at first, a broken heart is not a bad thing. You give up one love, substances, for another, God. Breaking off relationships with an addiction is always difficult, but even more so because that relationship turned you into an uncaring and insensitive person who hurt people.

Admitting this will break your heart, not just because you are ending a relationship but because of the wrongs you have done. That is part of the healing process. A broken heart is a humble heart, and being humble means you recognize that you need to change. Allow God to mend your broken heart in a healthy way.

■ *God, don't let me love drugs and alcohol more than You, because they hurt me and the ones I love.*

K.B.

WHERE IS YOUR HEART SET?

*The high places were not taken away, for as
yet the people had not directed their hearts to
the God of their fathers.*

—2 CHRON. 20:33

I had my heart set on going to that party!" Is that a
familiar phrase heard in your house? It is interesting
how we use the heart to convey that our hopes were set
on some particular event or thing. To the writers of the
Bible the heart was the center of the human spirit, from
which sprang emotions, thoughts, motivations, courage,
and action. It was so important that these writers believed that if a person's heart was right with God, the
rest of him was as well. The heart had the power to
direct a man toward or away from God. It was command
central, so to speak.

Where is your heart set? On your goal for recovery?
Or is it, like the people in today's passage, divided between God and some idol? Perhaps you have an idol—
such as an addiction—hidden in the back of your mind
that you retreat to when you feel bad. If you don't confront and deal with it, your recovery will be affected.
Sooner or later, that idol will show itself and betray your
divided heart. Don't delay; look deeply within yourself
and see if an idol is there. If there is one, talk to someone. You will be less likely to keep it if someone knows
and is willing to hold you accountable for it.

■ *Father, help me to set my heart on a healthy path to
recovery.*

R.M.

TEMPTATIONS OF YOUTH

Run from temptations that capture young people.
—2 TIM. 2:22 CEV

Between the ages of twelve and twenty-three, the hormones that cause growth and physical maturity are at an all-time high. The male hormone testosterone creates chest hair, facial hair, pubic hair, enlargement of the penis, rapid growth spurts, and other physical changes. It also causes the sex drive to be one of the most potentially difficult things about this stage of development.

The sex drive is strong at this stage of development, so sex is often on your mind. You can't help it, the hormones racing through your body affect you quite strongly. What you can help is what you do with your desires. Drinking and drugs lower your inhibitions, your ability to do what you believe to be right. When they are high or drunk, most teenagers are sexual.

You have made a decision to recover from chemicals, and because you are thinking more clearly you can make wiser decisions about your sexual activity. Unless you are ready to be a father, and most teen males aren't, it is important to think about the consequences of your sexual behavior. Bad choices about drugs and alcohol led to your need to enter recovery. Bad choices about sex could lead to consequences just as severe.

■ *God, You created hormones. Help me to cope with the desires my hormones cause.*

K.B.

Acting Free

Stand fast therefore in the liberty by which Christ has made us free, and do not be entangled again with a yoke of bondage.
—GAL. 5:1

Tony had been drug-free for months, but he was still acting like he was addicted. He struggled with talking about feelings, and he frequently changed the subject just to avoid talking about painful subjects. He wasn't truly free yet. He had all the ingredients for being free but hadn't made the behavioral changes to be consistent with his new status. He was like a slave who was suddenly freed by his master but wouldn't leave the safety of the plantation on which he was enslaved.

There is a certain safety and predictability about being enslaved. Every decision and aspect of your life is planned for you. Addiction isn't very different from slavery. Before long, it consumes you and you begin to make all of your decisions according to how your addiction can be satisfied.

Be aware that your former slavery to addiction will be alluring at various times throughout your struggle to be free. That doesn't mean you are losing ground; it just means that you need to reassure yourself that freedom is better than any kind of slavery.

■   *It is important to act in a way that is consistent with your freedom from drugs or alcohol.*

R.M.

THE SCAPEGOAT

*The goat shall bear on itself all their
iniquities to an uninhabited land; and he
shall release the goat in the wilderness.*
                                    —LEV. 16:22

In ancient Israel, there was a way to get rid of people's
sins. They would confess all their sins while laying
hands on a goat and then send it out into the desert with
their sins on its back, never to be seen again. Sometimes families do this too. There is often one person in
the family who is seen as the black sheep, or the bad
kid. This person often gets into a lot of trouble and acts
like the scapegoat. Often this person is addicted to
drugs or alcohol.

The family scapegoat thinks to himself, "If everyone
thinks I'm such a bad person, I'll just prove them
right." He screws up in school, drinks too much or gets
high, sometimes gets into trouble with the police, and
constantly feels angry. The family thinks, "See, we were
right; he is a problem child." And because everyone
believes it, nothing changes.

In order for the scapegoat to change his negative behaviors and addiction, he must first stop believing that
he is the black sheep. Otherwise he will not see that
change can happen. The things you believe about yourself make you act certain ways. When you believe negative things, you act in negative ways.

■ *Lord, help me to stop being the family scapegoat.
Help me to look at the good things inside me.*

                                                        K.B.

DO IT FOR ME!

"Did I conceive all these people? Did I beget them, that You should say to me, 'Carry them in your bosom' . . . to the land which You swore to their fathers?" —NUM. 11:12

I don't know what to do. How am I supposed to get better if no one tells me what I'm supposed to do!" These certainly sound like words of a person asking for help. Yet they came from a young man who had been in treatment two times and had worked his recovery program for well over a year. Why did he find it so hard to know what to do?

He was accustomed to being told what to do and to having people work his recovery for him. It seemed his recovery was more important to his parents, his girlfriend, and other friends than it was to him. Of course, his recovery was important to him, but he wanted everyone to do it for him.

It is characteristic of childhood to depend on others for your well-being. When we see a young person doing what a child does, though, we think it humorous or even aggravating. This is equally true during your recovery. In the early stages, you depend on others to point you in the right direction. There comes a point, though, when you must take over the controls and begin to act independently and risk making decisions on your own. So take the controls of your recovery and don't expect others to do it for you. That is the essence of growing up and growing healthy.

■ *Father, help me to grow up in my recovery and not expect others to do it for me.*

R.M.

I CAN'T DO IT!

Christ gives me the strength to face anything.
—PHIL. 4:13 CEV

No way, I can't do that!" We had just told Mike that he needed to tell his parents he had stolen his mother's ring to buy cocaine. All his peers in the group knew that Mike needed to talk with his folks, but he had tons of excuses ready for them.

"They'll never trust me again," he complained. They told him he needed to take that chance if he wanted to get better. "My mom will feel terrible that her own son could do such a thing," he tried. They told him his mother would feel worse if she found out later. "My dad will ground me forever," he moaned. They told him that was a chance he had to take if he ever was to face his responsibility.

After many excuses, one of the group leaders said, "It's not that you can't; you just *won't*." And that's what it came down to: Mike just simply would not do what he knew he needed to do.

You have the ability to do whatever is needed in recovery. Certainly you will feel at times that you don't have the strength or courage to make some of the tough decisions facing you. That's another reason you need a higher power. During times when you feel you can't, with God's help you can. Therefore, the next time you think you can't, it's probably just that you won't.

■ *Help me not to get* can't *confused with* won't.

K.B.

LOSING HEART

*"My son, do not despise the chastening
of the LORD,
Nor be discouraged when you are
rebuked by Him."* —HEB. 12:5

When I played basketball, my teammates often reminded me of how fortunate I was that the coach paid so much attention to me. Of course, this attention was in the form of yelling and screaming about what I wasn't doing! During those times it was really easy to get down on myself and think what a failure I was as a ballplayer.

Is that what happens to you when you are confronted with your mistakes during recovery? Do you give up? Do you say to yourself, "Oh, what's the use, I'm not ever going to recover anyway so why bother?" Why are you bothering to struggle to recover? You need to make an inventory frequently of your reasons to recover so that you can maintain your motivation.

Obstacles to your recovery are not there just to make you miserable. God very intentionally prepares you for the real test to come. You must put what happens to you into the perspective that it is from the Father's loving hand to help you recover. Things don't just happen to you. They are specifically designed for you by God to help move you along down the road to wholeness and health. So don't get down! God is helping you, just as my coach was getting me ready for the big game.

■ *Father, help me to not lose heart when I face obstacles in my recovery.*

R.M.

IT RUNS IN THE FAMILY

. . . visiting the iniquity of the fathers upon the children and the children's children to the third and the fourth generation.

—EX. 34:7

When therapists work with someone for the first time, they take a family history. You can almost always predict when someone has a problem with drugs and alcohol when you find relatives, often parents, who have addictions. You see, there is a biological part to the illness—it runs in the family.

Sometimes teens try to tell us their addiction is a genetic problem they can't do anything about. That's not true. That kind of thinking is meant to deny their responsibility for their choices. If someone is allergic to milk, it is his responsibility not to drink it. When he does, the allergic reaction is a consequence of his bad choice to drink milk.

If you come from an alcoholic family, your relatives have coped with their problems by drinking or getting high. This may have even been why you started abusing substances in the first place. Despite this fact, it is now your decision as to whether or not to continue. Instead of looking for scientific reasons to explain away your responsibility, make a choice to be different. Your choice may even affect whether future generations follow in your family's footsteps.

■ *Help me overcome family patterns to make better choices than the ones who came before me.*

K.B.

LOVE OR CONSEQUENCES

"As the Father loved Me, I also have loved you; abide in My love." —JOHN 15:9

What motivates you? If you abused substances for a long time, you likely were motivated by the consequences of your actions. When you made decisions, you might have asked yourself, "Can I get away with this and not get into trouble?" The consequences, or lack of them, of your actions determined the direction you chose to go. More likely than not you chose to do something illegal because you could get away with it.

In recovery, it is easy to let your motivation be the consequences of your actions rather than love for someone. The love of your body, yourself, and the love of others should be the motivating force behind your recovery. It is not so much that you will feel the pain of getting in trouble because of what you do. It is the fact that you will be letting yourself down. In addition, whether you know it or not people are watching you and your recovery process. It may prove to them that they, too, can have the same courage you have to change their addictive behaviors.

What is your decision? Will you be motivated by consequences, or will your motivation be respect for yourself and love for Jesus Christ, who called your body a temple of the Holy Spirit?

■ *Father, help me to be motivated in my recovery by respect for myself.*

R.M.

FAMILY SECRETS

"You will know the truth, and the truth will set you free."
            —JOHN 8:32 CEV

Bill had a problem. He had been in rehab and wanted to work on his recovery by honestly telling people where he had been and the things he had learned. His mother, on the other hand, was embarrassed about the treatment and felt he should tell people he had been in the hospital for tests. Basically, she was asking him to lie.

Families of addicts often keep these kinds of secrets. It's humiliating for them to admit that their child has a drug or alcohol problem, and they don't want anyone to know. Sometimes they try to keep other secrets too, which can be frustrating to someone in recovery trying to be honest and open about things.

You will have to stop keeping secrets if you ever expect your life to change. Recovery is about admitting mistakes to others and looking for help, instead of trying to do things on your own. This may mean that you have to talk honestly to your parents about the fact that keeping secrets and telling lies will only hurt you in the long run. While this may seem frightening at first, remember that with God even telling your parents that you can't keep secrets is possible.

■   *Plan to have a talk with your parents about family secrets that might injure your recovery.*

K.B.

WHAT KIND OF MASTERPIECE ARE YOU?

*Be diligent to present yourself approved to
God, a worker who does not need to be
ashamed, rightly dividing the word of truth.*
—2 TIM. 2:15

Recovery is a process, something God enables you to
do, and it is important that you remember you are participating and producing something. It is easier to keep
your focus on your work if you understand that your
recovery is the most important project you have ever
undertaken. Consider yourself a craftsman who is producing a masterpiece, something people will marvel at.
This work will give you the opportunity to help people
see the grace and power of God to change lives.

What does your masterpiece look like? Have you
been skimping on the attention to detail? Or cutting corners to get the job done sooner? If so you will be
ashamed of your work. You won't be likely to talk about
your recovery because you won't have much to talk
about. It really isn't something you are proud of.

Take pride in your recovery work. Pay attention to the
small details of your thought life and how you deal with
people. Attention to small details will contribute to an
increasingly beautiful masterpiece that will not only
look good but will also be good. When people look at
your life and the changes that have occurred, they will
marvel at what a masterpiece it truly is.

■ *Pay attention to the small details of your recovery.*

R.M.

A BETTER VIEW

Search me, O God, and know my heart . . .
And see if there is any wicked way in me,
And lead me in the way everlasting.
—PS. 139:23–24

Looking at yourself in a new way can be hard. You're used to seeing yourself as a happy-go-lucky stoner or a rebellious party animal. But in recovery, you're asked to look differently at yourself, to stop seeing yourself the way you did. When you try, you may find that your mind goes blank and you can't see yourself clearly.

When David wrote Psalm 139, he must have been going through something like this. He asked God to look inside him and notice all the thoughts and worries he couldn't see by himself. Because God knows what is inside you even better than you do, He can see problems before they become actual behavior that gets you into trouble. If you are willing, He will make you aware of the problems and prevent you from making dangerous mistakes.

If you go through recovery without trying to discover these inward patterns of thinking and feeling, you will never understand why you do the things you do. You will react instead of seeing danger coming and preventing it. Even though you may not be able to see these patterns clearly right now, God does, and He can help you to see them too.

■ *God, help me to see patterns in my life that keep me*
from walking the right path.

K.B.

THE BIG SCAM

*Now this I say lest anyone should deceive you
with persuasive words.* —COL. 2:4

Terry took pride in being a great scam artist. He could
scam the coat off anyone on a cold day. Scamming was
his way to avoid responsibility and also avoid the pain
and hurt deep within him. He had been hurt by an
absent father and a critical mother whom he felt he
could never please. He felt that he didn't matter, and he
was intensely angry. So he turned to hurting other people by scamming and manipulating them. To him, what
was even better was that they didn't even know they had
been manipulated. Manipulating people also came in
handy to cover his alcohol addiction.

Scamming had become a habit with him, and when
he finally got caught he wasn't sure what was truth and
what wasn't. That is the nature of deceit; you have to be
a genius to keep track of all the lies you have told others.
What Terry didn't realize is that the person he had done
the best scam on was himself. He had convinced himself that he was justified in manipulating people because they deserved it for being so dumb.

Beware of manipulating people to your advantage.
The price you pay may be scamming yourself into deceit and a web of lies that you cannot easily extract yourself from.

■ *Father, help me to always deal honestly with people.*
R.M.

SPLITTING YOUR PARENTS

*Children, you belong to the Lord. . . . "Obey
your father and your mother, and you will
have a long and happy life."*
—EPH. 6:1–3 CEV

Addicts pull scams on their parents. They go to Mom
and ask for something. If she says no, they go to Dad
and ask him. That's called splitting, tricking them when
you know the responsible thing to do is to accept "no"
in the first place.

Another scam is talking to one parent behind the
other parent's back. When angry at Mom, the addict
goes to Dad to complain and get Dad on his side. Dad
then yells at Mom. That's irresponsible too because
you're not dealing directly with the problem, you're
avoiding it.

A third kind of splitting is when Mom says, "Ask your
dad," you tell him that Mom said it was okay. Mom
never said it was all right, and so basically you are lying.
There are all sorts of splits someone can cause between
parents, and none of them is truthful or responsible.

You've decided you need to be more responsible for
the choices you make in life. Splitting parents is part of
the old you, the dishonest scam artist who always
wanted his way and would do anything, including lying,
to get it. Be honest with your parents; admit to splitting
them and ask them to help you not to do it in the future.
This kind of honesty is what recovery is all about.

■ *Ask your parents' forgiveness for splitting them and
for their help in not doing it again.*

K.B.

A QUICK TONGUE

Do you see a man hasty in his words?
There is more hope for a fool than for him.
—PROV. 29:20

When I was in high school, my friends and I prided ourselves on our ability to have a quick comeback to anyone who cut us down. We often cheered each other on in contests of who could come up with the quickest cut down—it was ruthless and sometimes very cruel. As I look back at those experiences, I realize that we were contributing to each others' poor self-esteem. Of course, none of us would admit that it hurt—we were too tough for that!

So how quick are you with your remarks? Speech is one of the best tests of how well someone is doing in recovery. It takes a great deal of inner strength to hold back a response. It shows me that the person I am talking with has thought about the impact his words will have on other people.

Some people object to this idea, saying, "I shouldn't have to watch everything I say around people. They know what I mean." Do they? I guess you have to decide how you want to interact with people. Do you want to build them up and encourage them as you talk to them? Or do you want to run roughshod over people and not even know that you are hurting them? If you want to encourage and build up, the answer to the first question is a resounding yes!

■ *Father, help me not to have a quick response to others' feedback.*

R.M.

SWEARING

*"Our ancestors were told, 'Don't use the
Lord's name to make a promise. . . .' But I
tell you not to swear by anything!"*
—MATT 5:33–34 CEV

I swear to God, I'm not lying!" Ever say something like
that? By calling on God to witness that you are not lying,
you call on a pretty high authority. Often this is the first
sign that you *are* lying.

Addicts are pretty untrustworthy people. After all the
scams they've pulled and lies they've told to get others
off their backs, their credibility is weak. So sometimes
they call God as their witness because they know that on
their own, nobody will trust them. That can be dangerous because if you call God as a witness to a lie or even
a half-truth, you make God out to be a liar.

Instead of swearing to God, you need to start being
a more trustworthy person, someone others will believe
just because they know you are telling the truth. If you
feel that you need to swear by God, that is a sign that
you don't feel you should be believed, and that means
you still have to work on being more honest. Trust takes
time to build, so start today. The first step is to stop
swearing by God or by anything. Just let your promise
stand for itself, and let your actions prove that you can
be believed.

■   *God, help me to become a more trustworthy person.*
                                                    K.B.

IRRITATING WORDS

A soft answer turns away wrath,
But a harsh word stirs up anger.
—PROV. 15:1

You probably never noticed that the people around you were angry while you abused drugs or alcohol. Their anger and frustration with you likely came from the irritating and harsh words you directed at them. Harsh words that are used as a comeback to another person's feedback are usually a clear indication that you don't want to hear what the other person has to say.

The way you handle others' emotions is a pretty good indication of how your recovery is going. When someone gets angry at you, do you get defensive and begin to look for reasons to put the blame on him? If you do, then you need to talk to someone about it because denial is taking root once again. If you run off at the mouth and defend yourself immediately, you may not hear and respond to that person's hurt or pain. If that goes on, you will contribute to a pattern of resolving conflict that will spiral back into abuse.

Keep your head when someone is angry. If you speak a "gentle word"—a word spoken in a normal tone of voice—you will be responding to the person's feelings rather than defending yourself from being attacked. Speak a gentle word, and you will make resolution possible.

■   *Father, help me to speak gentle words in response to others' feelings.*

R.M.

FINDING FAULT

*"Don't be hard on others, and God will not
be hard on you. Forgive others, and God will
forgive you."*
     —LUKE 6:37 CEV

Steve was incredibly critical. He was a master at put-downs and making fun of others. When he didn't like something about someone, or a person didn't live up to his standards of what was cool, he condemned that person.

Now, I knew something about Steve that is true of all who judge other people. They don't like themselves very much. Because they feel bad about who they are, they feel a need to make fun of others. They want to bring others down to their level. By acting so superior, they show that they don't feel very important.

Steve's attitude is harmful to recovery. Part of getting better is realizing how bad you are. Putting others down is just denying your own shortcomings. When you try to be superior by looking at others' faults, you overlook your own.

That's why it is important not to judge others. That is God's job, because He's the only one who can tell what a person is really like inside. Your job is to recognize and admit your own faults and shortcomings and work on them. Judging others probably means you're not looking at the things you need to work on; you're too busy worrying about others.

■ *The next time you feel the urge to make fun of someone, ask God to help you focus on your faults.*

             K.B.

SAY WHAT?

"Your words have been harsh against Me . . .
Yet you say,
'What have we spoken against You?'"
—MAL. 3:13

What a classic case of denial! God confronted Israel about the harsh things they had said against Him, and they said, "Say what?" The most common way people shift responsibility is to ask a question back to the confronting person. That is exactly what Israel did.

In dysfunctional families, that is called mystification—a fancy word to describe an interaction in which one person confronts another about some behavior and the person being confronted asks a question back, implying that the confronter is misguided. Of course, the person confronting is caught in a dilemma. Either he accuses the person of lying or gives up the confrontation.

What do you do when you are confronted? Do you, like the people of Israel, ask a question back to your confronter in an attempt to get him off track? How you take being confronted is a great indicator of how well you are doing in recovery. The person who can take confrontation calmly even if he is falsely accused is on a successful path to recovery. Staying calm and listening gives you an opportunity to resolve the issue at hand.

■ *Father, help me to keep my cool when I'm confronted.*

R.M.

DON'T EXPECT YOUR PARENTS TO FIX IT

He who spares his rod hates his son,
But he who loves him disciplines him promptly.
—PROV. 13:24

Jim's parents were afraid to say anything to him about his behavior. Even though they worried, they didn't want to make things worse by getting him mad at them. That was before he was picked up on a drunk driving charge. His father let him spend the night in jail, and the next day his parents brought him to the hospital for treatment.

Jim was furious. He told them he would change and it would never happen again. They had heard this before, and he hadn't changed. He told them they were making a big deal out of nothing. They told him jail wasn't nothing. Then he started yelling at them that it was their fault and they were the ones who really needed help. He drank because he couldn't stand being around them.

His parents *had* made a mistake. They had let Jim's problem go on for too long before doing something. Jim had gotten used to their taking care of things for him, and now that they were making him take responsibility, he was mad. He wanted them to fix it again.

Now that you are in recovery, stop expecting your parents to ignore problems or fix the life you've messed up. Begin taking responsibility for the consequences of your addiction.

■ *Help me to show my parents that I don't expect them to be responsible for my problems.*

K.B.

STAND FIRM

Be steadfast, immovable, always abounding in the work of the Lord, knowing that your labor is not in vain in the Lord.
—1 COR. 15:58

Why keep working? Nothing is changing. I haven't gotten anywhere!" Tom slammed his hands on his desk in his bedroom and put his head down.

Tom was frustrated with the slow progress he was making in overcoming a cocaine addiction. He couldn't see the progress he had made, however, because he spent so much time hoping his dad would notice the changes he had made and comment on them. He was slowly losing his struggle to overcome addiction.

You have, no doubt, heard countless times that the formula for standing firm in recovery is to give all of yourself to work on things you have the most chance of changing. You set yourself up for disaster if you depend on the affirmation of others as the test of how well you are doing in recovery. When you do this, you harbor expectations of others that they don't know you have. You want them to notice your progress, but they may not know you are looking for the feedback. Therefore, they probably won't applaud your work as quickly as you would like them to applaud—even if they do notice. Do you see the set up? They can't win, and you can't either.

Set yourself to work on recovery and don't waver from this task. You can count on the fact that your work will not be in vain, whether people notice or not.

■ *Don't depend on the praise of others to keep your recovery on track.*

R.M.

DANGEROUS PLACES

Do not enter the path of the wicked,
And do not walk in the way of evil.
Avoid it, do not travel on it.
—PROV. 4:14–15

An ounce of prevention is worth a pound of cure."
This saying means that a little preparation can avoid
spending a lot of time fixing things after making big mistakes. In recovery there is a need for prevention, and a
little planning can keep you from making big errors
later on. This is especially true when it comes to places.

Before you started recovery there were certain places
you went with friends to drink and get high. Some of
these might have been the park, the school parking lot,
parties, certain friends' houses, the mall, concerts, or
any place you regularly went. These places have become attached in your mind to memories of using substances, and when you go there you will feel cravings.
Maybe some of your old friends still go there to drink or
get high.

When you get serious about recovery you will realize
that you cannot handle being in these places for long
without feeling yearnings again. A good ounce of prevention would mean staying away from these places as
much as possible. Avoiding them might mean that you
avoid the danger of relapsing.

■   *Make a list of dangerous places in your life and*
    share it with someone else in recovery.

K.B.

WORRYING BEFORE "IT" HAPPENS

"Settle it in your hearts not to [worry]
beforehand on what you will answer."
—LUKE 21:14

I have noticed a trend among people who strive to re-cover from addiction: They worry well before an event ever happens. They seem to believe that if they don't worry, the event won't go their way. They may be able to do nothing about what they are worrying about, but they feel better when they worry because at least they are doing something!

Anxiety is a crippling emotion. It compresses time and puts you in a position to react to the upcoming event as if it has already happened. Instead of worrying about a problem when the time comes, as Jesus suggested to His disciples, we worry before and right up to the event. How prepared do you think we will be when the feared event actually confronts us? If you guessed that we would be poorly prepared you were right. Interestingly enough, the person who worries like this will perform even worse than the one who worries when there is a reason to worry.

Worry needs to be controlled in recovery. The solu-tion is not in the song lyric, "Don't worry, be happy!" The best reason not to worry is to remember that you will probably do worse if you worry. Tell yourself you will deal with whatever confronts you when you get to that time.

■ *Father, help me to let go of my worries and deal with the situation when I get there.*

R.M.

QUIET, GOD AT WORK

God is working in you to make you willing to obey him.   —PHIL. 2:13 CEV

Charles was ready to move on. I appreciated his enthusiasm; it was exciting to watch him change so quickly. But I knew that if he took recovery too quickly he might fail. While I was tempted to push him to work as hard as he wanted, instead I told him to slow down and listen.

"Listen to what?" he asked. "To what God is trying to tell you about what you should do next," I answered. This discouraged Charles; he thought I would tell him something deep and radical, that I would give him the keys to recovery. But I wasn't the one who would do the real healing work inside Charles—it was God.

It is tempting to work quickly. When you get a taste of something good, like recovery, you want more. But if you take on too much too quickly, you begin to think you're the one doing the work. Or you believe that your therapist or sponsor is giving you the answers. The truth is that only God can see clearly what your recovery will be like, and therefore He will be the only one who knows how to lead you at the right speed. When you rush through recovery, you take the chance of not hearing the messages God wants you to hear.

■   *God, help me to go slow and be willing to let You lead me in recovery.*

K.B.

THE PURSUIT OF TRUTH

Many of the Jews and devout [converts]
followed Paul and Barnabas, who . . .
persuaded them to continue in the grace of
God.
          —ACTS 13:43

Have you ever noticed that when a meeting ends people hang around to talk to the speaker? Sometimes they ask questions or want to thank the speaker; sometimes they even want to argue a point! Notice in the verse for today that some people hung around—and even followed—after Paul and Barnabas spoke to find out more about what they were talking about. Now that is motivation to know the truth!

Is that how motivated you are to know the truth about overcoming your addiction? It takes a great deal of motivation to be persistent in learning. It is not easy to learn new things. We often get casual about what we know, and won't seek new knowledge. Without new knowledge, though, we can't grow, and the recovery process will become stagnant and ineffective.

How are you pursuing truth? It could be going to a special meeting where a speaker is talking about an issue that is relevant to you. It could be going to a meeting of other teens who are in recovery. Whatever it is, you have to swallow your pride to be a learner. You have to be willing to admit you don't know everything and that you need and want more so that you can continue to grow.

■   *Father, help me to swallow my pride and be willing*
    to learn new things.

                                        R.M.

DO YOU REALLY MEAN IT?

I know everything you have done . . . . Since
you are lukewarm and neither cold nor hot, I
will spit you out of my mouth.
—REV. 3:15–16 CEV

There are three "temperatures" with which to approach recovery. Most people start out cold, denying that they need recovery. They are turned off to the work they need to do in order to lead a healthy life with God in the director's chair.

Hot persons recognize that their lives have become destructive and that they need to change. They buckle down and are eager to invest themselves in their program, looking constantly to live clean and sober lives, wanting to do whatever it takes to make their lives better.

Finally some in recovery are lukewarm, neither hot nor cold. They only go throught the motions to keep up the image that they're recovering. Obviously, they have no commitment to recover, and they will probably fail.

Cold people are turned off by suggestions that they need to change. Hot people are hard at work to please God and put Him in charge of their recovery. Both hot and cold persons are honest about their recovery and don't play games with God. Lukewarm addicts, however, do play games and are not totally honest. God says that this bothers Him a great deal, and He strongly prefers the first two kinds. Which type are you?

■ *God, I want to be on fire for recovery. Help me not to*
   become lukewarm to changes You bring in me.

K.B.

INDECISIVENESS

*Then we will no longer be infants, tossed
back and forth by the waves, and blown here
and there by every wind of teaching and by
the cunning and craftiness of men in their
deceitful scheming.* —EPH. 4:14 NIV

Being indecisive is a safety hatch. If you don't make a decision, you never have to worry about being wrong. But you won't get anywhere, either. Instead, you'll be floating without an anchor on an endless sea of values (things you believe to be right and wrong), getting caught up in whatever seems interesting. Without decisions—if you never put your anchor down and declare what you believe—you will remain adrift. This is a pretty dangerous position to be in. In order to recover from your addiction, you have to make decisions.

Indecisiveness is a characteristic of childhood. Children seem to be taken in by almost anything interesting or exciting. They don't seem able to discern what is good and what is bad. Of course, there is a good reason for that. They don't have the experience necessary to judge good from bad; therefore, everything looks good.

That's not how it should be in your recovery process. You need to determine your values for yourself. These values will help you determine what is good and what is bad. They will also help you make decisions that will help your recovery process. So don't let anyone tell you that something is good for you until you first decide for yourself according to the values you hold to be true.

■ *Father, help me to define my own values and to
make my decisions by them.*

R.M.

NO PAIN, NO GAIN

Suffering helps us to endure. And endurance builds character, which gives us a hope that will never disappoint us.
—ROM. 5:3–5 CEV

No pain, no gain," is a familiar saying. If athletes don't work their muscles hard enough, they will never get solid enough to last throughout the event they have trained for. You are training for just such an endurance event: recovery. It's not for the wimpy addict who wants to avoid hard work. No, this is a tough job.

At every stage of recovery you need to deal with pain. First comes the physical pain of withdrawal. Then you face the mental pain of admitting you're weaker than you thought. Next comes spiritual pain as you realize how far away God seems because you've pushed Him away. Finally, there's emotional pain as you begin to understand how much you've hurt yourself and others by your actions.

Although suffering *is* hard, and you've spent a lot of time trying to avoid pain, it is necessary to help you learn to last throughout recovery. Suffering builds endurance, which builds character, which builds hope for the future of your recovery. Instead of avoiding pain, start suffering gladly. The results of learning to deal with pain will make your recovery much stronger in the end.

■ *God, help me to experience pain and suffering gladly instead of learning how to be strong.*

K.B.

PERSISTENCE PAYS OFF

*Eternal life to those who by patient
continuance in doing good seek for glory,
honor, and immortality.* —ROM. 2:7

Persistence pays off. Award-winning actors and actresses once scrounged and took two-bit jobs until by persistence they got roles that made them famous. Athletes spend endless hours practicing their sport and rise to the top of their game. The list can go on: doctors, lawyers, and other professionals who have had to go through years of rigorous training to achieve a spot in their profession.

Recovery is that way as well. You will hit many potholes in the road as you grow and pursue health. It is important to remember that if you are traveling a smooth road you are probably not on the road to recovery. Instead, you are stagnating and losing ground.

Expect hassles and trouble. Expect obstacles in your path. That doesn't mean you are on the wrong path but that you are confronting life as it is; by your persistence you are learning and growing. Always remember that anything worth having is worth working hard for.

Be persistent in your recovery. Stick to the task you face in overcoming your addiction, and you will find benefits worth enjoying and sharing with others.

■ *Father, help me to persist in my struggle for freedom
from addiction.*

R.M.

How will you respond to hard times?

*As Stephen was being stoned to death, he . . .
kneeled down and shouted, "Lord, don't
blame them for what they have done."*
—ACTS 7:59–60 CEV

Stephen was arrested and imprisoned because of what he believed about God. Knowing that he was in danger, he had a couple of choices: He could either say that he didn't believe or stand up for his beliefs and risk the consequences. Stephen decided to stick with what was right, and he was put to death for his choice. Just before he died, he even forgave all those who wrongly attacked him. That's how sure he was of his beliefs.

You will eventually be faced with a similar choice. You will need to stand up for your recovery and the changes you are making, even though it may make you unpopular and you may lose some friends. Stephen was so convinced what he believed was right that he was willing to die for it. How convinced are you?

When the time comes for you to stand up for recovery, you certainly will not have to risk being put to death. But some of the consequences might be hard. When these hard times come, many addicts quit. That is because they weren't sure they wanted to change in the first place. You need to be positive that you plan to finish the recovery program you have begun. If not, you will quit the first time you are faced with standing up for yourself and your beliefs.

■ *Help me to be like Stephen and stand up for what I believe.*

K.B.

WEAK ENOUGH TO BE STRONG

*[They] quenched the violence of fire, escaped
the edge of the sword, out of weakness were
made strong.* —HEB. 11:34

The Bible is filled with paradoxes. It seems as if God takes delight in confusing us, so that we must look to Him to truly understand the world we live in. Often things are the reverse of the way we would expect. Weakness turned into strength—who ever heard of such a thing? It sounds absolutely crazy that in order to be strong we must first be weak. Sometimes we have to be shaken up in order to see things clearly. In order for God to help us, we must be willing to admit our weakness. Until that happens, we think that we are sufficient for ourselves and we don't need God. Our pride gets in the way of our seeing things accurately and understanding our complete dependence on God to make our recovery stick.

When you are ready to see just how weak you really are, you will be willing to reach out to others for the support you need in recovery. At that point you will see all the resources God has given you to accomplish victory over your addiction. You will wonder how you ever missed all this support! That is what happened to the saints spoken of in our Scripture for today. When they admitted their weakness God's power could truly be shown with clarity.

■ *Father, help me to admit my weakness and depend
on You to guide my recovery.*

R.M.

WORRYING ABOUT RECOVERY

"Don't worry about having something to eat, drink, or wear. Isn't life more than food or clothing?"
—MATT. 6:25 CEV

It all sounds so easy here in the hospital, but what about when I leave? I mean, it's so hard, I'm not sure I'm strong enough." When Tom said this to me, I knew he was serious about recovery. Some people leave rehab thinking they have it all together. That is dangerous, because they are certain to relapse. Only when you know it will be hard will you look for problems *before* they arise.

Tom was really worried. In fact, he was so worried that he didn't want to leave the safety of the hospital unit. He couldn't stop thinking about tomorrow and the possibility of failure. With this attitude, he wouldn't do well in recovery, because he would get stuck in his anxiety.

Anyone who takes recovery seriously will experience this apprehension. That is why the Bible says not to worry. You see, worrying is actually living in tomorrow, fearing what *might* happen. But most of the things we worry about never happen anyway. Besides, if you have put God in charge of your recovery, He will help you handle anything in the future. Your job is to focus on today, right now. If you can make it through the next day, you can begin fresh tomorrow. A lifetime of living clean *right now* will make for a solid recovery.

■ *God, teach me to focus on today's recovery and leave tomorrow until it arrives.*

K.B.

WHICH WAY?

*I have restrained my feet from every evil way
That I may keep Your word.*

—PS. 119:101

Recovery is very much like walking a path that is not at all clear sometimes. At times you will ask, "Which way am I supposed to go now?" How will you decide? If you are a hiker, the first thing you may ask yourself is "Where am I headed, and will the direction of this path take me there?" Let's translate that into recovery terms. You confront a situation that forces you to make a decision. You need to ask yourself, "Is this situation going to take me further down the road of recovery or away from it?" Your answer will determine your response to this situation. It is important to remember that the path you choose will also determine how successful you are in recovery. You may make better decisions that will help you grow and overcome your addiction.

Of course, you don't always have time to think out your response. You may have to think fast. What then? This is a little tougher. Make a list of as many trying situations as you can think of. Then ask that question of each situation, adding, "What if I were to face this situation?" If you do this, you won't be backed into a corner where you are pressured into a decision. That is a sure sign that you need to back off and think again."

■ *Father, help me to make good decisions to follow the path of recovery.*

R.M.

RUNNING FROM RECOVERY

But Jonah arose to flee to Tarshish from the presence of the LORD.   —JONAH 1:3a

After being confronted by every member of his family about the way his drinking had hurt them, Vince decided he needed to change. That first session was hard for him. He had watched each family member cry, as they stuck to their story. Realizing how bad things had become, he agreed to enter the rehab unit and start recovery.

But in the hospital it was harder than he thought. At first he believed recovery would take just a few weeks and then everyone would be satisfied and it would be all over. When he was pushed and made to look at attitudes and behaviors that kept him from getting better, he started getting angry and decided he didn't want things to get better after all. It was just too much work.

Basically Vince just put a few weeks into recovery, was discharged, and went back to doing the same old things. He wasn't willing to do the work needed, and instead chose to run from recovery. Don't be like Vince and kid yourself that you can easily change and make everyone happy. Recovery takes work, and many times you will feel like running away. But if you stick with it, the results will be well worth the work you put into changing yourself.

■   *Write down the reasons you began recovery. Keep reading over the list and continue your work.*

K.B.

TWO WORLDS

Do not love the world or the things in the world. If anyone loves the world, the love of the Father is not in him.

—1 JOHN 2:15

You live in two different worlds—the world of recovery and the world at large. The world of recovery is pretty focused. People who populate this world support you in your recovery, know the temptations you face, and confront you in a way that motivates, not discourages you. They are comfortable to be around; you don't have to be on guard all the time about what you say or about situations that might develop to threaten your recovery. This world is pretty safe.

The world at large is what you face once you leave the world of recovery. These people may not be sympathetic with your attempt to recover. They don't know the language of recovery and probably won't be careful of the impact of their behavior on your recovery. Sometimes it seems that they look for ways to sabotage your recovery.

Never forget that in spite of living in these two worlds you don't have to agree with the values of dysfunction you find in the world at large. You need to live in the world of recovery while you live in the other world. Don't try to live in both at the same time. If you do that you will most certainly fail. Sooner or later, you will have to choose. You can't live on the fence forever.

■ *Don't try to live in two worlds, but choose to be committed to recovery no matter what.*

R.M.

HAVING IT ALL

"What will you gain, if you own the whole world but destroy yourself? What would you give to get back your soul?"
—MATT. 16:26 CEV

Sam came from a wealthy family. He had grown up spoiled and thought he deserved the things that many people only wish for. For example, his parents bought him a car on his sixteenth birthday. He always had the best clothes and had lots of spending money. Even though he bragged a lot about the things he had, he still felt like something was missing.

Others looked at Sam's life and thought, "If *I* had all that stuff, *I* would be happy!" Sam, however, wasn't happy. Being spoiled, he believed he *deserved* the happiness he wanted. And so, with all his spending money, he started to buy drugs and alcohol.

At first getting drunk did the trick. When that stopped working he tried pot. Then cocaine, crack, acid, and whatever he could buy with the money his parents gave him. But even though he could afford anything he wanted, and always had friends willing to party with him, Sam still felt empty and unhappy after the high wore off.

What addicts can't understand is that having everything is not what makes you happy. Tons of money, great drugs, and intense partying do not fill the emptiness inside. The next time you start to get jealous, remember Sam. He had it all but still felt empty.

■ *God, nothing I try can really fill the hole in my soul. Please fill it with Your love.*

K.B.

BEATING YOUR HEAD AGAINST A WALL

Why should you be stricken again? . . .
The whole head is sick,
And the whole heart faints.

—IS. 1:5

Have you ever felt like beating your head against a wall? You might feel this way when you try to convince someone he is addicted. It is discouraging to realize you are not able to make a difference when the person doesn't want to change. You need to step back and take another look at the situation before beating on that wall again.

What puts you in this frustrating situation is your assumption that expending energy toward changing something will make it change. However, your thinking something should change doesn't mean it will. "Shoulding" is a great way to obscure your vision of reality. When you use the word *should* in your thoughts about change, you are comparing what is happening against an ideal situation. More often than not, reality is a far cry from the ideal. Therefore, you have now created a situation where you will automatically be disappointed and frustrated because reality does not conform to your idea of how it should be.

Let go of your demands for reality to be different and work with it. Drop your unrealistic expectations and begin to formulate strategies for changing things as they are presented to you, rather than demanding that they be different.

■ *Father, help me to surrender my demand for change in areas I cannot change.*

R.M.

ONE TOUGH DAY

I will sing aloud of Your mercy . . .
For You have been my defense
And refuge in the day of my
trouble. —PS. 59:16

David had been having one of those horrible days when nothing goes right. He had been turned down by a girl he asked out. He got a D on a test he studied hard for. One of his old friends, an ex-drug buddy, said some nasty things about him around the school. And to top it all off, he had another of those long fights with his mother about something stupid.

David's first thoughts were, "If it's this hard, why am I even trying to stay clean? I really could use something to make me feel right." He felt a tremendous urge from deep inside to get high. It was strong, and he really wanted it. Fortunately, another thought kicked in: "I'm about to relapse."

In Narcotics Anonymous groups, you can find a sponsor, someone you can phone when the urge to get high is strong. David called his sponsor, and they went out for coffee and to talk. He reminded David that when the desire to get high again becomes too strong, we can always call out to our higher power, God, for the strength to handle it. After some prayer and with the help of a friend, David was able to get past the cravings and remember that the problems of today last only until the sun goes down.

■ *Make a plan so that you'll know where to turn for help when you crave relief from substances.*

K.B.

THE POWER TO BE WEAK

Watch, stand fast in the faith, be brave, be strong.
—1 COR. 16:13

What shows true strength? Is it being able to lift a lot of weight? Is it never showing your feelings? Is it having people be afraid of you and your temper? What makes people think you are strong?

Have you ever known someone who, to prove just how "tough" he is, says, "Go ahead, hit me. Hit me with your best shot!" He wants others to think he can take their hardest hits and live to tell the story. It does take a lot of strength to keep your hands down and take someone else's hitting you. It is a demonstration of inner strength to resist the impulse to beat the other person to a pulp!

When you make the choice to develop inner strength rather than strength that can be seen by others, you are choosing health and recovery. This inner strength will help you to recognize your weaknesses and your need for God to help you with them. Weaknesses are no longer something to be feared, but rather something to embrace because they give you an opportunity to see God work in your life. Paul said, "If God's power rests on me and my weaknesses, then give me those weaknesses, because I will get to see God even more!"

■ *Father, help me to not be afraid of my weaknesses and be assured that You will help me with them.*

R.M.

AT LEAST IT'S NOT DRUGS!

Woe to those who rise early in the morning,
That they may follow intoxicating drink;
. . . Till wine inflames them! —IS. 5:11

In his attempt to prove to his parents that he really didn't need help, Henry told them, "Look, it's only booze. Lots of people drink, most of the kids I know. I could see you being worried if it was drugs." He tried to make things sound better than they were, but his parents and I could see what he was trying to do. It was denial.

There are lots of ways to fool yourself into believing that you are doing okay and really don't have a problem. One of those ways is to lie to yourself that alcohol is a better problem to have than a drug problem. When you are dependent on a substance, it doesn't matter what the chemical actually is; it's still a problem, and you are just as addicted.

Some in recovery try to convince themselves that they can handle drinking; it's just drugs that are a problem. This is denial too. The fact is that many addicts cross over from drug addiction to alcoholism. The actual substance you abuse is only part of the problem; the other part is the fact that you aren't able to cope with life without using something to make you feel high. Don't try to justify your substance abuse. If you use, no matter what chemical it is, you lose.

■ *Don't try to convince yourself or others that things are not as bad as they look; that's denial.*

K.B.

A SLAVE TO FEAR

You did not receive the spirit of bondage again to fear, but you received the Spirit of adoption by whom we cry out, "Abba, Father."
—ROM. 8:15

Fear flows through most of what we do. Why do you do what your peers want you to do even though you know you shouldn't? Why do you behave differently around certain people? Why don't people get up on their table in a restaurant and sing "Jesus Loves Me"? The reason is fear. Fear of rejection is often what motivates us to behave within certain limits. This fear motivates a lot of behavior. It is an awful feeling when someone doesn't like you, or when you sense that someone is displeased with you. It is so motivating that you may even attempt to conform or seek to make amends.

That same fear will stalk you throughout your recovery. Deciding to overcome an addiction means putting yourself in a position to be rejected by those who choose not to recover. That is why it is important to know the antidote to this fear.

The sure solution to the fear of rejection is relationships with people who will support you and encourage you in your recovery. These are people you can run to when you have been hurt, and you will find safety and encouragement. When you have a foundation of secure relationships to work from, it is a lot easier to handle rejection.

■ *Develop solid relationships with people who support and encourage you.*

R.M.

KINDS OF DENIAL

The truthful lip shall be established forever,
But a lying tongue is but for a moment.
—PROV. 12:19

You might think denial is simple—it is not admitting you have a problem. It's really more complex than that. In fact, there are many things a person in denial might believe:

"I don't drink more than any of my friends."

"What's wrong with an occasional buzz?"

"But I only do it on weekends!"

"I'm still doing O.K. in school."

"I can quit anytime I want to."

These are just of few of the statements we hear alcohol and drug abusers say all the time. They all have one thing in common: All are meant to get people off the addict's back. But even if they work, they help the addict put others off for just a little while. Eventually the problems created by substance abuse will become big enough that others will be able to see that something is terribly wrong.

If you really are serious about changing your life, watch out for denial. It's not as simple as it might seem. Be truthful with yourself and those who care about you. Let them know that you need help to make it. The longer you put off admitting this, the longer it will be before you can lead a clean and sober life.

■ *Help me to see myself as I really am. Break down my*
walls of denial so that I can see the truth.

K.B.

WHAT DOES YOUR RECOVERY LOOK LIKE?

Therefore I run thus: not with uncertainty.
Thus I fight: not as one who beats the air.
—1 COR. 9:26

What does your recovery look like? Are you taking a stroll? Are you running a 100-meter dash? Or are you in a marathon? People take different approaches to their recovery. Some are like sprinters. They push to get things "right" and are so driven that they drive everyone else crazy. This person eventually burns out and crashes.

Some people look like they are headed nowhere fast. They are out for a good time in recovery and aren't concerned about the finer points that make recovery strong. They assume that they are on the "right" path and will get there sooner or later. After all, why put yourself out?

The last type of person is the one who realizes recovery is a marathon and is committed for the long term. He knows there are mountains of discouragement to climb and setbacks, and at other times there is easy running. So he is careful to set a pace that he can keep up. At the same time, he is open to encouragement and feedback when he is losing ground.

Which of these persons are you like in your recovery? Remember that your recovery cannot be accomplished in a day or even a year. It's a life-long process that will bring the growth you want.

■   *Father, help me to set the pace for a healthy recovery.*

R.M.

A SCAM ARTIST'S STORY

Bread gained by deceit is sweet to a man,
But . . . his mouth will be filled with
gravel. —PROV. 20:17

It was pretty intense, the biggest rush I've ever had!"
Fifteen-year-old Bill sat across from me as he talked
about breaking into a friend's house. The friend had
trusted Bill enough to tell him that she was holding
$1,500 her boyfriend had made selling cocaine. If she
really had known Bill, she would never have given him
that information, but he had a way about him that made
people believe him.

"She deserved it; she was dumb enough to trust
me," he said. Something had happened to him since he
started using cocaine. His conscience, the part that tells
him what is right or wrong, had become weak. Like a
muscle, the conscience gets smaller when it isn't exer-
cised, and Bill's was so small it almost didn't exist.

"Anyway, it was drug money, so it really wasn't that
bad." He made one last try to convince me that his
actions weren't bad. But I knew better. I could see how
he was hurting himself by not listening to his guilt. The
more he got high, the more the things his parents had
taught him about good and bad were disappearing from
his mind. Bill had once been a pretty good kid, but now
he was a person that nobody could trust.

■ *How has your conscience slipped since you began*
using?

K.B.

AFRAID OF WEAKNESS

Though He was crucified in weakness, yet He lives by the power of God. For we also are weak in Him, but we shall live with Him by the power of God. —2 COR. 13:4

People spend a lot of time avoiding reality. It's quite easy to avoid reality. After all, that is why substance abuse is such a powerful addiction. It allows you to avoid reality even if for only a little while. It is powerful enough that you want to go back for more and more. That is what makes it so hard to recover from addictions. Recovery is the difficult process of trying to develop new ways of dealing with reality. One of these realities is the disturbing fact that sometimes we are weak and have limitations.

Are you afraid of your weakness? If you are, then you are afraid of a reality that all of us must deal with. It is important to understand that there are many things beyond our control, and we need to focus on things we can truly change. Having limitations isn't a permanent problem, but it is an obstacle you will always face. Even if you overcome one limitation there will always be another to face. That can sound pretty discouraging, but remember that you are not in recovery alone. In order to overcome, you will need to deal with limitations in your life as they really are, not the way you think they should be.

■   *Father, help me to deal with my weaknesses without fear.*

R.M.

REPAYING EVIL WITH GOOD

"If your enemies are hungry, give them something to eat. . . ." Don't let evil defeat you, but defeat evil with good.
—ROM. 12:20–21 CEV

Brad was angry and wanted to get back at the person who had wronged him. He was smart enough to know he couldn't go around beating up everyone he felt had done him wrong. Instead, Brad wanted to turn the others on the rehab unit against the guy and make him feel lonely and isolated.

Brad told me his plan, making sure it fit the rules of the unit. At first I agreed with his plan, but then I wondered why he wished to confront the guy. Was it because he cared or because he wanted to make the guy pay for what he had done? If Brad's goal was revenge, the plan would backfire and become a fight where each tried to hurt the other more.

When someone has wronged you, payback and revenge are *never* the answer. The plan you come up with needs to pass two tests. First, you need to leave revenge and payback to God. Second, you need to be certain that whatever you do is designed to help, not hurt the one you feel has wronged you. Brad's confrontation would only have made things worse unless Brad honestly wanted to help the other guy. Always repay evil done *to* you with good done *by* you. According to God, that is the best payback.

■ *Teach me, God, never to pay back one wrong with another.*

K.B.

LOOKING BACK SATISFIED

I have fought the good fight, I have finished the race, I have kept the faith.

—2 TIM. 4:7

I am happy I chose the path I did. I have come far, because I lived, breathed, and slept getting better." Those are the words of a young man who had successfully negotiated his recovery, and yet he knew that much of the path was still ahead of him. He wasn't afraid because he had learned the lessons necessary to take on almost any challenge. Even if he didn't know all that was necessary, he could learn what he needed on the path as he continued along.

Few feelings are more satisfying than looking back on good, healthy decisions. It is self-esteem building and feels just plain good. That's what Paul was saying. He had worked long and hard in his mission work, and he could look out from a prison cell and say he had fought the good fight.

Will those be your words in the future? Yes, if you are willing to make good decisions now. The important thing to remember is that the decisions you make today have value in the future. They are not "throw-away" decisions that will bear no fruit. That isn't to say that you must ruminate over decisions for days on end just to avoid making the wrong one. Make decisions, but understand that they will have lasting value.

■ *Remember that your decisions today will have lasting importance.*

R.M.

BUILDING ON THE ROCK

"Anyone who comes and listens to me and obeys me is like someone who dug down deep and built a house on solid rock."
—LUKE 6:47–48 CEV

Some houses are carefully constructed of the finest, strongest materials on top of solid foundations. They withstand tornadoes, hurricanes, and all sorts of storms without crumbling. Others are built quickly and cheaply. When storms come, they fall apart.

Recovery is like building a house. If you cut corners, you build a weak and shaky new life. The first time problems arise, the house caves in and you must start building all over again. People looking for quick fixes construct rickety lives that can't handle challenges.

Solid change means hard work and slow, solid progress. Take time, carefully working on your recovery to make certain that the results will last. Since God created you and knows you inside-out, He can stand by you throughout the construction process, making certain that the new life you are building will outlast the storms of life that are sure to come.

God also provides a solid foundation on which to build your new life. A life anchored to God will simply not blow away. As you work on recovering, consider carefully what you are building on, and make God the foundation of all the changes you start.

■ *God, assist me as I work on changing negative patterns that keep my life weak and shabby.*

K.B.

GOD ISN'T DEAF

*"I cried out to the LORD . . .
And he answered me."*
—JONAH 2:2

Few people in the Bible faced more adversity than Jonah. He created much of his own misery, but still he had a lion's share of problems. You can learn an important lesson from Jonah while you continue your pursuit of health. In spite of how you feel when you get discouraged, God is still listening. It seems that when things don't go our way, or a day seems to be filled with problems and hassles, God is the furthest away from us. But just the opposite is true. We get blinded by our problems, and we end up seeing God through our problems. When we do that He looks pretty dim and far away. We end up overwhelmed by the problems we face, and want to give up because we don't have the resources and God is a long way off.

The most important principle to master when you face adversity is to see your problems through God. By looking at your problems through God, you will begin to see opportunities to grow and learn more for the road ahead of you. That is what Jonah did when he uttered the prayer that is today's scripture—he said it in the stomach of a whale! Yet, God was still there, waiting for Jonah to admit his weakness and powerlessness over his situation, and to ask for His help.

■ *Father, help me to look at my problems through You.*
R.M.

THE LORD'S PRAYER

*"Keep us from being tempted and protect us
from evil."* —MATT. 6:13 CEV

If you go to church, you have probably said the Lord's
Prayer many times. In fact, you may not even think
about what you are praying. One line in this prayer is
important for those in recovery.

Temptation is one of the worst things about recovery.
You know that you need to stay clean, and avoid people
and situations that might drag you back into the addictive patterns. Yet you long for the old ways because they
were so much easier than trying to stay clean. There is a
battle inside you, and you feel torn between giving in or
continuing to fight.

Every time you say the Lord's Prayer, you ask God to
do two things. First, you ask Him not to lead you into
temptation. You beg him to keep you away from tempting situations that could destroy all that you have
worked so hard to achieve. Second, you ask God to deliver you from the evil one, to keep you safe when you
find yourself in dangerous situations.

From now on, when you say the Lord's Prayer, think
about what these two parts really mean. Ask God to
keep you from situations in which you are tempted to
drink or get high. Then ask for deliverance from danger
when you get into troublesome predicaments.

■ *Lead me not into tempting situations, and, if I am in
one, deliver me before I mess up.*

K.B.

ENVYING THE WRONG PEOPLE

Do not fret because of evildoers,
Nor be envious of the workers of iniquity.
—PS. 37:1

I work as hard as I can at recovery, but it's so hard. Tom has it so easy. Everything is going great for him. He doesn't have a care in the world. It's so unfair." Greg was really discouraged. He had been working very hard in treatment and was religious in attending support group meetings, but his friends who used drugs didn't seem to have the problems he was facing.

It's easy to cast an envious eye on those who seem to go merrily through life, never paying a price for their denial and refusal to deal with their problems. Why do you have to deal with yours? Couldn't you just quit, leave well enough alone, and everything would be fine? Just because someone is blind to the wounds in his life and his dysfunctional coping strategies doesn't mean it is right. You probably have already found the price paid for denying and ignoring the pain in your life.

Beware of comparisons; they will always lead to distorted thinking. There is nothing worth envying about someone who is in denial and continues in a self-destructive pattern of abusing drugs or alcohol. Maintain perspective on recovery. You are doing it for yourself, not to come out ahead in a comparison with someone else.

■ *Father, help me to maintain perspective on my recovery and not compare myself with anyone else.*

R.M.

DON'T BE AFRAID TO TELL OTHERS

"You don't light a lamp and put it under a clay pot or under a bed. Don't you put a lamp on a lampstand?"

—MARK 4:21 CEV

Zach knew life after rehab would be hard. His only friends were those with whom he had skipped school and gotten drunk. The memories they shared were of wild drinking sprees. When he got home, he would have to start over. I didn't believe Zach would make it.

But then he did some things that surprised me. He started going to Alcoholics Anonymous. I thought he might go once and quit, but he went three times each week. When he got different key chains for sobriety, he proudly wore them on his belt. He started telling people about his recovery. Before long, he had convinced the school administration to start A.A. in his school.

Zach made it in recovery because he told others his story. He believed that something which had made him feel better and think clearly, should not be hidden. Before recovery he was a mindless burnout who was always in trouble. Now he had become respected, even by the authorities he was always getting into trouble with before.

When you try to keep your recovery a secret, you don't have the support you need to make it. Don't be so afraid of failure that you don't tell anyone. When you talk about your recovery, you're not only helping yourself, but you might also save another addict.

■ *God, give me courage to tell my story to anyone who can be helped by it.*

K.B.

SEEING CLEARLY

It is better to go to the house of mourning
Than to go to the house of feasting.
—ECC. 7:2

Sometimes you can see things much clearer when you are serious or even sad. I'm not proposing that you get depressed just to see things more clearly. But grieving or feeling sad over not doing things just right isn't always bad. These feelings have an interesting way of getting us to focus on the real issues we would otherwise avoid.

How often have you heard people talk about their substance abuse problem at a party? Why not? Usually the reason is that they don't want to talk about things that are "depressing." They want to continue to avoid reality. That is why substance abuse is so enticing. It is a great way to escape the uncomfortable realities in our lives.

It is important to put reality in its proper perspective or your recovery will be short-lived. Reality doesn't change much. Substance abuse is a way to change reality, but it actually distorts it. Your treatment is meant to help you learn new ways to deal with reality so that it is not always so depressing. When you have learned these ways, you won't have to run from reality, but can deal with it and get on with the real fun in life.

■ *Father, help me to deal with reality as it is, and not avoid the uncomfortable things in my life.*

R.M.

A NEW PERSONALITY

God's Spirit makes us loving, happy, peaceful. . . . Because we belong to Christ, we have killed our selfish feelings and desires. —GAL. 5:22–24 CEV

Chad discovered something important about himself. What he found out shocked him and lowered his self-esteem. Several of his A.A. buddies had confronted him and told him that he was full of pride and sometimes said things to put others down. They also said that he got angry when he didn't get his own way.

Deep inside, Chad knew they were telling the truth, but had a hard time admitting it. As part of his recovery, he had to start making a list of things about himself that kept him acting like an addict, like scamming, not looking at himself truthfully, pretending he had it together when he didn't, and putting others down to make himself look good.

Somehow, hearing others say these things felt worse than just thinking them inside. As we talked he shared that he was afraid he was so bad there was no way he could ever make it in recovery.

There is good news for Chad, and for you. When you turn your life over to God and ask for help in recovery, something begins changing deep inside. The old personality becomes uncomfortable, and you wish to find new ways to act. That is God, slowly giving you a healthier and more controlled personality.

■ *Lord, help me not to get discouraged when the old me doesn't feel right anymore.*

K.B.

Oh, I Can Do It Tomorrow!

Do not boast about tomorrow,
For you do not know what a
day may bring forth.
—PROV. 27:1

How many times have you said "I can do it tomorrow"? We think that by putting it off, a job will become a little bit more palatable tomorrow. The fact is that the job is bad no matter which day you do it!

Putting things off in recovery is deadly. It will pick up speed and carry you along without your realizing it. Suppose you decide to miss your support group meeting just one night, saying to yourself, "Oh, I can miss it this once. What harm will it do?" So you do whatever you decided was more important than your meeting. The next time your meeting comes along, you will probably find it a real struggle to go back. You have crossed a line that watered down your commitment to attending your meetings. The more times you cross this line, the easier it becomes to cross it again and again.

Don't put stock in what you can or can't do "the next time." The opportunity to change the trend of avoiding responsibility might never come because you have begun to make it less important. It takes a great deal of courage and strength to stick by a commitment no matter what. That might mean even being "religious" about it, so that you can have a tomorrow to plan for.

■ *Father, help me not to put off for tomorrow important things I need to do today.*

R.M.

RUNNING TO WIN

*You know that many runners enter a race,
and only one of them wins the prize. So run
to win!* —1 COR. 9:24 CEV

You know the story of the tortoise and the hare. The tortoise plods along to the end and never quits. The rabbit takes off fast and then naps, only to wake up and see that slow tortoise crossing the finish line. Recovery is like that.

People who abuse alcohol and drugs come to expect instant relief. Quickly the high takes over and they don't have to deal with much. Therefore, they expect recovery to be the same way, quick and easy. Like the rabbit, many decide to take a rest from recovery and relapse.

Those who succeed at recovery are like the tortoise. They know that it will be a long, slow journey and that they will have to make it by carefully taking one step at a time. These individuals sometimes feel tired, but keep working at it. Sometimes they may feel like giving up, but they keep trying. Sometimes they envy others who seem to move so rapidly and find instant relief, but they keep thinking one day at a time.

In the end, careful and slow-moving people win the prize: sobriety. While they may have worked much harder, their lives show the results. And they have learned a valuable lesson: nothing that comes quickly in recovery is really worth it. True growth and maturity take time.

■ *Do you feel like a clumsy turtle in your recovery? You're doing the work that will win the race.*

K.B.

DON'T GIVE UP

Let us not grow weary while doing good, for in due season we shall reap if we do not lose heart.
—GAL. 6:9

Anything worth having is always hard. Anything easy to get isn't worth much." That is true of recovery. It is by no measure easy; it is hard work. Because it is so difficult, you will sometime want to throw your hands up and say, "I give up!" Remember that anything worth having is worth working for. You've worked for other things you really wanted. You didn't mind the hard work because what you wanted was important enough to expend the energy.

Some people seem to have a timer in their heads, set to go off when they think they will have spent enough time on one job. When their timer does go off and they see they have more work to do, they get discouraged. Their time limit has expired and they're ready to play, but they can't leave the job yet.

Recovery is worth the hard work. It takes little or no strength to give up. It takes a lot of character and inner strength to endure. Today's passage makes clear that there is a harvest of benefits if we don't give up in doing what we need to do to keep going in our recovery.

■ *Remember that recovery is a lifelong process. Don't put a timer on it and expect to complete the process.*
R.M.

I'M NOT SURE I'M READY TO CHANGE

He gave himself to rescue us from everything that is evil and to make our hearts pure. He wanted us . . . to be eager to do right.
—TITUS 2:14 CEV

Are you ready to change? For some the answer is yes, for others no. Giving up old, comfortable ways of coping with problems is scary because it means doing new things you might not feel ready to try. What does change mean? What is in your future? Since you can't predict it, the future is totally uncertain, and that can make change frightening.

Usually when someone has a choice between doing something he knows he can do well or something new, he may not succeed at, he will choose the thing he knows. But when it comes to addictions, the old ways are the danger you're trying to stop. So you face the unknown, not sure whether you want to proceed.

God sees your choice and understands your uncertainty. Because He wants to rescue you from your unsatisfactory past and to help you make better choices for the future, He is a good place to start. Perhaps you don't know whether you want to change. He will give you the desire to do it when you ask. If you wait until you feel like it, you will never begin. Take the first step right now. Ask God to give you the desire to do what is right.

■   *Lord, make me ready to change.*

K.B.

IMPRESSED WITH YOURSELF

Shall words of wind have an end?
Or what provokes you that you answer?
—JOB 16:3

Small things matter in recovery. They indicate where you are in your recovery overall. One of those "small things" of recovery is the way you interact with and support people. Job had an interesting bunch of friends during his trials. They advised him on a host of problems they perceived he had. What was obvious as they talked was how important they thought they were. They were sure their advice was earth-shattering and awe-inspiring. They showed little humility.

Beware of long-windedness when people ask you for advice. Don't have a lofty view of yourself. When we talk to people, we are sometimes talking to ourselves as well. After all, there are two people in a conversation, and there are two people listening—you and the person you are talking to.

Our speech and the way we talk are dead giveaways of what we think of ourselves. Be sure to indicate that you have found things that work for you, but may not work for the person you are advising. Give that person the right to not take your counsel. Each of these suggestions indicates a humility that needs to be central to your recovery. When you get overly confident and proud, you set yourself up for relapse.

■ *Father, help me to talk in a way that keeps my pride in its rightful place.*

R.M.

T.G.I.T.W.

"If you are as humble as [a] child, you are the greatest in the kingdom of heaven."
—MATT. 18:4 CEV

Many years ago a guy in my high school had some letters written on his jeans, T.G.I.T.W. One day I asked him what they meant. He told me they stood for The Greatest in the World. While he was a pretty good guy, I didn't think he was *that* great!

It did get me to think a little about what really made someone the greatest. In recovery, greatness is not measured by how rich, how good-looking, or how smart you are. It's measured by whether you can stay sober one more day. Staying that way means you need to work your recovery program. And working your program means you have to do something very important: stay humble.

When Jesus' disciples asked who would be the greatest in heaven, he said something pretty deep. He told them they needed to stay humble, like little kids. Children don't go around bragging all the time; they just enjoy life minute by minute. Greatness is measured by your ability to recognize that you are not some special, wonderful person. It comes by being humble, as little children.

■ *God, keep me humble as a little child.*

K.B.

FOOLISHNESS

Foolishness is bound up in the heart
of a child,
But the rod of correction will drive
it far from him.

—PROV. 22:15

Children make decisions based on thin air sometimes. Their actions are whimsical and impulsive. They give very little to their actions; whatever hits them is what they do.

How would people characterize the way you are managing your recovery? Would they say you have made some pretty foolish decisions lately? If this is true, maybe it's time to grow up and begin to use what you know. In our treatment programs, we often refer kids to what they learned in the beginning. They are given tools to use throughout recovery. At times, though, they set aside these tools and lapse into old behavior. They should have known better, but they chose not to use the tools they developed, and they go on impulse alone.

The solution is to get back to basics. Go back over some of the materials you were given in treatment. Talk to someone who can remind you of the basics of expressing your feelings when they arise, being honest, and admitting your need for God to guide your recovery. Getting back to the basics isn't admitting defeat; it is doing what you have to to get moving again in your recovery.

■ *Father, help me to use the tools I have been given to progress in my recovery.*

R.M.

BACK TO BASICS

How can you be so stupid? Do you think that by yourself you can complete what God's Spirit started in you? —GAL. 3:3 CEV

In organized sports, every once in a while a team makes dumb mistakes. At half-time or after the game, the coach will give a talk on mastering the fundamentals. He tells the team that they have forgotten the basic building blocks of the sport and that next week they will have to work on relearning the simple things they have messed up.

Sometimes it is good to review the fundamentals of recovery. After you've been working for a while, it is easy to forget the simple things you learned in the beginning, things like admitting you are powerless, or that you need God's intervention, or that you should stay humble. Once you fail to remember these basic parts of your recovery program, nothing else will work.

Spend some time today thinking about the important things you learned early in your recovery. Think about how they can be taken for granted because they now seem so simple and basic. Remember that what may seem simple on the surface, is really the foundation of any good recovery. If these steps are forgotten or neglected, all of the building you have done on this foundation will crumble, and you will find yourself right back where you started.

■ *God, help me remember the basics so that the rest of my recovery will have a strong foundation.*

K.B.

A SIGN OF GROWTH

[He] is under guardians and stewards until
the time appointed by the father.

—GAL. 4:2

I am often asked, "How do you know when you are growing?" You will grow in recovery if you concentrate on working your program and remaining committed to using the tools you have been taught. Often you don't notice that growth because you concentrate so hard on practicing the "right" things. How many kids have said to you, "Oh, by the way, I have grown two inches this month"? Not many, I would guess. We often don't pay attention to growth until it has already happened and we look back and notice that something has definitely happened.

There are some signs of growth that you can notice in yourself that may be encouraging for you to see. One sure sign of growth is being able to run your recovery unsupervised. In other words, you don't need someone looking over your shoulder all the time. When you can keep on track and call people when you need to without being prompted, you are growing. The need for supervision and constant direction is a characteristic of childishness in your recovery. If you can see areas in your life that need examining and go after them with energy, that is a good indication that you are growing up and growing healthier.

■ *Father, help me to see areas in my life that need attention and deal with them unprompted.*

R.M.

WHICH WAY NOW?

*Your ears shall hear a word
behind you, saying,
"This is the way, walk in it."*
—IS. 30:21

It is common in recovery to wonder about what to do next. You can't always be certain that what you want to do is the right thing. In fact, it's good that you sometimes wonder about which way to go, because that means you are honest enough to know you can easily mess up.

As you become more truthful with yourself about the wrongs you have done and the hurt you have caused others, something exciting will start to happen. Your conscience will become stronger. God works through your conscience by helping you to recognize right from wrong. When you are committed to allowing God to lead you, He is able to push your conscience to tell you when you are about to make a mistake.

It is always dangerous to trust yourself too much, and it is important to get feedback from others on a regular basis. On the other hand, as you progress in recovery you will begin, partially because of others' caring confrontations, to hear God's voice speaking to you from your conscience, directing each step through recovery.

■ *God, strengthen my conscience. Direct my journey through each step of recovery.*

K.B.

WHY WORRY ABOUT THE REST?

"If you then are not able to do the least, why are you anxious for the rest?"
—LUKE 12:26

In recovery, people tend to worry about things that don't matter. They get distracted with areas that catch their attention, but they aren't ready to deal with them yet. Then they dive in and fail, and wonder why. For example, you may not be ready to go to a party because you know that it will be a sure set-up for failure. It's okay to allow yourself to grow in your recovery.

It's like developing a new skill, something you have never done before. Take a sport like racquetball. First, you learn the rules of the game. Next, you master the basics of keeping the ball in play without killing yourself running into the walls of the playing area. Once you have mastered the basics, you must practice. Increasingly, you will gain skill as you play. However, let's say that you decide to challenge the best player in the area to a game. You get slaughtered, and you feel dejected and discouraged. The problem is that you have taken on someone who is better than you, and you have attempted to do things that you weren't ready to do at your skill level.

Recovery isn't much different. You must allow yourself to be new to "the game," and learn the ropes before you take on more advanced jobs.

■ *Allow yourself to grow in your recovery and take on things that you are ready for.*

R.M.

FEAR WILL SINK YOU

When Peter saw how strong the wind was, he was afraid and started sinking. "Lord, save me!" he shouted.

—MATT. 14:30 CEV

Until they realized it was Jesus, the disciples were terrified of the person walking toward them on the water. Bravely, Peter tried to walk over to meet Jesus. Peter took a few steps, got scared, and began to sink. If Jesus hadn't reached out to save him, Peter would have drowned.

Until you put God in charge of your recovery, you were stuck in the middle of the stormy sea of addiction without a way back to solid ground. With God's help you were able to start walking across to the safety of the shore. As long as you continue to trust and keep your eyes on God, you won't sink and drown.

There will be times when you begin to doubt and start thinking, "This will never work." Immediately you will start sinking, because you aren't trusting the One who can keep you from getting in over your head. Even during these times, God will be right there reaching out to you, waiting to grab your hand and pull you out of the sea of addiction.

There is no need to be afraid or to doubt. God is the Master of even the most furious sea of addiction. Grab the hand He is reaching out and be pulled to safety.

■ *God, if I begin to sink, remind me that You are reaching out to pull me to solid ground.*

K.B.

PAIN IN PERSPECTIVE

For our light affliction, which is but for a moment, is working for us a far more exceeding and eternal weight of glory.
—2 COR. 4:17

It is important to put the pain you experience during recovery in perspective. Maybe there is a good reason for it. It is small in comparison to the end result of living a life pleasing to God and drug-free.

When I played basketball, more than once the coach told me, "No pain, no gain!" As with many clichés that we throw at each other, there is a lot of truth in that phrase. The pain and struggles you go through in your recovery give you the staying power you need to hang in there. Pain in recovery is never without purpose. It is a down payment on a lifestyle of recovery.

Is the pain you experience from a bad decision you made? Don't lie down and have a pity-party. Learn from it. Ask yourself, "What did I do wrong here?" And "What can I do differently to avoid it next time?"

The pain you feel may be from a good decision that people around you don't approve of because they are still immersed in dysfunctional behavior. This isn't "bad" pain. It tells you that you are on the right track. If you don't meet resistance from the people around you who are abusing, then you aren't actively pursuing recovery.

■ *Father, help me to keep my struggles for recovery in the proper perspective.*

R.M.

OWNING UP TO YOUR MISTAKES

*If you have sinned, you should tell each other
what you have done. Then you can pray for
one another and be healed.*
                    —JAMES 5:16 CEV

There's something pretty cool about sharing mistakes
and dumb choices of the past with someone else. Recovery is all about looking at yourself and admitting you
can't handle your addiction on your own. The moment
you start feeling you've got it under control, pride steps
in and you fail.

As long as you stay humble and admit that you're
weak, you keep moving in a healthy direction. The best
way to stay humble is to let others know what you're
really like inside. That kind of honesty will help others
to know what you're up to and will assist them in pointing out things you need to change. At the same time, it
will keep you from getting too proud of yourself.

No one in this world is perfect. We've all made mistakes. Unless you share with others what you're really
like, you pretend you're someone you're not. While it's
hard to tell others your deepest secrets, fears, guilt, and
regrets, it will free you from hiding things about yourself. And when you hide things, you go right back
where you started: in denial of the truth.

Be open. Share the truth about yourself with at least
one other person. When you get the load of secrets and
shame off your back, you will be much lighter, walking
down the road to recovery.

■   *God, don't let me hold back the truth about myself.
    Keep me from falling back into denial.*

                                                    K.B.

CONSEQUENCES OF PUTTING THINGS OFF

Woe to you who put far off the day of doom,
Who cause the seat of violence to come near.
                                    —AMOS 6:3

I sure wish I hadn't put off talking to someone. If I hadn't, I would have been able to avoid the relapse that put me back so far."

It is painful when you realize how dearly you've paid for putting things off. That is what Terry was realizing as he told me about a recent situation he couldn't get out of with his friends. Some of his friends called him up and put him on the spot, asking him to go with them to a party. Instead of putting them off, making them wait for his decision while he called his sponsor, he put off his recovery and decided to go to the party. He thought he was strong enough to resist any temptation. But his friends hadn't been honest with him about their plan for the evening, and he ended up not being able to get home without them.

It is important to understand that you will frequently confront the choice to remain consistent with your goals for recovery or to put that choice off. At first, putting things off looks pretty harmless—as Terry thought going with his friends would be. But he didn't pay attention to the feeling that he needed to call his sponsor to talk about whether he was making a good choice. If he had, he might have avoided the consequences he now faced.

■   *Never put things off related to your recovery that you can do now.*

                                                    R.M.

LOOKING FOR THE FIRST HIGH

*"Come," one says, "I will bring wine,
And we will fill ourselves with
intoxicating drink."* —IS. 56:12

Bert talked to us about his alcohol and drug abuse, and how things just kept getting worse until he didn't feel much of anything when he used. "In fact," he said, "toward the end, I was using just to feel normal. I just couldn't handle the misery I felt when I wasn't drunk or high."

He started drinking to feel good. Eventually drinking lost its thrill for him. He moved on to pot, which also worked for a while, but like booze it stopped making him feel high. He then tried harder drugs, but eventually nothing made him feel like the first high.

Most addicts keep searching for that first high. Even after they realize that chemicals aren't giving them that high they keep trying. In the end they must use larger and larger amounts just to keep from feeling any kind of withdrawal effects; they avoid pain but don't get high. Overdoses often are the result of someone's trying to use enough to feel high.

Next time you long for that first high, remember that it never comes back. The only thing that does come back, time after time, is the emotional pain you've been putting off and the physical effects of withdrawal.

■ *God, help me to stop looking for what I can never get back and focus on staying high on life.*

K.B.

ASSUMING TOO MUCH

*You do not know what will happen tomorrow.
For what is your life? It is even a vapor that
appears for a little time and then vanishes
away.*
—JAMES 4:14

One thing that sets teens up for failure is their tendency to assume that nothing will change from one day to the next. When they think this, they end up frustrated and angry that everything is going wrong. Part of the reason for this is not that the day hasn't cooperated with their plans (which it never does!), but that their expectations have been too inflexible to conform to what a day typically presents. You see, you must plan for the unexpected because it is sure to happen. By assuming that nothing is going to change, you either accidentally or intentionally place yourself equal with God because He is the only one who knows what tomorrow will bring. You may never have thought of it that way, but if you think about it you'll see what I mean.

The phrase "one day at time" holds a lot of truth. To assume that tomorrow will be the same as today is not taking one day at a time. It is putting off what you can do today for tomorrow with the assumption that you can predict that you will be able to do what you had planned. Be careful not to place too much emphasis on tomorrow. You can still plan, but grab today while you have it. You will never have it again!

■ *Father, help to grab today and make it count for my recovery.*

R.M.

FAITH LIKE A TINY SEED

*"If you had faith no larger than a mustard
seed, you could tell this mountain to move
from here to there. And it would."*
—MATT. 17:20 CEV

Robert began to have doubts about some of the changes he was making in recovery. "Look, how can believing in a higher power that I can't see or hear make things better?" It was a question of faith; Robert wanted to use his senses to believe in God, to see, hear, taste, touch, or smell God. It was difficult to believe in something he couldn't experience with one of his five senses.

This kind of doubt can hold us back in recovery. Now, God is big enough to handle your doubts; He knows you well. The problem is not God; it's us. Faith is believing in something even though our senses can't directly detect it. And there are lots of things we've never seen firsthand but we believe in, like the ozone layer.

A mustard seed is one of the smallest seeds on earth. Jesus said that if we have only a tiny bit of faith, like the puny mustard seed, we can do things so amazing that they are humanly impossible, like making mountains move. Recovery from drug and alcohol abuse might seem like an impossible mountain, but with a wee bit of faith, like a tiny seed, it will happen.

■ *God, I have faith that You can do something miraculous to help me stay clean one more day.*

K.B.

INVINCIBILITY

> *"I am, and there is no one else besides me.*
> *I shall not sit as a widow,*
> *Nor shall I know the loss of children."*
> —IS. 47:8

One of the myths of youth is that you are invincible, that bad things happen to everyone but you. So when a friend who had a relatively successful treatment program relapses, you may say to yourself, "That will never happen to me!" You develop a false sense of security as to how well things are going and how well you are doing. That is exactly what the people of Israel thought as well. Things were going well, and they "lounged in their security" and were unable to defend themselves against a marauding army.

There is a useful message for you in the passage for today. Never get caught by the myth of invincibility. If you believe that the bad things that happen to others will never happen to you, you are sure to make them happen. If your friends can relapse, so can you. This is particularly true when you get secure in the success of your recovery. Recovery never carries itself along. It takes work and vigilance to watch out for the little things that trip you up and turn into a major relapse.

■ *Father, help me not to think that I am invincible and assume that I am safe from relapse.*

R.M.

THE WILD BROTHER

"Father, I have sinned against God in heaven and against you. I am no longer good enough to be called your son."
—LUKE 15:18–20 CEV

The younger of two brothers was a party animal. He asked his dad for his half of the money and took off into the world to live wildly. After all the money was gone and his friends had disappeared, he was left to find a dead-end job that paid next to nothing. He was forced to suffer the consequences of his actions: loneliness, guilt, and depression.

When he finally sobered up, he realized he had screwed up so much that anything was better than where he stood. He decided to go back to his dad and apologize, but not with your typical "I'm sorry." He realized that he didn't deserve his father's forgiveness, and so he said, "I'm no longer good enough to be called your son."

There comes a time when an addict is far enough along in recovery that he understands just how bad the things he did were. A simple "I'm sorry" apology does not begin to make up for the hurt caused by his actions.

When you reach this point in recovery, it's comforting to know that the story ends well. The father was so excited that his wild son had returned to his senses that he threw a big party to welcome him home. No matter how far down you slip, God will welcome you back with open arms.

■ *Don't let guilt ruin your recovery. God will forgive you for things you have done.*

K.B.

THE USEFULNESS OF ADVERSITY

Before I was afflicted I went astray,
But now I keep Your word.
—PS. 119:67

Adversity is much more than hassles and pain. It is very useful for your recovery to get your priorities back into order. They need ongoing care in order to be maintained and kept in functioning order. That is where adversity comes in. In the verse for today, the writer makes it pretty clear that the adversity he faced was useful to get back on the track he was purposing to follow.

Peace and quiet in our lives have a way of putting us to sleep. When we are asleep, figuratively speaking, we are much less responsive to our needs and the temptations we face. A sleeping person isn't much on decisions, is he? It is important to remember that not all adversity is bad. It is often specially designed by God to get your attention or wake you up, and give you an opportunity to reorder your priorities before you fall off the edge of your cliff of relapse.

Another thing to remember is that often you will experience adversity because of a wrong decision you have made. In this case, adversity is essential because you can learn from the bad decision and not make it again. So remember to look at adversity as something you may be able to use rather than complain about.

■ *Father, help me to see adversity as something I can use to avoid mistakes in the future.*

R.M.

GETTING BUSTED

Why should a living man complain,
A man for the punishment of his sins?
—LAM. 3:39

In the hospital unit where I work, smoking is not allowed. So when I walked by Jerry's room and smelled cigarette smoke, I was surprised. I was a little disappointed, too.

Jerry didn't want to be in the hospital; he felt his drug problem wasn't that bad. His parents did, especially when the school told them their son was skipping three or four days each week and getting high with friends. But as Jerry's head cleared up, he could admit that things weren't so good, and he had done great work. And then I smelled the smoke.

Naturally Jerry got in trouble. And he acted like I was the one who had done something wrong for busting him. That was part of Jerry's addiction. He had trouble taking responsibility for things he did wrong, and that was why he was acting like it was my fault for getting on his case. A major part of recovery is admitting when you mess up and taking the consequences for your own mistakes, *not* blaming everyone else.

Next time you get busted for doing something wrong, make an adult decision. Take responsibility for your actions. Until you begin to admit mistakes and deal with the consequences, you are still practicing addictive behaviors.

■ *God, help me to take responsibility for my actions instead of getting mad that I got busted.*

K.B.

ADVERSITY WITH A PURPOSE

But He knows the way that I take;
When He has tested me, I shall
come forth as gold.
                              —JOB 23:10

I've paid my debt! I've worked hard at recovery. It just isn't fair that it isn't getting easier yet." John interpreted the adversity he faced as an accident, and that God had said "Oops" when this problem hit him. God knows you better than you know yourself. He knows exactly what you need to come through recovery successfully. Seeing adversity as a mistake, as something out of the ordinary, sets you up for more frustration than had you just dealt with what was before you. The problem is that reality is often a drag. It presents you with a bewildering array of frustrations and hassles. You get into trouble when you begin to think that "normal" is peace and that hassles and frustrations are "abnormal."

Perspective makes a big difference when it comes to handling adversity. You need to see the adversity you face in your recovery as something God has designed especially to help you grow and become healthy. Remember, you are still in the process of becoming healthy, and that takes time, patience, and endurance. Seeing adversity as something to help you grow will help you further down your path to health.

■   *Father, help me to see the adversity I face as You help me to grow.*

                                                            R.M.

WHAT IF GOD IS TOO TOUGH ON ME?

If you think you can stand up to temptation,
be careful not to fall. . . . [God] will show
you how to escape from your temptations.
—1 COR. 10:12–13 CEV

Sometimes recovery can be lonely. You wonder whether anyone else has ever felt the same cravings you have. You wonder whether you can handle all the things you need to in order to recover. Most of all, you wonder whether God will come through when your temptation is strongest, if He will help you deal with it all.

You are not alone. All addicts have wondered the same thing. There is no temptation you will go through that others have not experienced in their own recovery. Those cravings and longings are shared by thousands of other addicts and alcoholics, and people definitely understand. But best of all, God understands.

Because God knows you inside and out, He comprehends how hard things are and will not allow more than you can handle. Every time things feel too hard, God will provide an escape route for you to take. You don't have to go through recovery lonely and isolated, trying to avoid relapse on your own power. You have others who have been there, and a God who can be trusted to safely get you through any situation.

■ *Others have felt the same cravings you have, and*
God has come through for them.

K.B.

THE ILLUSION OF TOMORROW

"Come," one says, "I will bring wine,
And we will fill ourselves . . .
Tomorrow will be as today."

—IS. 56:12

Never put things off for another day. Procrastination leads to laziness, and laziness leads to relapse. Keep in shape and ready to take opportunities as they come. If you don't, if tomorrow is better you won't be in any shape to take advantage of it.

Before initiating your treatment you may have thought you had to "go for all the gusto." After all, you never know about tomorrow. But what if you won't have a tomorrow? By assuming that tomorrow will always come, you set yourself up for more procrastination. With more procrastination comes a lack of preparedness to take advantage of the opportunities you have during the day.

Never presume upon God's grace. He doesn't have to give you another day. Each day is a gift from God, given to you to continue on in your quest for health and wholeness. Never take it for granted. Tomorrow will always be an illusion unless you make today count.

Remember that each day gives you a chance to prepare for the next. It is painful to realize that an opportunity is before you, but you can't take it on. Don't let that happen in your recovery. Always take each day as a gift, and use it to prepare for the next.

■ *Father, thank You for today as an opportunity to pursue healthy behavior and lay a foundation for the future.*

R.M.

A GOD WHO UNDERSTANDS

And now that Jesus has suffered and was tempted, he can help anyone else who is tempted. —HEB. 2:18 CEV

How can God understand me? He is somewhere up in the sky, and I'm here on earth. He doesn't have to go through all the stuff I do!" You may be wondering the same thing. Turning your recovery over to God might feel like trusting someone to care for something he doesn't know anything about—like loaning your car to your six-year-old sister; because she doesn't know how to drive, she will probably wreck it.

This is not the case. God sent his Son Jesus to earth to live among humans and to experience life just as we do. Because Jesus was totally human, He experienced all the pain and temptations we feel. He was tempted in the wilderness by Satan. He was made fun of, beaten, and eventually killed.

Through it all, even though He was just as human as you or I, He handled it. He did so because He depended on His higher power to be in charge of His life on earth. Certainly God can understand what you experience when temptation, pain, unhappiness, or other hard situations happen in your life. He's been there. And because He knows exactly what it's like, He can be trusted not to wreck your life.

■ *Lord, You were tempted, so You know what I'm going through. Help me deal with hard times in recovery.*

K.B.

FAMILIAR WITH WEAKNESS

We do not have a High Priest who cannot sympathize with our weaknesses, but was in all points tempted as we are, yet without sin.
—HEB. 4:15

It is consoling to remember that God understands our weaknesses. That doesn't mean He doesn't expect us to be responsible for our actions or to keep trying to overcome our problems. You may not understand just what it is like for someone to understand your weaknesses while at the same time expecting a lot from you. In your mind you may tend to split these qualities. Either you have come into contact with someone who understands, but doesn't expect much from you, or you know someone who expects a lot from you, but has little or no understanding of your weaknesses. This person may just pass your weaknesses off as "excuses" not worth listening to. God isn't like that. As our scripture passage for today makes clear, He is completely familiar with human weakness because, though He was without sin, He lived thirty-three years in human flesh.

When you mess up and let yourself down, and let God down, don't beat yourself up as an act of repentance. You don't need to. God understands. He still expects you to get up and try again, but He understands. Your best approach to recovery is to give yourself the same kind of grace God gives you when you don't reach your own expectations.

■ *God understands your weaknesses and wants us to keep struggling with your recovery.*

R.M.

THE FIRST TEMPTATION

*When the woman saw that the tree was good
for food . . . she took of its fruit and ate. She
also gave to her husband . . . and he ate.*
—GEN. 3:6

God told the first man and woman that they could eat
fruit from any tree except one. They did the one thing
they were not supposed to do.

While the world is a very different place today, there
is at least one thing that has not changed. When we
know we are not to do something, we want to do it even
more. Even though there are lots of other things we *can*
do, what we think about most is the thing we shouldn't
do.

Addiction is like that. Even though there are other
things to think about, what you think about most are
drugs and alcohol. You wake up in the morning and
think about it, you go to school and think about it, you
think about it at home, at work, at play, everywhere.

It is important to remember that thinking too much
about one thing is dangerous. You begin to block out
other things and focus only on the craving for substances. Addiction prevents you from seeing so many
other wonderful chances for fun and growth. When you
find your mind staying too long on your cravings for
alcohol and drugs, remember that there is more to life
than the things you can't have. Watch your thoughts;
they can get you into trouble.

■   *There is more to life than alcohol and drugs. Spend
more time thinking about these things.*

K.B.

USE WHAT YOU KNOW

As for you, continue in the things which you have learned and been assured of, knowing from whom you have learned them.
—2 TIM. 3:14

Recovery is often a series of returns to truths you've always known. To grow and stay fresh in his ministry, Paul always kept refreshed in the things he knew to be true.

Timothy was a young pastor who needed encouragement to keep focused on his ministry. He sometimes forgot to use the lessons he had learned from doing the tasks before him. Under the most trying circumstances, we tend to forget to use tools that at one time effectively kept us on track.

One of the tools guys often forget most quickly is that of being honest about their feelings. It is easy to fall back into the unfeeling, tough image that surrounds you no matter where you go. A lot of your friends will be uncomfortable when you begin practicing what you've learned about expressing your feelings and will resist your doing this. You will be confronted with a choice between staying current with your feelings or giving in to your friends and keeping your feelings to yourself.

One of the ways to get through this is to be discriminating about who you can safely share your feelings with. That way you don't shut down altogether, but instead, you maintain your health.

■ *Father, help me to use what I know and not forget to use the tools I have been given.*

R.M.

ACTIONS SPEAK LOUDER THAN WORDS

*Anyone who doesn't breathe is dead, and
faith that doesn't do anything is just as dead!*
—JAMES 2:26 CEV

It's not enough to believe in God. It's not enough to quit using chemicals to cope with problems. Those are just the beginning of recovery. To make sure that you really are changing deep inside, your whole life needs to change in ways that you may not understand.

When you turn your life over to God, you trust Him to make these changes. As you grow closer to Him and give more control over to Him, old desires become more and more uncomfortable. A new desire takes their place—the desire to do what is right in God's eyes. You will find that attitudes and behaviors you never even thought much about become troublesome and unnecessary.

On the other hand, each time you start feeling like you need to change something you are faced with a decision. Do I change it, or do I ignore it? A true man of action isn't satisfied with just talking about his problems; he jumps right in and makes the needed changes. Simply believing in God is not what true faith really is. Faith means that when God shows you something that needs to be different, you change it. After all, your actions really do say more about you than the words you speak.

■ *God, give me the strength to change about myself whatever You show me needs changing.*

K.B.

COASTING

*Then I looked on all the works that my
    hands had done
And on the labor in which I had toiled;
And indeed all was vanity.*
                                    —ECC. 2:11

Have you ever tried to walk up an escalator the wrong way? It takes a great deal of effort to walk against the downward motion of the stairs. It's funny to see small kids try this stunt; they don't have the strength to overcome the stairs and end up right where they started.

That picture is accurate of recovery. You face downward forces as you attempt to overcome addiction. Friends, family, daily stresses, and internal turmoil pull you back down to the place where you started— addicted. You must never coast in recovery. You have to make it an ongoing practice to pursue your recovery; even if you aren't pursuing it hot and heavy, you have to keep moving or the forces will continue to pull you down. Don't be like the foolish rich man who thought he could rest on all he had achieved and done to carry him along in his partying. Don't be like the guy who thought tomorrow would be like today, and he would be as rich then as he was now. Unless you continue to work at recovery you won't make further ground. In fact, you may lose ground.

Develop an attitude of growth and learning. If you do, you will be on the right course that will keep you moving in your recovery.

■   *Father, give me an attitude of learning in my recovery so that I won't coast and lose ground.*

                                                            R.M.

APATHY

"Vanity of vanities," says the Preacher;
"Vanity of vanities, all is vanity."
—ECC. 1:2

Apathy is a word that describes the inner feelings of addicts before recovery. Someone who is apathetic is totally bored. Everything inside is empty and dark, and nothing seems to mean anything. It's all jumbled and confused. To cope with those feelings, thrills are needed, and that's why many start drinking or getting high in the first place.

Unfortunately, the feelings of emptiness and boredom return after the substances wear off. And when you start the recovery process, since you aren't getting high or drunk anymore, you still need to deal with the apathy you feel. To make things worse, the one thing that makes life interesting, the substances, can't be trusted to bring relief anymore, so things seem doubly dull.

Relax. Even though you may feel this way at first, and sometimes even after being in recovery for quite some time, it's going to get better. As you slowly find things to replace the need for kicks and thrills—safer things that don't threaten your life or health—the boredom will begin to fade. That's part of trusting God, too. You even need to trust Him with the dull ache of that inner apathy.

■ *Show me, God, alternate ways of dealing with my feelings of apathy.*

K.B.

COMMITTED TO RECOVERY

*I discipline my body and bring it into
subjection, lest, when I have preached to
others, I myself should become disqualified.*
—1 COR. 9:27

Recovery is sometimes incredibly exhausting and difficult. It will push you to the limits both emotionally and physically. Paul's words are pretty radical. Slaves have no other choice but what their master wants. Imagine that recovery and the work it involves are your master. You will need that kind of commitment for success in your recovery. It is an extreme level of commitment, but at the same time it gives you strength to make decisions. It helps you to set priorities. Paul was willing to do anything, including enslaving his body to His will, to follow Jesus. Are you willing to do that for your recovery? It may help you develop the focus you need to succeed.

An athlete, when training for an event, subjects everything in his life to the sole purpose of preparing for his sport. You need this kind of single-mindedness to follow the path to recovery. This kind of focus will also help you make difficult decisions about the people you hang out with and whether to listen to your parents about a situation you are facing. It takes a great deal of focus and commitment to do anything, including enslaving yourself to your recovery, to regain your health.

■ *Father, help me to keep my focus on growth during
my recovery and not waver from that path.*

R.M.

NOTHING SEEMED INTERESTING TO ME

I said in my heart, "Come now, I will test you with mirth; therefore enjoy pleasure"; but surely, this also was vanity.

—ECC. 2:1

William had been in recovery for about six months, and we were reviewing his progress. "You know, I can remember when nothing seemed to make me feel good. I mean, before I starting using, there were all these hobbies I had, and they all got so boring," he recalled. The more he got into drugs, the more time and energy they took; he let all his interests just drift away.

A way to tell how bad a person's chemical abuse has become is to ask him what he does for fun. When the addiction is still in the early stages, the addict can think of a few things that are interesting, and he may have a few hobbies. But when he has been using for a while, it is difficult for him to say what is fun, because most of his free time is spent thinking about getting high or drinking.

In recovery, an addict loses his prime source of entertainment, substances. Now he is left with nothing to do for fun. And so, in order to learn how to start living a clean and sober life again, he needs to find new things to do. What about you? Now that you are in recovery, do you have any safe yet fun interests in your free time? Without good, clean fun you'll start wishing for the old days and thinking about using again.

■   *Make a list of things that interest you that don't involve substances. Pick one and have fun again.*

K.B.

A WISE FRIEND

To do evil is like sport to a fool,
But a man of understanding has wisdom.
—PROV. 10:23

Who will support your recovery? The person who delights in the things you do that show progress in your recovery. He will get excited about your victories. At the same time, he will have the courage to challenge you to continue your recovery. When you begin to slow down or make decisions that hobble your recovery, he will be quick to confront you. Don't shrink from his feedback. He is a rare friend who is brave enough to risk your rejection by telling you the truth.

People who will not help you in your recovery wink at the things you do to hinder your progress. They make it easy for you to set your recovery aside for another day. Beware, these people will only undermine your commitment to overcome addiction and make it easy for you to compromise your values. They aren't helping you. In fact, they are enabling more addictive behavior. Beware also that they will get their feelings hurt when you tell them you can't hang out with them because they are hurting you.

A truly wise friend is willing to help you accomplish your goals, even if it means losing your friendship or changing himself.

■ *Father, help me to know who is a wise friend and cherish his friendship and not shrink from it.*

R.M.

GET A SPONSOR

Where there is no counsel, the people fall;
But in the multitude of counselors there is
safety. —PROV. 11:14

You're in a boat in the middle of the lake without a paddle! How can you row to shore? Recovery is like that at first. You give up the things you once used to cope with life, alcohol, and drugs. You avoid places where chemicals are. You have no friends because all your old ones are still getting high and drunk. It can be pretty scary at first, and you need someone to talk to.

If you try to recover on your own, you will trust yourself too much and probably will begin using substances again. There are places to turn for help. You might turn to an addictions counselor, someone trained to help you recover. He or she will listen to you and will be able to give great advice as you struggle with your new life.

You might choose to go to Alcoholics or Narcotics Anonymous. There you will find recovering alcoholics and addicts who know exactly what it is like to be where you are. They will help you find a sponsor, someone you can call anytime you feel the urge to use substances; your sponsor will help you continue your recovery program.

Don't try to do it alone; you will certainly fail. Talk to someone who understands what you are going through.

■ *God, help me to find someone to talk with who understands what I am going through.*

K.B.

BRUTAL HONESTY

For neither at any time did we use flattering words, as you know, nor a cloak for covetousness—God is witness.

—1 THESS. 2:5

It takes guts to be honest, particularly when you know it may not be to your advantage. Anyone can be honest when it's convenient, and that doesn't say anything about his character. On the other hand, if you are honest even when you know it won't help—that is a sign that you are committed to brutal honesty.

Paul was honest when he went to the church in Thessalonica. He may not have had an awe-inspiring appearance or wowed anybody with his ability to speak, but he didn't flinch from showing the people who he was—warts and all. That is exactly what made him stand out from the rest of the prophets who wandered into town. He was honest, no matter what—and that was unusual.

Are you willing to risk being brutally honest with a friend who has asked for feedback about his abusive behavior? Even more important, are you willing to be brutally honest with yourself when you begin to see signs of relapse? If you are, then you are in a good position to continue your quest for health. It is indeed scary to confront signs of relapse in yourself, but your commitment to recovery can carry you through to the other side.

■ *Father, help me to be brutally honest with others and with myself.*

R.M.

JUST ONE MORE CHANCE

They lied to Him with their tongue;
For their heart was not steadfast with Him,
Nor were they faithful in His covenant.
                                              —PS. 78:36–37

I promise I'll never do it again; just give me one more chance." Have you ever tried that one on people? Chances are, you really meant it but before long, you were going back on your promise. Most teens say this when their parents decide they have had enough and are going to do something about what is going on.

Addicts make lots of promises, but the drugs are in control. As long as your decisions are really being made because of your dependency on drugs, no promise will last. Just one more chance is really a scam to get your parents to let you off the hook.

You've had lots of chances. Before you used substances, you had a chance to say no. The first time you got high or drunk, you had a chance to never do it again. Many times since then, you have had chances to stop. In spite of all these chances, here you are working on recovery.

Just one more chance is a phrase you need to avoid. Don't try to get out of dealing with the consequences of your chemical abuse. Instead of trying to get parents or others to give you a break, start living your life responsibly. Your actions got you here; let your actions get you out.

■   *Lord, help me listen to what others are telling me*
     and take responsibility for what I have done.

                                                          K.B.

MISSING AN OPPORTUNITY

"They all . . . began to make excuses. The first said to him, 'I have bought a piece of ground, and I must go and see it.'"
—LUKE 14:18

Probably no feeling is more desolate than realizing you have missed an opportunity to move further down the path to recovery. You feel awful when you realize that the opportunity will not return just to give you a chance to get it right the next time. This opportunity could be to say no to a friend who frequently asks you to go with him to parties you know you shouldn't go to. It could be telling someone about the decision you have made to go straight and live a drug-free life.

You may use a missed opportunity as an excuse to give up, feeing you will never make the right decisions for recovery. After all, if you are not moving in recovery you don't have to worry about making poor decisions. You just don't make any!

But you need to understand why you missed that opportunity. What made you pass it by? Were you afraid of what others might think? If so, you need to deal with that fear. Talk to someone you trust and resolve that fear. Or pray that God will help you resist and learn from it.

Keep moving in your recovery, even if you make mistakes and miss opportunities. In spite of this you will continue to learn and grow toward health if you take this kind of risk.

■ *Father, help me to take the risk of missing opportunities in order to grow more.*

R.M.

WHAT DOES IT TAKE?

The foolishness of a man twists his way,
And his heart frets against the LORD.
—PROV. 19:3

One night Rob and some friends were sitting around drinking and smoking joints when some guys drove by and yelled at them. Rob and his buddies yelled back, hopped in their car, and chased them.

When they reached a local hangout, they all jumped out of their cars and yelled some more. Everyone was drunk, no one was thinking too clearly, and they started fighting. Trying to seem tougher than he felt, Rob pulled a knife and accidentally stabbed one of the guys. He later died, and Rob went to jail.

His pastor told me that when he visited Rob, the boy seemed eager to change. He recognized that his substance abuse had gotten him into trouble. A year later some friends of Rob's told me he was out of jail on probation; however, he was drinking and using drugs again.

Clearly even jail wasn't enough for Rob. Although his probation agreement stated that he must remain clean, Rob chose to use. Drugs were more powerful in Rob's life than his good sense. Even murder and jail couldn't keep him straight. Don't believe that you've finally learned your lesson. Recovery is something you need to work on every day; once you quit working, the chemicals will take control again.

■   *God, keep me from giving up on recovery and going back to my old ways.*

K.B.

EXCUSES, EXCUSES

"Ah, Lord GOD!
Behold, I cannot speak, for I am a youth."
—JER. 1:6

Jay thought he was God's gift to women. He could overcome any obstacle; any problem he could solve, and any girl he could charm. His addiction to cocaine kept his opinion of himself at a high level. Then he got caught shoplifting. He began to understand that he needed to change, not simply because he was caught stealing, but because he realized he was destroying himself and his relationships with others. So he went into a hospital program and began his recovery.

He wasn't ready for the difficulty of overcoming his addiction. He was filled with excuses and reasons for not doing well. He'd say anything except that he was afraid. He was afraid of people thinking he was a failure at overcoming his addiction. He was afraid of disappointing his parents and hurting them any more. He was afraid of feeling worse than he already did. So his excuses were a way to avoid the pain of change.

Sometimes recovery hurts. It isn't easy, and it takes more effort than you may have to give. That is why you need a source of strength beyond yourself. God is waiting and willing to help you in your weakness. You need only to recognize that you are indeed weak and need His help.

■ *Father, help me to accept the pain of change without using excuses.*

R.M.

DANGEROUS REMINDERS

Let God change the way you think. Then you will know how to do everything that is good and pleasing to him. —ROM. 12:2 CEV

George came to therapy on time each week for his session. He had been drug-free for three months, and he seemed to be doing quite well. That's why I was a little surprised when he came to our session wearing a black T-shirt with a picture of a pot leaf on the front.

I asked why he was wearing clothes that told others he was still part of his druggie past. He said it was a shirt that he liked a lot and didn't want to get rid of yet. After talking with him for a while, I discovered that he also had a bong, some rolling papers, and some seeds lying around his bedroom. While he wasn't using, he was setting himself up for relapse simply by the temptations he allowed in his room.

Like George, you may have kept things from your past that could tempt you to get high or drunk again. Beer posters on your wall; left-over drug stuff like coke spoons; pictures of yourself when you were using; clothing with drug and/or alcohol themes—all of these are dangerous reminders of your past that could tempt you to use in your future. Keeping these around is like hanging on to a past you are trying to change. You need to avoid those things if you wish to stay clean and sober.

■   *Though it may be hard, get rid of things that could tempt you to relapse.*

K.B.

SWEATING THE SMALL STUFF

"He who is faithful in what is least is faithful also in much; and he who is unjust in what is least is unjust also in much."

—LUKE 16:10

Trust is probably one of the most hotly contested issues between parents and teens. For the teen, it is a mark of maturity that he always looks for ways to prove he can be trusted. The problem between parents and teens is over the way this trust is gained. Most teens expect to be trusted, and if they blow it, it can then be taken away. On the other hand, parents expect teens to be trustworthy in small things, indicating that they can be trusted with "big" things.

Your success in recovery is very much like what parents look for in trustworthy behavior. If you pay attention to the small things of recovery you will succeed because you concentrate on things people won't notice. It also shows your motivation for recovery. Are you recovering for yourself, or are you recovering so that people will notice?

The "small" stuff of recovery is those aspects most people don't notice, but that build a strong recovery process. They include honesty, patience, a willingness to share with others your feelings and thoughts, and an ongoing pursuit of God in your life. These things are not readily noticeable to people. Remember, though, the question: Who are you recovering for, yourself or others?

■ *Sweat the "small stuff" of your recovery and keep your pride in place to build a solid recovery.*

R.M.

THE SERENITY PRAYER

A wise man is strong,
Yes, a man of knowledge increases strength.
—PROV. 24:5

God, grant me the serenity to accept the things I cannot change. . . ." In your recovery there will be certain things you can do nothing about. Drugs and alcohol will always be there. People will always tempt you; some will not accept the changes in you, and others will not forgive you when you ask them to. These things are beyond your ability to change.

". . . the courage to change the things I can. . . ." You have much work to do to change things about yourself. You will always need your higher power—God—during this whole process. He will work in you and with you to stop old patterns that kept you addicted, and help you to develop newer, healthier patterns if you allow Him to.

". . . and the wisdom to know the difference." Some people refuse to admit that not everything can be under their control. They try to change people and things and become ever more frustrated because they can't. Only a wise person admits that he can't fix everything. Unless you know the difference between things you can change and things you cannot, you will become angry and resentful. It is important to work one day at a time, and try to change only yourself. Leave the rest to God.

■ *Grant me the serenity to accept the things I cannot change, the courage to change the things I can, and the wisdom to know the difference.*

K.B.

REAL HUMILITY

I say, through the grace given to me, to everyone . . . not to think of himself more highly than he ought to think, but to think soberly. —ROMANS 12:3

How do you judge your worth? We all have some criteria by which we measure our worth and value. It may be how well we perform a sport. It may be how well we are liked by others. It could be our ability to keep people happy and peace in our family. It is important to find a way to judge your worth based on something that doesn't change.

Imagine walking into a room with a ruler. Measure the dimensions of the room and report them to a friend. The friend takes his ruler, which is different from yours, and comes up with different measurements. Who is right? The same is true of our worth. Everyone judges his worth by a different yardstick, which changes according to the people he is around. If I am around one set of people, I feel like a real dope because they don't value me. If I am around other people, I feel good about myself because they value me. Who is right?

The source of real worth is our standing before God. He values us in a way that doesn't change. That makes us able to exhibit real humility based on God's evaluation of us. We can count on the fact that His evaluation won't change, and we will be valued and precious in His sight because He has said so.

■ *Father, thank You for loving me and allowing me to look at myself realistically without fear.*

R.M.

FORGIVING YOURSELF

Have faith when you pray for sick
people. . . . The Lord will heal them,
and if they have sinned, he will forgive
them.
                              —JAMES 5:15 CEV

John had asked God thousands of times to forgive the things he had done while using. He really felt terrible, like there was a load of guilt on his back that he didn't think he could handle much longer. Every time something bad happened, John told himself that it was because of all the bad things he had done, and that he must deserve it. He felt like God couldn't forgive him.

Was it really God who couldn't forgive John? I didn't think so and told him that. In fact it seemed to be that John couldn't forgive himself. He suffered from something we call False Guilt, guilty feelings that are no longer needed because God has completely erased the wrongs. The opposite, True Guilt, is the result of something you've done wrong, for which you have not asked forgiveness.

Think about your own life. You've done lots of things wrong. If you've asked God for forgiveness, it's done. Next you need to go to the person you've wronged, ask for his or her forgiveness, and try to make amends. If you've done all that and still feel guilty, you aren't forgiving yourself.

■   *God, help me to recognize false guilt in my life and*
    begin to forgive myself.

                                                    K.B.

FEELING DEFEATED

Moses said to God, "Who am I that I should go to Pharaoh, and that I should bring the children of Israel out of Egypt?"

—EX. 3:11

Moses had great status in Egypt before he ran away to the desert after killing an Egyptian. He thought he would be doing his fellow Hebrews a favor, but instead he was resented. He banished himself to the desert, afraid for his life. He felt defeated because his people did not recognize him as a worthwhile deliverer of them. No doubt he spent his time watching sheep and feeling sorry for himself. Then he spotted a burning bush that wouldn't quit burning, and he found himself talking with God. When God told him to return to Egypt and deliver his fellow Hebrews, Moses used the excuse of incompetency. The fact was that he felt defeated and unable to do the job.

By using this excuse you get people to feel sorry for you. How could they possibly expect someone as pitiful as you to accomplish the monumental task of recovering from addiction? Defeat is a smoke screen to keep others from holding you responsible for your behavior. Obstacles and difficulties are to be expected in your journey toward recovery. Don't use the excuse of defeat to keep from trying. God will bless your efforts even though you may stumble along the way.

■   *Feeling defeated is not an excuse to keep from trying and working on your recovery.*

R.M.

ALLOWING GOD TO WORK

Be humble in the Lord's presence, and he will honor you.
—JAMES 4:10 CEV

Frank had done a fantastic job identifying his strengths and weaknesses. He had looked at himself honestly and had dealt with his past. The result was the first moral inventory he had ever completed. There would be others as he changed and saw new things in himself, but for the present he had done the best job he felt he could.

Reviewing his list, he said he felt bad about a lot of the things on it. I assured him that was normal; when you start looking inside honestly, you are bound to see things you don't like about yourself. In fact, his feelings indicated that he was being honest with himself about the wrongs he had done. Instead of blaming anyone else, he was starting to take responsibility.

Furthermore, the guilt and regret he felt made him aware that he and God had a lot of work to do. When you ask God to change you, you need a certain humble attitude as you approach God to ask Him to work with you to weed out the bad and strengthen the good. Until you feel sorry for the wrongs you've done, God cannot work to change you. If you don't feel bad enough, you won't feel a need to be changed, and you will resist God's work.

■ *God, give me a humble spirit. Prepare my heart to be ready to change.*

K.B.

DON'T EXPECT MUCH!

Moses said to the LORD, "O my Lord, I am not eloquent . . . I am slow of speech and slow of tongue."
—EX. 4:10

It is always interesting to me that when a person is asked to do something he is sure he can't do, he will find a million reasons why he can't do it. The bottom line is that even though he may have never attempted such a task, he doesn't want to try and fail. The threat of failure is enough to convince him to not even try.

That was the approach Moses used when God told him to go to Egypt and deliver His people out of bondage. Moses used the excuse that God needed someone who was articulate and a brilliant spokesman to deliver the people, and since Moses was neither of these, God must have been mistaken. Moses was afraid of facing the people and failing. He wasn't up to feeling worse than he already did.

You may have had a dozen different excuses for not trying to recover from your addiction. All of them probably were related to the question "What if I try and fail?" When you fail, it doesn't mean you are a failure. It means you made a mistake, and mistakes can be avoided. So if you relapse or make a bad decision, remember that you are allowed to make mistakes as long as you remember to get back up and get going again. Don't use it as an excuse to not try anymore.

■ *It is important to view failure as an event rather than who you are.*

R.M.

Finishing the Job

God is the one who began this good work in you, and . . . he won't stop before it is complete on the day that Christ Jesus returns.
—PHIL. 1:6 CEV

Ken felt as if recovery was taking forever. At fifteen, a few months seem like years. Even though he was doing all the things that had been suggested, he still felt like getting high from time to time. He wanted God to take away all his addictive behaviors and attitudes, and he wanted it done quickly.

Ken and I talked about how he had become an addict. His brother had been using for years, and Ken looked up to him. Even before he got high the first time, he had been thinking about it for over a year. As things fell apart in his family, he turned to drugs to feel better and to get back at them. The angrier Ken got, the more he used; the more he used, the angrier he got. In other words, he hadn't become addicted overnight; it had taken a long time.

While recovery seemed incredibly slow and difficult for Ken, it was important that he try not to push God to move faster. Sometimes it can take years to undo problems you've been developing for a long time. God knew what He was doing, and was doing it slowly. Maturity and growth cannot come overnight. But God always completes any task we ask Him to, even when it seems too slow for us.

■ *Lord, help me to be patient when recovery work seems to take too long.*

K.B.

WALK, DON'T RUN

If we walk in the light as He is in the light, we have fellowship with one another, and the blood of Jesus Christ His Son cleanses us from all sin.
                                                    —1 JOHN 1:7

Pacing is critical in running. If you treat a marathon like a sprint, you are sure to lose because you'll burn your energy early in the race. Likewise if you treat a sprint like a marathon, the other runners will be getting medals while they wait for you to cross the finish line. The winner is the one who can measure his resources according to the demands of the race. The marathoner who conserves his energy while running will have energy left to win the race.

Pacing is important in recovery as well. Some guys take on recovery like a sprint, but they crash and burn because they expect too much and don't pace themselves. Others handle recovery like a Sunday stroll and betray their lack of motivation by their pace.

See changes coming and slow down so that you can handle obstacles. A stressful time might approach in your life, like having to take exams at school. Slow down and make difficult decisions about your use of time— going to support group meetings and studying. There is nothing foolish about slowing down to talk to someone about your problems. Don't worry; you'll get back up to speed soon if you slow down when you need to.

■ *It is important to take time to walk in your recovery to handle the obstacles effectively.*

                                                    R.M.

FALLING AWAY

"[They] gladly hear the message and accept it. But they don't have deep roots, and they believe only for a little while."
—LUKE 8:13 CEV

Alex started projects but never finished any. He would get interested in something, put all his energy into it, and then get bored and start something new. Like many addicts, he had little ability to tolerate boredom; as soon as something lost excitement for him, it became a total drag.

One day he decided that he was smoking too much marijuana. For perhaps the first time, he admitted to himself that he was losing control of his life. So he decided to quit. He jumped quickly and excitedly into recovery, going to several N.A. meetings. He liked what he learned, found a sponsor, even memorized the 12 Steps.

But as you may have already guessed, he soon got bored. The initial excitement wore off, and Alex decided to try something different. Even before what he learned had a chance to make a difference, he was back to looking for new thrills.

It takes time for real change. Since addicts have little patience and easily become bored, many fall away from their first attempt at recovery. You, too, may become unhappy with the process. It is important to remind yourself that this boredom is a pattern you are trying to change, and stick with it despite the feelings.

■ *Let the seeds of change that I am now planting in recovery grow and bear the fruit of my work.*

K.B.

PLANNING FOR THE FUTURE

The plans of the diligent lead
surely to plenty,
But those of everyone who is hasty,
surely to poverty.

—PROV. 21:5

It is important to plan for the obstacles you will face in the future. This is one thing that few guys spend time thinking about. Even after they begin their journey into recovery, they hang on to thoughts of invincibility. They continue to think that bad things happen to other people and never to themselves. When obstacles hit, they stumble, feel bad that they stumbled, and quit. Pride blinds them from seeing that they are human enough to have problems like everyone else.

It is crucial that you plan for obstacles. Sometimes when you plan like this you feel that you are getting down on yourself, or you think the worst. You might feel that if you think of the bad things you will face, you will make them happen. That couldn't be further from the truth. The more situations you can come up with that might present obstacles, the better prepared you'll be.

Think of worst case scenarios and ask yourself "If this happens, what will I do?" Be as specific as you can when you are planning. Use the approach "First I will do this. . . . Then, if that works I will do this. . . . If that doesn't work I'll try _____ instead." Get the idea? The more you do this, the more successful your recovery will be.

■ *Plan for obstacles in your path so you can be prepared to act when they come up.*

R.M.

DEVELOPING NEW INTERESTS

Do not incline my heart to any evil thing,
To practice wicked works
With men who work iniquity.
—PS. 141:4

Now what do I do for fun?" asked Tim. It was a good question. His idea of a good time had been going out with friends and getting stoned. Any time they thought of something to do, it always involved drugs. Tim realized that without drugs to occupy his time, he didn't know how to have fun anymore.

Any time you make radical changes in your life, you have to adapt your whole life to fit with the changes. When you start recovery, you give up drugs and wild partying. Suddenly you are faced with the loss of the one thing you thought of as fun and exciting. It is time to develop new interests.

Look around. There are lots of things to do that are clean and don't involve drugs or alcohol. Ask your parents. Ask your sponsor, if you have one. Ask your school counselor or youth pastor. Because you've only had fun while drinking or getting high, you've forgotten that there's a whole world out there filled with excitement and adventure. Start developing new interests.

■ *God, help me to find new ways to have fun that don't harm my recovery.*

K.B.

WHERE IS YOUR HOPE?

Those who wait on the LORD
Shall renew their strength. . . .
They shall walk and not faint.
—IS. 40:31

Without hope most people could not survive. Concentration camp survivors consistently report that what got them through their horrible experience was the hope of seeing loved ones again. That hope carried them through to the end. Hope helps us to take some pretty bad circumstances and look forward to something better.

Hope plays a critical role in recovery as well. Without it, most people who strive to overcome addiction give up. They hope that through struggles and pain, they will one day be able to say they are recovered addicts. However, if you place your hope on something that changes, you are sure to be disappointed.

On whom does your recovery depend? You? The support of your family? In the last analysis, it is God who will ultimately bring you into complete health and recovery. If you place your hope on Him, you will never be disappointed. The future can disappoint us, but God never disappoints us. He may not do what we have in mind, but He will accomplish His will for us if we surrender control to Him. The more we try to prove how independent we are, the less likely we are to depend on God to bring about the change we are seeking.

■ *Father, help me to surrender my control to You and hope in You for my complete recovery.*

R.M.

REMEMBER THE POSITIVES

Anyone who belongs to Christ is a new person. The past is forgotten, and everything is new.
　　　　　　　　　　—2 COR. 5:17 CEV

While making out his moral inventory, Tom got really depressed. He began to see himself as a hopeless piece of junk, a guy who never did anything good. So I asked him to read his list to me. Then it all made sense—you see, his list included nothing good about him; it was all negative.

No person is completely negative. There are positives even in the worst addict's life, although he can't always see them. While it *is* very important to be honest about the negatives in your life, you also have to look at your strengths. To be completely honest with yourself, you have to look at the good, as well as the bad.

As you make your list of character traits, you will be tempted to look either too much at the bad, which will make you feel guilty and depressed, or focus too much on the good, which is pride. These two extremes are dangerous because you're not looking at the whole picture. Honesty is the only way to balance the two. If you're not balanced, you can't finish your inventory. If you won't look honestly at yourself, you will fail in recovery.

■　*God, show me things I need to know about myself in order to progress in recovery.*

　　　　　　　　　　　　　　　　　　　K.B.

A CAT OR A LION?

*The slothful man says, "There
is a lion outside!
I shall be slain in the streets!"*
—PROV. 22:13

Do you know anyone who always finds reasons for not doing something? His imagination knows no bounds in finding excuses. You might be that person. Your parents ask you to take out the garbage, and you say, "It's too late, and I have to get to bed, you know." Or, "Aw, come on, Mom, it's raining out and I don't want to get wet." Sound familiar? There are jobs we like to avoid, so we find every reason to get out of doing them.

When we encounter a job that involves a lot of responsibility our first response is often fear—that we won't do a good job, that we will let others down, that we will feel bad about ourselves because we are sure we will do it poorly. In a way we turn the job into a roaring lion that we need superhuman strength to overcome. Have you done that with your recovery? Have you made it so big that you can't possibly overcome your addiction?

When guys face adversity in recovery, they often take the attitude of the sluggard in today's passage. They become fearful of the cat that has suddenly turned into a man-eating lion. Don't allow that to happen. Recovery is a day-by-day process. Don't turn it into something so big that you are sure to fail.

■ *Father, help me avoid finding reasons to not recover.*
R.M.

BEING CONTENT

*I am not complaining about having too little.
I have learned to be satisfied with whatever I
have.*   —PHIL. 4:11 CEV

Inside all addicts is an emptiness. Trying to fool yourself into not feeling it by getting high and drunk doesn't make it disappear. But most addicts keep trying bigger and better highs, hoping they will work. Of course they don't and so they are left feeling discontented and dissatisfied.

Discontentedness can be dangerous. People try all sorts of things to make themselves feel better. But things don't cut it anymore than drugs and alcohol do. That is because things cannot make a person feel any more or any less satisfied; they just temporarily cover up the emptiness.

You have everything you need in life when you have a relationship with God. He promises to meet all your needs, so looking for things to meet your needs is really looking for something to replace God. Part of any solid recovery is learning to be content with what you have today. No physical object can do that for you; it is something you must learn and practice. Accept the fact that you are who you are and that you have everything you really need. Be content with who you are.

■   *God, teach me to keep me from looking to things to
fill the emptiness only You can fill.*

K.B.

NEVER SATISFIED

"Consider your ways! . . .
You eat, but do not have enough;
You drink, but you are not filled
with drink."

—HAGGAI 1:5–6

Thrill seekers look outside themselves for excitement and satisfaction. They need stimulation and change. If nothing is happening, they are bored. Thrills keep them alive and feeling something. However, what they feel is not the real thing. It is contrived and artificially induced. What keeps thrill seekers always seeking more excitement is the need to not explore what they really feel. They run from it by looking outside themselves for stimulation and excitement.

A sure sign of problems in your recovery is never feeling satisfied. It is a restlessness that may be especially strong when "nothing" is happening in your world. Of course, it isn't the "nothing" happening as much as the "something" happening inside you that you may not want to deal with. So you turn to external things—food, clothes or other material things, money, or even drinking and abusing.

What prevents this slide into relapse? You need to do what God instructed His people to do: "Give careful thought to your ways." Keep an eye on what you are doing. Write about your day or talk to a friend about your frustrations so you can stay on top of feelings you might run from.

■   *Father, help me to give careful thought to my ways so*
    that I can find inner satisfaction.

R.M.

A FISHERMAN'S TALE

Jesus said to them, "Come with me! I will teach you how to bring in people instead of fish."
—MARK 1:17 CEV

Fishing may be the most relaxing sport. You sit in a boat, with the waves lazily lapping at the sides. The warm sun beats down on your back. You cast your line and slowly reel it back. If you're lucky enough, you may even catch a fish.

The key to fishing is patience. If you expect instant results, you will be disappointed, because fish have a mind of their own. So you wait and relax, casting and reeling.

Talking to others about recovery can be a lot like fishing. You know others like yourself who could live a much better life if they only knew what you have learned. But they have minds of their own, and must make the decision to change for themselves. That's why patience is important.

If you get frustrated and quit, you might miss out on helping another addict find what you have. So relax. Be patient with others and remember your own path to recovery. Chances are you lived in denial for a long time before you came to your senses and made the important decision to start recovery. Cast your line by telling others about what you have found. Reel them in as they become more interested. Never give up; the next cast may be the big catch.

■ *God, help me to tell others of my recovery, and help them to understand their need for change.*

K.B.

PUSHY FRIEND

He who is slothful in his work
Is a brother to him who is a great destroyer.
—PROV. 18:9

Do you know how much guts it takes to be the kind of friend who pushes you to stretch yourself beyond the limits of what you thought you could do? A friend who pushes you also risks your anger, and even your rejection. When I was a kid, I used to love to watch the movie about Brian Piccolo and Gale Sayers, who was a great running back for the Chicago Bears. He was the model for all future running backs in the league. It seemed that no one could tackle him. His friend Brian Piccolo was a somewhat ordinary fullback. He didn't gain as much yardage as Sayers, and did most of the blocking that would often free Sayers for long gains. They were fast friends. They trained together and had the guts to push each other—not because they wanted to make each other miserable, but because they cared deeply for each other.

You must decide what kind of friends you are going to surround yourself with. Will they be the kind of people who have the inner strength to push you to reach for the highest you can give, like Brian Piccolo, or are you going to choose friends like the brother in the passage for today, who is slack and cuts corners and doesn't expect much from you? It's not an easy choice.

■ *Father, help me to find the kind of friend who is*
willing to push me.

R.M.

BAD EXAMPLE

*"It will be terrible for people who cause even
one of my little followers to sin."*
—MATT. 18:6 CEV

John usually came to sessions alone. This week, at her
request, he had brought his mother. She was worried
about him. While he didn't use drugs anymore, something else was happening.

John's deep unhappiness was no longer being covered up by drugs. Now he snapped angrily at others.
His younger brothers and sisters were starting to imitate
him as well. The screaming, hurtful comments, put-
downs, and defiance had increased in the house because his siblings were acting like him. John got angry
at her for saying this and started pointing out things she
and his dad needed to change.

Without chemicals to make him feel better, the real
John started to come out. He took his misery and unhappiness out on others in the family. But because he
was so angry, he refused to see how he was affecting
others and instead chose to point the blame at his parents.

Your behavior affects others. While it is great that
you aren't using anymore, you still have a lot to change.
It is important not to bring others down with you; that
will only make things worse because everyone will be
miserable, not just you. Recovery *is* hard; don't make it
harder by giving others a bad example to follow.

■ *Make me aware of the ways I influence others, especially those who look up to and admire me.*

K.B.

IF ONLY . . .

> *Oh, that they were wise, that they*
>   *understood this,*
> *That they would consider their latter end!*
>   —DEUT. 32:29

People rise and fall in their struggle to overcome addiction. You might bump into guys who remain openly defiant about their drug-abusing lifestyle and are unwilling to hear about where they are heading. You might attempt to tell them you have been where they are heading, and it isn't really much fun. But, to your dismay, they won't listen. You might say to yourself, as God said of His people, "Why couldn't they have listened to me and understood what will happen to them if they keep up the way they are going!"

When you meet someone like that, be sure to do some discerning of your own. Look back on where you have come from and learn from his pride and arrogance. What turns you off about his unwillingness to listen is an enemy to your recovery. If you allow it to be unexamined, it will rise again. So when you talk to someone like this, remember to take a look over your own shoulder and ask, "How is my pride these days?"

Remember to give that person the right to reject good advice. Only after he has felt the full consequences of his behavior will he be ready to listen to you. Stay close, be a friend, and be ready to give advice when he is ready to hear it.

■ *Father, help me examine my motives and pride*
  when I confront someone who is not ready to change.
                                                      R.M.

WHAT WILL THE NEIGHBORS THINK?

*"Be angry and do not sin": do not let the
sun go down on your wrath.*
—EPH. 4:26

Every time Brad did something wrong, his mother
asked him the same thing, "What will the neighbors
think?" Like the time the police busted up a party he
was having, when his father yelled at him on the front
lawn, or more recently when he went into rehab. It irritated him that his mother lived her life for the neighbors
and expected everyone else in the family to also.

He knew from A.A. that you can't do things just to
impress or please others; you do what is right because it
is the right thing to do. Each time his mother worried
about what other people thought, Brad felt guilty and
manipulated.

Because he was feeling angry, and because he was
working on being more honest about himself and his
problems, Brad decided to talk with his mother about
this. Afterward she didn't change much, but Brad had
done something important. He had taken responsibility
for his feelings by talking directly to the person he was
irritated with.

You can learn two things from Brad's story. First,
don't attempt recovery just to impress others. Second,
when you have a problem with others, go to them and
try to work it out. They may not change, but you've
done the right thing.

■ *Lord, help me to approach someone I have negative
feelings about and try to work things out.*

K.B.

DOOMED TO REPEAT IT

Remember the days of old,
Consider the years of many generations.
Ask your father, and he will show you.
—DEUT. 32:7

Have you ever heard the phrase "Those who don't know the mistakes of history are doomed to repeat them"? It is a worthy idea that you should keep in mind throughout your recovery. You need to keep in the forefront of your consciousness just exactly how you got to where you are today. Can you recount what went into your addiction, what happened to force you to seek treatment, what happened in treatment, and the course of events since being in treatment?

The people of Israel had a strong tradition of recounting history to their children so that they would never forget their heritage and special position as the people of God. When you begin to lose motivation you will need to remember why you chose to recover from your addiction. You may be able to do this yourself, or you may need someone to tell you why you decided to overcome your addiction. It is important that you never forget why you are doing what you are doing so that you will have purpose and motivation for the road ahead. It is pretty easy to get casual about recovery. So take some time today to remember how you got to where you are today, and recommit yourself to the plan you have undertaken.

■ *Remember to review where you have come from in your recovery and where you are going.*

R.M.

HOW MANY TIMES SHOULD I FORGIVE?

*"If he sins against you seven times in a day,
and seven times in a day returns to you,
saying, 'I repent,' you shall forgive him."*
—LUKE 17:4

Peter wanted to do what was right, but when his father hassled him about school for the third time that week, he exploded. He had asked his father to lighten up, and told him that he really was trying. His father had even agreed to start trusting Peter to study more, but still kept getting on his case.

To top it all off, Peter *had* been studying more, and he knew his next report card would show it. That was why he came to his next session so angry. "Why should I forgive him?" he asked. "He just keeps doing it." He felt frustrated and discouraged that all his work seemed to prove nothing to his father.

When you allow anger to build up, you become resentful and start destroying your recovery. Deep inside, Peter knew he should forgive his dad. Yet he didn't feel he could keep forgiving over and over if his dad refused to do his part.

You can never put a limit on forgiveness. If you really want to work at recovery, you can't afford *not* to forgive someone, even if he keeps doing the same things. Even though it's quite hard, the growth and maturity will be well worth the effort in the long run.

■ *God, teach me how to forgive even when people keep doing the same things I've asked them to stop.*

K.B.

A FORGIVING FRIEND

"Greater love has no one than this, than to lay down one's life for his friends."
—JOHN 15:13

It takes a great deal of courage to accept forgiveness from someone. It takes humility because it is an admission that you have done something wrong. It takes security in oneself because there is a sense of acceptance in spite of the pain of a mistake made. You have found a valuable friend who is able to forgive you and still remain your friend.

Forgiveness is an incredible act of love and sacrifice. Your friend (or you as a friend) is helping to restore your relationship. It is a true act of love to say "I forgive you" and be able to let go of the grievance and move on in your relationship. He could say, "No way am I going to forget what you did to me. I'm just waiting for a good opportunity to pay you back!" It doesn't take much character to be that kind of friend. But he who forgives acts differently from everyone else and is to be cherished and appreciated. By forgiving you, he is demonstrating his commitment to you as a friend. He is willing to "lay down" his emotional life for you, so that your relationship can be re-established. It also is a reminder of what he will help you to reach for in your relationship with him and others.

■   *Father, help me to appreciate my friends who forgive me when I mess up.*

R.M.

FORGIVING OTHERS

When people sin, you should forgive and comfort them, so they won't give up in despair.
—2 COR. 2:7 CEV

It's funny how sometimes people get so angry. Someone wrongs them, and they hold on to the angry feelings, refusing to forgive. It's also very controlling, because the other person can't do anything about it. In a way it's similar to revenge, like saying, "I'll get them back. I won't let them ever forget what they did to me."

There is a dangerous side effect to this kind of payback. After a while, the other person stops caring if you forgive him or her. Since you're not going to give in, since you're determined to be in control, why bother trying anymore? That means you're left holding the bag; you're angry and bitter, but no one cares. It backfires on you.

People will hurt you sometimes. You have to decide whether you want to go through the rest of your life angry at them, getting them back by not forgiving them. If you do, you'll eventually lose that relationship. Too much of this, and you'll be a lonely, bitter person. Forgiveness not only mends relationships, it also keeps you happy and friendly.

■ *Lord, help me to forgive others and to mend broken relationships.*

K.B.

A TIME TO LISTEN

She had a sister called Mary, who also sat at Jesus' feet and heard His word.
—LUKE 10:39

Are you hungry for new information about recovery? Do you take time to listen to those who want to help you succeed in recovery? Mary was that kind of person. She recognized that Jesus was a well-spring of truth and was willing to take time listen to Him. She dropped everything, including helping Martha with dinner, to listen to Him. She is the picture of devotion to learning.

You need to be a devoted student of recovery. When you hear of an opportunity to learn more about recovery, don't pass it up. It will keep you sharp and thinking about how you can continue to improve. If you don't keep fresh your understanding and knowledge of yourself and your recovery, you will grow stagnant, and stagnant conditions take a lot more effort to change. Recovery is a lot like a car: It is easier to maintain a speed than to start moving.

However, you could be like Mary's sister, Martha. She was so busy with things to do that she missed her opportunity to sit at Jesus' feet and learn truth from the source of all truth. What an opportunity! Don't be too busy recovering from your addiction to stop and learn new things that will help you succeed in the future.

■ *Father, help me not to be too busy to stop and learn new things about my recovery.*

R.M.

LET GOD CHANGE YOU

*We pray for God's power to help you do all
the good things that you hope to do and that
your faith makes you want to do.*
—2 THESS. 1:11 CEV

What will recovery do to me? I don't want to be a
nerd," stated Chris. He had a fear that if his life started
changing, he wouldn't be completely satisfied with the
results. He wasn't certain he wanted to trust God without
knowing what he would become. He wanted all the
answers right away.

You can't be certain where God will lead you in recovery. You do know that the way your life was didn't
work and things fell apart. When you were in control of
the process, you didn't do such a hot job. Maybe the
things you wanted, and may still want, aren't the things
that will make your life better in the long run.

God is not going to make you unhappy or miserable.
He's not going to turn you into a person you aren't satisfied with. God takes the person who's already there and
makes him better. He's got big plans for you, plans you
never even thought of. Right now you may not understand them, and may not be sure that's what you want.
But God doesn't screw up the way humans do, and He
can be trusted to not only make great changes in your
life but also to help you feel good about the changes He
is making.

■ *God, make me the person You want me to be. Help
me to trust You even if I don't know the end results.*
K.B.

THE UNEXAMINED LIFE

I thought about my ways,
And turned my feet to Your testimonies.
—PS. 119:59

Can you imagine driving a car blindfolded? That is exactly how many attempt to conduct their recovery. They keep moving, never bothering to see if they are heading in the direction they want to go. The only thing that counts to them is that they are doing something related to recovery. That may prove to be a good approach at least in terms of commitment, but you can have a lot of movement and produce little. It would be much like the contraption that has a lot of bells and whistles, cranks, and moving parts, but it isn't worth much since it really doesn't accomplish much. It looks interesting, but that is about all.

It is important to slow down and look at just how you are doing in your recovery. Are you heading in the direction you intended? Or are you getting hung up somewhere and don't know why? You need to ask yourself such questions, or find a trusted friend who isn't afraid to challenge you to keeping moving. Without this, you are sure to get somewhere and realize that it isn't what you had in mind. Managing recovery is much like taking a journey; on occasion you need to stop, survey your progress, and plan for the road ahead.

■   *Father, help me to take time to examine my path and plan for the road ahead.*

R.M.

BEARING GRUDGES

"You shall not take vengeance, nor bear any grudge . . . but you shall love your neighbor as yourself: I am the LORD."

—LEV. 19:18

Colin was trying to work on his list of wrongs he had done to others. Hard as he tried, he kept seeing the wrongs others had done to him. He was having difficulty focusing on himself and being responsible. Thoughts of getting even with others for what they had done to him were much easier than dealing with the pain he had caused them.

Soon he quit working and began drinking again. He didn't want to take responsibility for himself. He seemed to prefer being a victim, blaming and planning revenge. The fact that he didn't want to deal with his wrongs showed that moving on in recovery would be too difficult.

It is far easier to feel wronged and be angry than to admit having wronged someone else. The anger keeps hurt and guilt away by keeping you focused on others rather than on yourself. But it also blocks any future work in recovery because it stops you from dealing with guilt and hurt. Until you begin to look honestly at yourself, you will continue to be in denial. But when you choose to take responsibility for yourself and the wrongs you have done to others, you can start forgiving yourself, making amends to those you've wronged, and begin growing again.

■ *God, don't let me hold grudges. Help me instead to be responsible for what I've done to others.*

K.B.

OBSTACLES TO GROWTH

Since therefore it remains that some must enter it, and those who to whom it was first preached did not enter because of disobedience.
                                        —HEB. 4:6

Are you stubborn? Do you hang on to an idea even if it will hurt you? Do you hang on to a request to go to a party after your parents have already said no? Stubbornness can both hurt and help you. The healthy part of stubbornness leads to persistence and endurance in a given task. That is a needed part of recovery. Without a little stubbornness, you won't follow through on extinguishing your addiction.

Stubbornness can also be a weakness. It acts a lot like blinders on a horse, which make sure the horse keeps his eyes on the road. Stubbornness focuses attention on what you want and not on what you need. As you continue on this stubborn path, you get farther away from being able to choose what you need rather than what you want. For example, you need to stay away from drug-abusing friends, but you want the right to choose whomever you want for friends. Which will you choose?

Beware of stubbornness and wanting your own way. It will be an obstacle to your recovery, keeping you from determining what you need to do and enabling you to choose things that will hurt you. They key to growth is knowing the things you need and choosing them.

■   *It is important to not be so stubborn that you won't choose what you need to do to stay healthy.*

                                                    R.M.

LIVING IT UP!

I came so that everyone would have life, and have it in its fullest.

—JOHN 10:10b CEV

All of John's life his parents had taken him to church. Every Sunday morning he went to Sunday school and church. Sunday night he went to youth group. Wednesday night they went to church too. And often, during the other days, his parents had him attend special church functions. Because he was abusing chemicals, he found everything except drugs boring, and especially church since he felt his parents were controlling him by making him attend.

Now it was time for him to make a decision about recovery. Would he allow God to be his higher power? Because of his feelings about church, he feared that living a life for God would be dull and boring. So he resisted allowing God to take control of his recovery.

Our God is not dull. In fact, He is exciting and unpredictable. He doesn't want your new life to be boring either. His whole reason for dying on the cross was to make life full, rich, and exciting—but not in the way an addict considers exciting. Before you reject God as being boring, consider carefully the verse above. Would an uninteresting God want your life to be lived to the fullest?

■ *God, I'm afraid that living for You won't be exciting. Help me to see that You want me to be happy and fulfilled.*

K.B.

YOU CAN'T FOOL GOD

"Foolish ones! Did not He who made the outside make the inside also?"
—LUKE 11:40

It is pretty easy to forget that you are working your recovery program for you and you alone. There is only one other who truly knows how your recovery is going, and that is God. You may be able to fool people about how you are doing, but in the long run you are only fooling yourself. Trying to fool others has a boomerang effect—you end up believing your own lies and you'll have a one-way ticket to relapse.

It is important to keep in mind that recovery is something that, though you need to be accountable for how it is going, is between you and God. If you strive to be honest and share your feelings and thoughts with Him, you will find success in recovery. This success will result because you will also want to share your feelings and thoughts with others who can help you. Being honest with God, whom you can't fool anyway, will produce a healthy desire to be honest with other trustworthy people too. Before long, you will develop a healthy cycle of sharing your feelings and concerns with God and others, and you'll find the support you need to be consistent in your recovery process.

■ *Be honest with others and with God so you can get the support you need to keep going.*

R.M.

IT'S NOT FAIR!

Are we saying that God is unfair? Certainly not! . . . Everything then depends on God's mercy and not on what people want or do.
—ROM. 9:14–16 CEV

I don't get it. I give my recovery over to God, and then this happens." Marty had gotten a speeding ticket on his way to our session. He was running a little late and so he thought he would make up the time by driving a little faster. He didn't notice the policeman by the side of the road until he saw flashing lights in his rearview mirror.

"How can God let this happen to me? It's not fair," he complained. Marty really was trying to learn how to turn things over to God. But he seemed a little confused about how God works in a person's life. When you do something wrong, there are consequences, and they're your fault, not God's. It's not a question of fairness at all.

God is completely fair; in fact, He's better. He allowed us to avoid the biggest consequence of all, eternal death, because of His Son's death. Therefore when we mess up and suffer the consequences, there is no reason to say God's not fair. Instead we need to learn how to deal with our responsibilities and stop looking to God to get us out of mistakes He didn't make.

■ *Forgive me, God, for blaming You for my mistakes. Help me take responsibility for my actions.*

K.B.

TRUSTING GOD

"Let us be strong for our people and for the cities of our God. And may the LORD do what seems good to Him." —2 SAM. 10:12

You will meet guys who treat their recovery this way. They will say, "I just trust God to lead me in my recovery." This is often just an excuse to not do any work in their recovery because they are afraid of failing. A true definition of manhood is the ability to face the work ahead and at the same time trust that God will also make good on His promise to heal you of your addiction.

It takes strength and courage to face the unknown and trust God to bring about what He has promised to do in your life. Why is this so courageous? Because of the strength it takes to let go of the steering wheel of your recovery. God has a plan in mind to accomplish your growth and healing, and you don't know the specifics of that plan. So you have to continue to struggle and work in recovery, and watch and see how God brings it about through a variety of experiences, both trying and exhilarating.

Are you ready for such a loss of control? Do you trust God enough to do what He has promised? Or do you want to play God because you don't want what God may have in store for you? God is worthy of your trust.

■ *Father, help me to trust You to heal me and work hard to overcome my addiction.*

R.M.

NEVER STOP PRAYING

Always be joyful and never stop praying.
Whatever happens, keep thanking God
because of Jesus Christ.
—1 THESS. 5:16–18 CEV

It had been a tough week, and Sean was feeling discouraged. He looked depressed and beaten down, and seemed to be losing hope that things would ever feel good again. I reminded him of some very positive changes he had made in the past months, but even that didn't seem to help much. And then I asked him if he had talked to God lately.

Sean hadn't. He told me he felt distant from God, like somehow God was too busy or not interested in his recovery. "When things get this bad," Sean confided, "I don't feel much like talking to God." Sean had let his relationship with his higher power take second place to his feelings of hopelessness. It wasn't God who moved away; it was Sean.

When things are going good in recovery, you feel on top of the world, and you are excited about the things God is doing in your life. When things start going bad, often the first thing you neglect is your relationship with your higher power. It is easy to forget that God's strength is the foundation of recovery when life takes a turn for the worst. When things go bad, that's when you need God the most.

■ *Lord, I need You, my Higher Power, to depend on.*
Help me to make talking to You my first thought.

K.B.

THE DANGER OF LOOKING BACK

But Lot's wife looked back and she became a pillar of salt.
—GEN. 19:26 NIV

When things get rough in recovery, every guy has a tendency to look back at the "good ole' days." It is natural to second-guess ourselves when we begin to struggle in any endeavor and wonder if we made the right decision. But looking back slows our progress. This is particularly true of recovery.

When you face adversity, look for someone you can talk to. That is what people who are supporting your recovery are for. They are there to stand with you when you struggle and to help you regain the focus you temporarily lost. They will also help you focus your sights on the goal ahead—health.

Don't let your pride get in the way. You have to remind yourself that you will do whatever it takes to recover, even if that means leaning on someone else for a time. It is not a sign of weakness to depend on someone else to get back on track. If you aren't willing to find help and, instead, keep looking back, you may convince yourself that you made the wrong choice and go back to your old way of living. Then, it will take twice the effort you have already expended to get back to where you are now.

■ *Father, help me not to look back except to remind myself that I am committed to recovery and don't want to go back.*

R.M.

CONFRONTING OLD FRIENDS

"You shall not hate your brother in your heart. You shall surely rebuke your neighbor, and not bear sin because of him."

—LEV. 19:17

Now that you've started your new life, you've learned a lot of things that are helpful to you. You've learned that the way you were living had a lot of unpleasant consequences. Being clean and sober helps you to see more clearly the problems caused by your chemical abuse. It also helps you see what others are doing to themselves as they continue to abuse substances.

Sitting by and watching friends continue to make a mess of their lives is quite hard. Unless you say something to them, you are actually helping them to continue in their addiction. Doing and saying nothing is enabling.

You have a responsibility, because of your friendship, to confront them with the consequences of their alcohol and drug abuse. While they probably will not listen, and might even get angry, you need to say something. Tell them about the changes you are going through. Let them know there is hope. Don't sit by and let them make a mess of their lives as you once did. Caring means sharing, so talk to them about their chemical abuse.

■ *Help me, Lord, to confront an old friend about his substance abuse. It's worth risking a friendship.*

K.B.

BEING QUESTIONED

*"Now prepare yourself like a man;
I will question you, and you shall
answer Me."* —JOB 40:7

When someone questions you or your motives, your first response is to get defensive. Of course, when you get defensive you are only confirming in the other person's mind that you are probably guilty. Therefore, it takes real courage to be able to take being questioned and not get defensive.

The man who pleases God is willing to take being questioned. He even welcomes it because he knows that it will make him think. It will force him to examine his own motives and keep a healthy perspective about himself and how he is doing.

The coward is the man who upon being questioned gets defensive and attempts to shift the focus from himself onto the person questioning him. In that way, he doesn't have to answer the question and look at things he is afraid of.

Don't be afraid of questions. You can say, "I really appreciate your asking that because I need to think about this." That may sound canned and "not you," but being questioned isn't always bad. It doesn't always mean that the questioner assumes you have done something wrong. Instead, he may simply be asking for the reason you did something. So be careful when you answer questions.

■ *Don't get defensive when you are questioned; it may be something you need to think about.*

R.M.

THANKING THOSE IN CHARGE

Be thoughtful of your leaders who work hard and tell you how to live for the Lord. Show them great respect and love because of their work.
—1 THESS. 5:12–13 CEV

Most addicts have negative feelings toward people in charge. Parents, principals, police, counselors—any authority figures—are avoided. Addicts focus on getting high and drunk, so they cut themselves off from people who could help. They choose to be angry and resentful of caring adults. As part of their recovery, they need to work on those bitter feelings.

Some of the adults you resented really cared about you. They tried to warn you, then tried to stop you, and finally insisted you get help. The more they tried to help, the angrier you got. Now you need to recognize that they can help you get away from dangerous impulses and addictive behaviors and can direct you to healthier living.

As your attitudes change about a lot of things, you'll see that you need to be thankful to those authority figures who cared enough to insist you change. If you've let resentment build up toward them, it's time to start tearing it down. If you've done wrong to them, it's time to apologize and make things right. You can't afford to push away those who care and have worked hard to help you find health and sobriety. Begin today to start thanking them for the work they did to get you where you are today.

■ *God, work in me to change my attitude about those in authority. Help me to thank them for caring.*

K.B.

Choosing Your Battles

Stand therefore, having girded your waist with truth, having put on the breastplate of righteousness.
—EPH. 6:14

Tommy was a happy little boy who loved to imitate his dad. One day, his dad gave him a hammer. This was a great gift because Tommy's dad was a carpenter and loved to make things around the house. Tommy couldn't wait to try out his hammer—on the couch, on the cat, on the dog, on the dining room table, on just about everything that would stand still. To Tommy, everything was a nail.

Sometimes guys aren't much different with their recovery. Everyone they come into contact with presents them with an opportunity to try out their new knowledge about recovery. They make no distinction about whether the person is ready to hear what they have to say. To them, everyone needs to hear what they have learned.

It is important to choose your battles wisely. Don't fight with everyone about his or her need for recovery. You may win the battle and lose your relationship. Or worse yet, you may lose both the battle and the relationship because you are so intent on winning your point. You need to give others the right to not recover. You may be instrumental in their decision to recover because you have maintained your relationship with them.

■ *Father, help me to choose my battles wisely in sharing with people about my recovery.*

R.M.

LIFTING THE BLINDFOLD

*Only Christ can take away the covering that
keeps them from seeing.*
—2 COR. 3:14 CEV

Denial continues throughout recovery. At first you
deny that you have a problem. Then you have to start
seeing the negative patterns of behavior that keep the
substance abuse in your life. After that comes a denial
of how the chemicals hurt friends and loved ones in
your life. Finally you have to start taking full responsibility for the things you have done, instead of just blaming
others.

Every time a wall of denial is broken down, there is a
new opportunity to see things in your life as they really
are, instead of just looking at them in the old ways. It's
as if you have a blindfold on, but as you turn your life
over to God, He is able to slowly remove the blindfold to
see things more clearly.

On your own power, you are stuck. Because you have
seen things the same way for so long, it is very difficult
to change your way of looking at them. Many addicts
have a hard time moving through recovery, because
they don't let God lift the covering and help them see
things as they really are. Each time you get stuck in
recovery, or get tired of the process, it means you need
to take another step, but you can't understand yet. God
opens your spiritual eyes so that you can move on to
become the person you really want to be.

■ *God, lift the blindfold of denial so that I can look
clearly at the changes I need to make.*

K.B.

A CLOSE CALL

If anyone's work is burned, he will suffer loss; but he himself will be saved, yet so as through fire.
—1 COR. 3:15

Crisis response teams specialize in dealing with close calls. They train day in and day out to know how to respond in a crisis. The key to their success is knowing the kind of crises they have to deal with. Crisis response teams are often specific in their function. That limits the amount of knowledge they must understand, thus they respond more effectively.

In recovery, it is important to prepare for the unexpected. You will need to be your own crisis response team. That doesn't mean you have to know everything about recovery and deal with your crises alone. It does mean you should work to have the ability to figure out what is wrong and how to respond to it.

How do you do that? You need to always learn about recovery. Throughout your recovery you will meet people who have a better understanding of recovery than you do. You need to take time to talk to them and ask questions so that you may be better prepared for the unexpected in your life.

You also need to know your resources. Know who you can call on for help for a particular problem. It is important that you develop a support system to fill in the gaps when you don't know what to do.

■ *Develop a support system to help you respond effectively to crises in your life.*

R.M.

I HATE CONFRONTATIONS!

It is better to hear the rebuke of the wise
Than for a man to hear the song of fools.
—ECC. 7:5

At the hospital unit where I work, a time is set aside every day for peers to confront the negative behaviors of others. Most people hate it, because they have to sit quietly and hear about what they are doing that is hurting themselves and others.

Let's face it, nobody likes to hear what he or she is doing wrong. That's especially true when you've been trying your hardest to do what is right. But unless you are able to sit and listen to the mistakes you are making, how will you ever know what to change?

Many relationships are based on dishonesty. People say only nice things to your face, and save the negatives for behind your back. It's easier that way, because you don't have to deal with the things you've done wrong. But it doesn't help much when it comes to looking at yourself honestly.

In the long run, it is better to hear honest confrontation, even though it sometimes hurts, than to have others pretend everything is fine. Don't avoid relationships where the other person is honest enough to point out your mistakes. Those relationships will help you grow the most.

■ *Teach me, God, to appreciate confrontations even though they are difficult and sometimes hurt.*

K.B.

A WORTHY MAN

"If he proves himself a worthy man, not one hair of him shall fall to the earth; but if wickedness is found in him, he shall die."
—1 KINGS 1:52

What is a "real man?" Is it someone who is tough and doesn't get hurt? Maybe you think a real man is a guy who can charm women and get them to go home with him. Solomon suggests a definition of a real man in today's passage. A real man does right and deals with people honestly. All the other definitions are sorry imitations of what it is to be a real man in God's eyes.

You may say, "That doesn't sound like much. I can do that." But look closely at the day you have just completed. What was it like? Did you bend the truth a little to make people think you were a nice person? Did you inflate what you could do with a girl to make sure she would be impressed? Did you cheat on a test and get away with it? Did you get away with coming in late, and scammed your parents into thinking you couldn't help it? It isn't as easy as it sounds to be someone who does what is right. It takes a great deal of courage to do something wrong and admit it, but that is what a "worthy" man does. He is strong enough to "take the heat" when he messes up; he admits his wrong and allows himself to feel bad. He then uses that feeling of guilt to motivate him to set right what he has done wrong, and he gets on with life.

■ *Father, help me to be a real man in Your eyes and do what is right toward others.*

R.M.

MAKING THINGS RIGHT

"If . . . someone is angry with you, leave your gift there in front of the altar. Make peace with that person, then come back and offer your gift to God."
—MATT. 5:23–24 CEV

Often I hear people say, "If they're angry at me, they need to tell me. It's not my job to deal with their feelings!" Big mistake. If you know someone is angry about something you've done, it *is* your responsibility to try to work things out. That's called making amends.

In recovery you work on accepting responsibility for your own actions. After all, your mistakes got you in trouble, not others' responses to your mistakes. A big part of accepting responsibility for things you have done is to apologize to those you have wronged and then try to make things right. This is true even if you feel they shouldn't be angry at you. It is not up to you to judge whether the other person's feelings are right.

When you know someone is mad at you and you don't do anything about it, you put distance between yourself and God. That is because God is pushing you to take responsibility for your mistakes, and you are ignoring Him. By now you know that you need God on your side if you are ever going to make it. So when He reminds you of someone you have hurt, listen and humbly approach that person to make things right.

■ *Help me remember people I've wronged and give me the courage to make amends whenever possible.*

K.B.

USING OTHERS

They will exploit you with deceptive words;
for a long time their judgment has not been
idle, and their destruction does not slumber.
—2 PET. 2:3

When you abuse drugs and alcohol, you learn to exploit other people to attain your ends, which usually results in more drugs to use. There is a mentality that is required in order to treat people like objects.

In its most unvarnished state, using people is greed. Its underlying belief is that your satisfaction and gratification are more important than a person's worth. You may not have thought of this when you were treating people this way, but your behavior betrayed this approach to people. It is easier to treat people as things when you fear their rejection and disappointment. By treating them this way, you can keep your emotional distance and can be sure you won't get hurt.

So now you are recovering from addiction and are trying to treat people as people, and not use them. If you treat people humanely, though, you risk being hurt. By this time you have learned more effective ways to cope with being hurt. One of these is to talk about it with the person who has hurt you. In this way, you are not left with your hurt, and you can be free to create a new habit of treating people the way they should be treated—with the respect you expect from them!

■ *Father, help me to treat people with respect and not use them.*

R.M.

Restitution

"I will give half of my property to the poor.
And I will now pay back four times as much
to everyone I have ever cheated."
—LUKE 19:8 CEV

Sid realized he had to make restitution. That is, he had wronged someone, and he needed to make things right. He remembered stealing a diamond bracelet at a party. He had been drunk that night, and didn't remember the things he'd done the next day.

He woke up and discovered the bracelet in his pocket. Feeling guilty and not wanting to admit he'd stolen it, he gave it to his girlfriend. After they broke up he forgot the whole incident. But now that he'd been sober for some time, things were coming back, like stealing the bracelet.

One important step of recovery is paying others back for the damages you have caused them, and Sid wanted to take this step. In Sid's case, this meant he needed to either get the bracelet back, admit he'd taken it and apologize, or repay the person from whom he'd taken the bracelet. Until he took this step, he'd be living with the guilt of his actions that night.

In your life you have done wrong to others because of your addiction. It is your responsibility to go to them and make restitution for the damages you caused. Avoiding this step will block your progress and hurt your recovery.

■ *Grant me the courage to make restitution to those I've cheated or harmed by my actions.*

K.B.

GIGO

We have thought, O God on Your lovingkindness,
In the midst of Your temple.
                                        —PS. 48:9

In my graduate training, I had to learn how to program a computer to do certain tasks. It is important to understand that computers are really dumb machines. They will do only what you tell them to do and not a single thing beyond that. Computers can be programmed to do incredible things at an incredible speed, but they are no match for the human mind.

Some students would write a program that was an endless loop of commands. The computer would mechanically and faithfully carry out those commands, but it would not be able to get out of the loop because it wasn't programmed to. We would joke about the computerese term GIGO, which means "Garbage In, Garbage Out." That is pretty descriptive of what happens with the computer. If you supply it with garbage, it will be more than happy to supply you with garbage in return.

That is what happens with your mind as well. If you fill it with garbage—addictive substances, pornography, and so on—sooner or later it will begin to push some of the same stuff out of you. On the other hand, if you fill your mind with things that are excellent, praiseworthy, true, noble, and pure you will produce good stuff.

■   *Father, help me to fill my mind with healthy things*
    that will not contaminate it.

                                        R.M.

GOD LIVES IN YOUR BODY

Surely you know that your body is a temple where the Holy Spirit lives. . . . So use your body to honor God.
—1 COR. 6:19–20 CEV

It's my body, and what I do with it doesn't harm anyone else," said fifteen-year-old Brett. He was trying to get me to see that if he wanted to get high or drunk or do anything it shouldn't matter to anyone else. Obviously, he was trying to come up with a good argument that people should leave him alone to make decisions for himself.

Now, that might seem like a good argument on the surface. But for those who are serious about working a recovery program, it doesn't work. When you commit your life and your recovery to God, He actually moves in and starts working from the inside out. So what you do to your body not only affects you, but also affects the higher power you've invited to help you change.

Furthermore, since God is by far the most important guest you'll ever entertain, you have a duty to make the place you've asked Him to live in a great place. After all, when you invite someone over to your house, you don't want to make him sit next to smelly garbage. Don't do that to God. Make your body a place where God is an honored and respected guest. Take care of it.

■ *Lord, help me to clean up my body so that You will not be offended and can enjoy Your stay.*

K.B.

BEING TESTED

"I brought him to Your disciples, but they could not cure him." —MATT. 17:16

There will be times, and may have been already, when people will test or question your motives and abilities. It is aggravating to be questioned. I imagine that is how the disciples felt when they attempted, but were unable to heal a man's son. How humiliating to have the man announce to everyone how incompetent they were! Their abilities and faith were being questioned.

The most common response to questions or tests is anger. You are angry that someone does not believe you. You also feel hurt that someone wouldn't trust you. These two emotions—hurt and anger—are a pretty powerful combination. This combination will not instill hope in the person questioning you. If you act upon these emotions, you will probably blow up and prove the other person right. He or she can then walk away saying, "See, I knew this kid wasn't getting any better. Did you see how he blew up at me!"

When someone doubts the effectiveness of your recovery, don't get mad. Use it as an opportunity to show just how much progress you have made by controlling your anger and honestly telling him how you feel about the comment. You will see for yourself just how far you have come.

■ *Father, help me to control myself when others test me or doubt my recovery.*

R.M.

BEING CONSISTENT

Try your best to please God and to be like him. Be faithful, loving, dependable, and gentle. —1 TIM. 6:11 CEV

Mr. and Mrs. Peterson looked quite frustrated. They couldn't trust their son, Jeff. They would make deals with him, only to find out later that he had gone back on his end of the bargain. They couldn't believe a word he said.

Jeff meant to keep their agreements, but things would come up, and he just wouldn't think about his parents; he thought only about getting high. Jeff had a problem all addicts have—inconsistency.

Most addicts aren't hard-core druggies; in fact, many are good people. But drugs have become more important to them than their dependability. Even after they stop using, that old inconsistency continues, and they aren't reliable.

In recovery, you need to learn how to be trustworthy. That's hard because for some time now you haven't cared that much if people trust you. But now that you are trying to be different, you need to work on doing what you say you will. That means sticking to the rules, admitting when you've messed up, and working on recovery every day. Being a consistent, dependable person is the way to rebuild the trust you are looking for.

■ *Lord, help me apologize for not being dependable and work on becoming more reliable.*

K.B.

LIVE WISELY

*See then that you walk circumspectly, not as
fools but as wise.*   —EPH. 5:15

Our society has various definitions of what is manly or
masculine. We have the stereotypes of John Wayne and
Rambo, of Clint Eastwood or Van Damme. Each of these
men through the roles he played defined what manhood
was. Generally, the message is a disregard for the rules
of society in order to get the "bad guy." This disregard
for proper behavior is what makes us cheer for them,
because they are doing things that we would never have
the guts to do. Interestingly, one element is missing in
these characters: the quality of wisdom. Few characteri-
zations of manhood portray a man who is wise and careful in his dealings with people. That is seen as gutless
and wimpy.

You are no doubt influenced by these images of manhood in your clothing, behavior, and other forms of expression. Yet these expressions of manhood are often
opposed to a good recovery. Being wise and careful are
qualities you need for a good recovery. You need to
hang on to the idea that being careful and living in a
way that is wise for your recovery shows your true
strength, even though others may not see it that way.
Don't let others define your masculinity for you. Strive
to do things that will show inner strength.

■   *Father, help me to be strong enough to live my life
wisely.*

R.M.

WANTING TO DO RIGHT

I know that my selfish desires won't let me do anything that is good. Even when I want to do right, I cannot. —ROM. 7:18 CEV

Early in his recovery Bob's first thought every day was to get high. Then he would remember that he was in recovery and that today was a new beginning, the first day of his recovery. Still, all day he thought about the good times he had when he was using. Then he reminded himself that recovery was more important. It was like breaking up with a girlfriend—he just couldn't stop thinking about it and sometimes wished he could have it back.

Now that's powerlessness! While he knew he needed to be different, at the front of his mind most often was getting high. He constantly felt on the edge of giving in. He wanted it badly, but knew it could never be.

Your body will play tricks on you. It is so used to going through life with the aid of substances that it will remind you constantly of its desire to deal with life through chemicals. You will find yourself thinking that maybe you can now control it, or maybe just a little couldn't hurt, or even that no one would know if you used only once. That is the old you speaking, the part you have given to God because you can't handle it alone. Continue to give those desires to God, asking Him to change them.

■ *Take control of my selfish desires and change them into a desire to work on recovery.*

K.B.

PARTING WORDS TO A SON

*"I go the way of all the earth; be strong,
therefore, and prove yourself a man. And
keep the charge of the LORD your God."*
—1 KINGS 2:2–3

When you attend a funeral, do you think about things
you have never thought about before? It really isn't all
that comfortable to be confronted with death and also
our own mortality. People often say the most important
things of their lives when they are facing death. That
was certainly the case with David as he faced his death.
He thought about what he could tell his son Solomon to
guide him in the years to come. David said to the future
king of Israel, "Show yourself a man!"

Take these words to heart as you strive through your
own recovery from addiction. David told Solomon:
"Observe what the Lord your God requires." Be a man
of principle, who isn't afraid to follow his values. The
true meaning of masculinity is to be strong enough to
follow your values in the face of resistance and temptation. Masculinity isn't the number of girls you go out
with. Masculinity isn't being tough and not showing
your feelings. Masculinity is following your values in
spite of what the crowd does. David knew that Solomon
needed strength to be true to his God and right values.
God knows what you need for recovery: "Be strong,
show yourself a man."

■ *Father, help me to be a man of principles and values
that I am not afraid to follow.*

R.M.

CHANGING YOUR GOALS

The others think only about what interests them and not about what concerns Christ Jesus. —PHIL. 2:21 CEV

An addiction happens when someone becomes so focused on getting high or on drinking that everything else takes second place. The addict's pleasure comes before anyone or anything else. His main goal in life is to satisfy the desire to use substances. Thoughts, actions, attitudes, and behaviors all center around getting, using, and enjoying the high.

Something changes when recovery starts. The goal is no longer getting high and finding pleasure. It isn't even staying clean and sober. Rather, it is doing what God wants done. The addict's focus changes from substances to God.

In many ways this is much simpler. Instead of making all sorts of complicated plans to purchase substances, use them without anyone finding out, and then moving on to the next high, you can simply look to God to do what is best in your life. Trying to find pleasure from chemicals is a never-ending battle, because it leaves you feeling empty and wanting more. Trying to find pleasure in serving God *does* work because it fills the emptiness that drugs and alcohol cannot. Plus, it brings real happiness.

■ *I want to make serving God, not my own pleasure, my new goal in life.*

K.B.

FINISHING WELL

"This man began to build and was not able to finish."
— LUKE 14:30

The key to success in any race is to keep your mind on the end. Runners need to conserve their energy so that they will have enough left at the end of the race to win. Runners who don't plan ahead this way don't win very often. Instead, they are the ones who usually look very good in the early part of the race, only to fall apart near the end because their energy is spent.

Recovery is very much like a race. Of course, the race is a marathon and not a sprint. As a matter of fact, it is a life-long marathon in which you will always need to keep in mind that there is indeed an end, and that you must pace yourself to finish well. Don't drag yourself over the finish line in the end. Rather, finish strongly with God's help because you have watched your emotional resources closely and used them when the demand was there.

So the key is to watch for situations you need to focus your energies on and focus with all your heart. Then watch for situations where you can keep moving but rest while you are moving. That way you can conserve your emotional energy and use it to finish well.

■   *Father, help me to conserve when I need to and push myself in my recovery when I need to.*

R.M.

ACTING LIKE A BABY

You are acting like the people of this world. . . . You are like babies as far as your faith in Christ is concerned.
—1 COR. 3:1 CEV

I caught Paul doing something he promised he would not do. When I pointed it out to him, he got angry and argued with me. So I held my ground and pushed him to look at what he had done. When he saw that I wasn't going to let up, he crossed his arms, turned sideways in his chair, looked up at the ceiling, refused to talk, and pouted.

For a moment I was pretty mad. This guy was seventeen years old but was acting like a baby. Instead of allowing me to help him by pointing some things out, he gave me the silent treatment and pouted.

But then I remembered he had been using chemicals since he was twelve and was probably stuck emotionally at that age. Unfortunately for Paul, I would have to push him only as much as a twelve year old could handle, not like the seventeen year old he was. That meant his treatment would go that much slower.

Think for a moment about the way you respond when you get in trouble over the way you act. Can you handle being treated your age? Or must you be handled like a child? Unless you want to go through life being treated that way, maybe there is room for improvement.

■ *God, help me to act in such a way that others respect me and don't baby me.*

K.B.

WHEN THE NOVELTY WEARS OFF

"Because lawlessness will abound, the love of many will grow cold."   —MATT. 24:12

Have you ever noticed that no matter what job you take on, you soon get tired of it? I remember when I first went to work for the railroad. I had the job of changing the railroad ties every day. It was back-breaking work, but it was fun because I could actually see the fruit of my labor after the day was done. Before long, though, the novelty of working this hard wore off and it became a real drag. I got bored and was ready to quit.

Recovery is a lot like that. At first, you feel like you can conquer the world. Things are going great, until you begin to tire of the job you have undertaken. You think to yourself, "Isn't it about time that this was over? I'm getting pretty tired of this." This is the time you need to watch yourself closely because you are a sitting duck for relapse. You begin to tire more easily as you struggle on in your work of recovery.

The best way to regain some of the energy you lost in working your program is to take some time and look back. You may even want to describe in the form of a letter to yourself just how far you have come. The joy may not return immediately, but you may be able to reestablish momentum that will keep you going without relapse.

■   *Watch out for relapse when the novelty wears off and review how far you have come and keep going.*

R.M.

I'VE PUSHED GOD OUT OF MY LIFE

Nothing can separate us from God's love. . . .
Nothing in all creation can separate us from
God's love for us in Christ Jesus our Lord!
—ROM. 8:38–39 CEV

Randy had relapsed the previous night. After three months of working hard to stay clean, he went to a concert and took a hit off a friend's joint. Realizing he had messed up, he figured, "Since I've already done it, why not just enjoy the high?" So he smoked several more joints and got totally wasted.

The next day he felt miserable. By the light of day he understood what he had done, and his guilt was tremendous. After all the hard recovery work he had done, because of one night, he was right back where he started. To make things worse, he felt he had let God down. Now he believed there was no way God could possibly trust him, and that God would be so angry He would no longer be part of Randy's recovery in the future.

Randy was wrong. Nothing we do can separate us from God's love. Although Randy made two big mistakes—taking the first hit and then telling himself a lie so that he could get high—that wasn't enough to push God away. Randy would have to start over and again put God in charge of his recovery, but God was more than willing to take His place as soon as Randy asked.

■ *Thank you, God, that my mistakes are not too big or too bad to separate me from Your love.*

K.B.

LIVING IN DARKNESS

"People who do evil hate the light and won't come to the light, because it clearly shows what they have done."

—JOHN 3:20 CEV

What is it about looking back over their lives that makes some people so frightened? It's because they must search their conscience and deal with the wrongs they have done. Some of their secrets are shameful and embarrassing, and often people would rather live in darkness, denying that those things ever happened.

People in denial are afraid of exposing their secrets, and so they choose never to deal with the past. They are doomed to forever make the same mistakes because they refuse to learn from their negative experiences. They live in darkness, locking up important memories that could help them change and finally be happy.

You may also be running from the light. When you ask God to be in charge of your recovery program, there is no doubt that He will want you to look at these shameful and embarrassing secrets. You must be completely certain you want this to happen. If not, you will again push these secrets back into the darkest corners of your mind and will start living in denial. Unless you are willing to allow God to make these secrets clear so that you can deal with them, your recovery will come to a complete stop.

■ *God, prepare my heart to be ready to deal with things I have hidden from myself and from others.*

K.B.

MAKING MISTAKES

There is therefore now no condemnation to those who are in Christ Jesus.

—ROM. 8:1

What happens when you make mistakes? Do you clam up and pout? Do you get angry? Do you blame someone else? Do you make sure it doesn't happen again? Your response to mistakes says a lot about how you will handle recovery, because recovery is filled with mistakes. I'm not trying to depress you. Instead I want you to understand that making mistakes isn't all that bad. Of course, no one goes out of his way to make mistakes, but a lot can be learned from mistakes. As a matter of fact, many of the inventions we take for granted resulted from mistakes. We have benefited from these mistakes because these inventors weren't afraid to look at their mistakes as an opportunity to learn more about how to reach their goal.

That is what you need to do in your recovery. You will probably learn more from your mistakes than you will from doing everything right—that is, if you don't make mistakes out to be major catastrophes and black holes of despair. When you adopt this stance toward mistakes, you won't have to condemn yourself in order to do a better job. Instead, you can assure yourself that you will do what you must to avoid it in the future, and at the same time learn from it.

■ *Father, help me not to be afraid of my mistakes and condemn myself for them, but learn from them.*

R.M.

YES, BUT . . .

Moses answered and said, "But suppose they will not believe me or listen to my voice; suppose they say, 'The LORD has not appeared to you.'"
—EX. 4:1

We do all we can to slither out of responsibility. One of the most classic ways addicts avoid taking responsibility for their recovery is to find reasons to fail. In today's passage, Moses did what we might call "Yes, butting." He kept coming up with as many reasons as possible to get off the hook of being responsible. God told Moses to go back to Egypt to deliver His people, and Moses said, "Yes, but what if they don't believe me?" Why didn't he just come out and say, "I don't want this job! Find someone else!"? Thankfully, Moses didn't do this, but accepted the job God had for him.

Do you "yes, but"? Do you find reasons to not do what you have committed to do? It is important to look at God, who will support you during recovery, not at your own weaknesses. I'm not saying you shouldn't express your feelings and frustration during recovery. Everyone gets frustrated and tired of working a recovery program. But if you focus on your weaknesses you will fail because you are depending on yourself. Look at your circumstances through the filter of God's power, and you can accomplish anything, including recovering from your addiction.

■   *Father, help me to look at my recovery through the filter of Your power.*

R.M.

GIVING UP YOUR RIGHTS

Don't cause problems for someone with a weak conscience, just because you have the right to eat anything. —1 COR. 8:9 CEV

I know my rights. I can do that if I want to! Who are you to tell me to stop?" We had just confronted Mike on some behaviors he was acting out. They were not against the law, but weren't helpful to others who were trying to work on their recovery programs. Mike got angry and started yelling about his rights and how America is a free country and so on. It was obvious that he wasn't as motivated to change as others were.

On one level, Mike was correct. He did have certain rights. On another level, he was wrong. The things he was doing were hurting others around him. By focusing on his rights he did not look at what he was doing to those who wished to change. It was his attitude he needed to change.

When someone points out a negative pattern, attitude, or behavior in your life, you will probably become angry. You'll wonder what right they have to tell you to change. But be careful; focusing on your rights will keep you from looking at the real causes of the problem. You have a choice to give up your rights, too. If practicing your rights is hurting others, or even your own recovery, you may wish to decide to temporarily give up that right.

■ *God, show me when my rights are less important than my need to change.*

K.B.

TOO MANY FRIENDS

A man who has friends must himself be friendly,
But there is a friend who sticks closer than a
brother.
—PROV. 18:24

Is it possible to have too many friends? I think it just might be. It is easy to have a lot of friends and have no one who really knows us, who really knows how we are doing and can't accuse us of losing ground or doing poorly in our recovery. We can hide in the crowd of people we surround ourselves with.

Are you strong enough to have a friend "who sticks closer than a brother"? It is scary to have someone know you that well. More often than not, you have made sure that no one has gotten that close because you are sure he won't like what he sees if he knows you "up close and personal."

It takes strength to be vulnerable with someone. But the only way to find the true meaning of friendship is to have someone know you that well, and to find out that he won't reject you. As long as you attempt to keep everyone at arm's length, you will never experience such a feeling. We have been taught that it is not "manly" to have a close friend who knows us so well. But a real man has the guts to be vulnerable enough to have a brother who sticks close to him.

■ *Father, help me to be vulnerable enough to allow*
someone to know me like a brother.

R.M.

SHARING THE MESSAGE

God was in Christ, offering peace and forgiveness to the people of this world.
—2 COR. 5:19 CEV

It's not enough to work on recovery alone. Sure your life is turning around, and things are getting better, and that's great. But other people are hurting just as you were, stuck in their addictions and powerless to stop. Most of them, though they won't admit it at first, feel totally out of control and miserable just as you once did.

An important part of any recovery process is letting others know about your changes and the wonderful things you are discovering. You help others, just as someone once helped you. But you also help yourself.

When you make a stand, others know that you mean it, that you are for real. They watch you as you change and see that something is different. They ask you about the things you are saying and doing. This means you have to be on your guard to really do the things you are talking about. This keeps you honest and working on recovery.

If you are serious about recovery, don't try to do it in secret. If you do, you will hide something good from people you might have helped, and you give yourself too much freedom to relapse. When people are watching, you will be on your best recovery behavior.

■ *Today, tell at least one person about the changes you are making in your recovery.*

K.B.

THE BUDDY SYSTEM

Two are better than one,
Because they have a good reward
for their labor. —ECC. 4:9

When I went to camp as a kid we were always instructed to have a buddy when we went swimming. It was a great way to have someone nearby to help you out if you got into trouble.

A buddy system isn't just for children, though. From what I hear, it is a cardinal rule for scuba divers to always dive with a partner. That way if anything goes wrong for one person, the other can help him out or get help for him.

Somehow people have gotten the notion that asking for help is a sign of weakness. That notion is very dangerous for recovery. It lays you wide open for problems when you are attempting a job alone that is dangerous to your well-being. Recovery isn't an easy thing to undertake and succeed at. You will need a friend to help you and to watch for trouble that you may not see.

It is a valuable lesson to understand that there is no shame in leaning on another person when you need help. It is a sign of pride and stupidity to want to do your recovery alone.

■ *It is important to have a buddy go with you in your journey through recovery.*

R.M.

YOU RECOVER, HELP ANOTHER

*He comforts us when we are in trouble, so
that we can share that same comfort with
others in trouble.*   —2 COR. 1:4 CEV

The group just sat there looking at each other, but no
one said much. Finally one member spoke up and said
what everyone was thinking. "I know I have a lot of work
to do, but I don't see how talking about it to others who
are just as bad off as I am can help." Many in group
recovery sessions wonder that.

Instead of explaining, I pushed him to talk about why
he was in the rehab unit. So he told his story. As soon as
he began talking, others' eyes lit up; it was clear they
could understand what he had been through. Several
began to tell their story and made comments like,
"Wow, I thought I was the only one who felt that!" That
was the beginning of an intense group session.

It's not always the brilliant professionals who can
make a difference in an addict's life. Sometimes just
hearing what others have been through and sharing
your own story can be much more helpful than expensive advice from a therapist. Because you have abused
chemicals and now want to change, you can offer something valuable to others in your situation: understanding
and comfort. Telling your story may just be what another person needs.

■   *Lord, let me help someone else with the story of my
recovery and the changes I'm making.*

K.B.

CAN'T LISTEN WHEN YOU'RE TALKING

*"Listen to this, O Job;
Stand still and consider the wondrous
works of God."* **—JOB 37:14**

In recovery, guys and their parents have trouble talking to each other at first. They all are so busy trying to make their points that it is impossible for them to listen to each other. It often takes someone from outside the family to get them to listen to each other.

Listening is a lot harder than you think. It isn't just hearing what is said and repeating it back. Any parrot can do that! Listening means hearing what another person has said and showing that you have heard. It means you have digested it enough to paraphrase what was said. And the person can say back to you, "Yes, you know what I mean." That takes a lot of practice and close attention. Is it worth the effort?

Listening is an incredible self-esteem boost to people. It tells them they are important enough for you to hear what they say even if you don't understand or agree. It takes a great deal of courage and integrity to do such a thing. It helps you, too. Practicing listening to people puts you in the position of learning more about yourself and remaining open to feedback. If you hone your skill to listen to others, when they are ready to give you feedback, you can hear them out.

■ *Father, help me to listen to others and be ready to receive feedback when they give it to me.*

R.M.

BE CAREFUL OF YOUR SELF-TALK

Keep your minds on whatever is true, pure, right, holy, friendly, and proper. Don't ever stop thinking about what is truly worthwhile.
—PHIL. 4:8 CEV

I'm such an idiot, even a retard could see that," said Jake. He had made a simple mistake and was putting himself down for it. I asked him if he talked to himself that way often. Naturally he hadn't thought about it much, and so we started to explore his self-talk.

We all go through life saying things to ourselves in our thoughts. When a person feels bad about himself, his self-talk is critical and negative. When someone is constantly criticized and put-down, after a while he begins to feel worse and may even start to hate himself. If you are the person doing the criticizing, it is with you all the time.

Quit putting yourself down. Instead of dwelling so much on the negatives about yourself, start saying more positive things about you. After a tough day say things like "Good job!" Focus on the good things you've done. While you may think you need to put yourself down to keep from messing up, this isn't true. Start treating yourself the way you want others to treat you.

■ *Each time you make negative comments about things you've done, stop and think something encouraging.*

K.B.

THE PAIN OF FAILURE

*"The rain descended, the floods came, and
the winds blew and beat on that house; and
it fell. And great was its fall."*

—MATT. 7:27

We learn about ourselves when we face failure. We find out what motivates us to do what we do. One response to failure is anger and rage because things didn't go the way you expected. This is a helpless, powerless anger that lashes out at anything nearby.

You need to ask yourself why something is so important that you get enraged over it. Often the answer is that failing is a real blow to your self-esteem. So no matter what you undertake, the results are a test of your worth. If you fail, you are a failure. If you succeed, you are a success. Life and reality don't usually cooperate in giving us successes all the time.

If you can find security and worth in how God looks at you as priceless and of great value, you may be able to take failure better. When you look at yourself through God's eyes you will see that you are already a success, and there is nothing that can change that. So when failure strikes, you can say to yourself, "It's okay. I don't like to fail, but it doesn't mean I'm a failure. It does mean that I have to change a few things in order to get it right the next time."

■ *Father, help me remember that my worth is secure in Your eyes, and when I fail I am not a failure.*

R.M.

LIFE OF THE PARTY

*The righteous should choose his friends
  carefully,
For the way of the wicked leads them astray.*
                                              —PROV. 12:26

Until he started drinking, Joe didn't have many friends, and those he did have he thought were nerds. He was lonely and didn't like himself very much. One night at a party, he again found himself watching more popular people drinking and having fun, and he decided to give it a try.

For the first time in his life he got drunk. Since he had no inhibitions and didn't care how he acted, he discovered he could have a good time and even make people laugh. Next week at school, several of the popular people patted him on the back and talked about how much fun he had been. Joe was hooked. Because he had found a cure for his personality that brought him friends, he kept drinking until it became a problem.

Though his drinking caused problems, he feared what he would be without it. He didn't want to become a boring nerd with no popular friends.

Joe needed to know that the fun person he was when he drank was the same person he was before he started. Drinking and drugs only bring out parts of your personality that are already there. It *was* possible for him to be outgoing and popular; he just needed to do it without chemicals. He gave too much credit to substances for the person he already was inside.

■ *Do you believe chemicals made you a better person? Be who you really are; chemicals won't improve your life.*

                                                          K.B.

FOOLISHLY WISE

Professing to be wise, they became fools.
—ROM. 1:22

A lot of guys have the wrong idea about their recovery. Their focus is all wrong. They think that if they pursue the things that will produce behavior that makes them look recovered, they can say that they have recovered. They are focusing on external evidence that proves they are recovered. But this proves nothing other than they can perform all the "right" behaviors. Actually they are getting farther and farther away from recovery and health.

Pursuing only behavior doesn't produce change. You have to change on the inside, which people won't see. Focusing on inside change will produce a recovery that lasts a lifetime. It is important that you not settle for behavior only—it isn't enough. You can fool anyone into thinking you are "wise" in your recovery, but be an absolute fool in how you make decisions regarding your life.

Focus on "small" things in your recovery like honesty, integrity, compassion, and doing the right thing. These will form a solid foundation from which to build a solid recovery process. Then, at some point in the future, someone may approach you and say, "I see the changes you have made and admire you. Tell me how you did it."

■   *It is important to pursue the small things of recovery instead of "looking" good in recovery.*

R.M.

WHAT WILL YOU GAIN?

"What will you gain, if you own the whole world but destroy yourself or waste your life?"
—LUKE 9:25 CEV

Bill knew what he wanted out of life was to be rich, have an easy job, and drive a nice car. That all sounded good, but he had no plan to get there. He just expected it to happen.

On a piece of paper we drew two columns and labeled "Goals" and the other "Behaviors." Under Goals, he wrote, "money, job, and nice car." On the other side, he listed the things he had been doing before rehab: "skipped school, ran away, and got high or drunk every day." Then I asked him to help me understand how those behaviors were helping him reach his goals.

Looking at the list, Bill realized he was a long way from where he wanted to be in the future. He had never really thought about how he was going to reach his goals; he just lived for the fun of today. Even if, by magic, he had reached his dreams, there was no way with his addictions that he could have enjoyed them.

What good is it to reach your goals if you're going to destroy yourself or waste your life? You must first allow God to help you get your life in order. Once that happens, you will not only be closer to your goals, you might even enjoy them when you get there.

■ *Help me, God, to get my life in better shape.*

K.B.

TRUE POWER

When He suffered, He did not threaten, but committed Himself to Him who judges righteously.
—1 PET. 2:23

How can you show true power throughout your recovery process? Will it be to resist temptation? Will it be to consistently attend support group meetings and be accountable to the group for your behavior? It is impossible to have power in recovery if you don't have a purpose.

Jesus was often called meek. This doesn't mean He was a milquetoast or a push-over. Instead, His meekness was power under control, directed in a fashion that is constructive and continues growth. Look at the picture painted of Him when He cleaned out the Temple of the money-changers. Also notice, though, that He was following a purpose for such actions. This purpose was to do His Father's will to cleanse the Temple of the filthy practices that had turned it into a "den of thieves."

For your recovery to be successful and growth-producing you must maintain a vision of your purpose. If you can keep in mind the purpose of putting yourself through such situations as setting limits on friends who are abusing drugs, you will be able to proceed successfully and feel confident of your path. It will give you true power to act assertively and that will facilitate your growth and recovery.

■ *Father, help me to focus on the purpose I have committed to in my recovery from addiction.*

R.M.

HEALING FAITH

Jesus touched their eyes and said, "Because of your faith, you will be healed."
—MATT. 9:29 CEV

What makes recovery successful? Faith in a higher power. It has little to do with how strong you are or how good you are; rather, looking to God and depending on Him to lead in directions that you never considered before makes your recovery successful. It's trusting an unseen force that is greater than yourself and stronger than your addiction.

Several times Jesus told people that their faith had healed them. One man trusted that Jesus could heal his daughter even though Jesus had never seen her. Another woman just touched Jesus' clothes believing they would heal her, and they did. The two blind men in today's passage believed that all Jesus had to do was say the word and they would see again.

Throughout Jesus' earthly life he performed many healing miracles. Each time the person believed Jesus could do it, and he did. You are looking for some healing too. You have a condition, addiction, that is ruining your life, and you want things to be different. Start believing that God can and will work in you to change things. Allow yourself to trust, to have a healing faith.

■ *I turn my life over to You so you can begin the healing process in me. Help me to have healing faith.*

K.B.

LOOKING BACK

*"Only fear the LORD, and serve Him in truth
with all your heart; for consider what great
things He has done for you."*
—1 SAM. 12:24

It is easy to forget where we have come from and the great things God has done for us. We get so caught up in our job in that we lose sight of the progress we have made. I once took a bicycle trip through England. For part of the trip, I had to cross a range of low hills that were as much as five miles long. I would get so absorbed in the climb to the top I didn't even bother to look back and see how far I had come. I only wanted to complain about how hard the ride was. Yet few feelings in my life compare to the way it felt to reach the top. Looking back, I could see the curve that gave me fits when I approached it or the steep incline I was sure I'd never make. They were all put into perspective from my perch at the top.

There is a time during recovery when you need to sit back and look back at how far you have come. You might be surprised at the ground you have covered. Besides that, you will also see just how faithful God has been through your progress in recovery. You will recall the times you were sure you wouldn't make it through the temptation that faced you, and you were able to. These will be good memories of the great things God has done for you. Cherish them.

■   *Thank You, Father, for Your faithfulness to me and
the progress I have made.*

R.M.

THANKING GOD

*The man could see, and he went with Jesus
and started thanking God. When the crowds
saw what happened, they praised God.*
—LUKE 18:43 CEV

Jesus, while walking down the road, saw a blind beggar and healed him. The man, who could now see, got so excited that he followed after Jesus, thanking God for his vision. Everyone around was so impressed that they too started praising God for the miracle that had just happened.

You are also experiencing God's work in your life, just like the blind beggar. God is opening your spiritual eyes, so that you no longer have to live blindly in denial and follow your desires. Every day you are learning new things because you are letting God show you things that are necessary for recovery. By now you must be pretty excited!

When someone does a nice thing for you, it is good to thank him. In your case, God is healing you from a burden of addiction that you couldn't get rid of by yourself. When was the last time you stopped and thanked God for the work He is doing in your life? Don't take God for granted. When you are thankful, others see this and can share in your happiness, and it may help them to be closer to God, too. Take time today to thank God for the growth and changes He has helped you to make.

■ *God, thanks for guiding me through recovery. I appreciate the work You are doing in my life.*

K.B.

A FAITHFUL FRIEND

I have sent Timothy to you . . . who will remind you of my ways in Christ, as I teach everywhere in every church.

—1 COR. 4:17

One of the greatest resources for recovery is a faithful friend. He will be willing to take the flak from you when he confronts you about inappropriate behavior. There are few people who will be committed enough to your recovery to hold you accountable for behavior that risks your recovery. It takes a great deal of courage and concern to be able to confront a friend who is making bad decisions and to lovingly encourage and prod him toward more healthy behavior. The person who is willing to do that is indeed a faithful friend whom you need to hang on to.

A faithful friend also will be quick to remind you of the basics of recovery. He will know what it takes to overcome an addiction, and can tell you what you need to hear. He may not even know that he is helping you with the "right" word, but God knows and uses this person in your life to keep you on track. As a matter of fact, this type of friend is often an effective tool that God uses in your recovery. Be sure to tell this friend just how much you appreciate his courage in helping you and standing with you through your recovery.

■ *It is important to have friends who will support your efforts to recover.*

R.M.

DON'T GET CORRUPTED!

If someone is trapped in sin, you should gently lead that person back to the right path. But watch out, and don't be tempted yourself.
—GAL. 6:1 CEV

Peter was doing quite well in his recovery. For over a year he had been sober, and he worked hard at staying that way. He had started reaching out to others, trying to spread the message of God's healing power. So far, so good.

However, Peter got cocky, proud of his accomplishments, and started holding himself up as an example for others. He started spending more time around others who weren't in recovery and slowly drifted away from the things he knew were right. Instead of drawing others into recovery, he eventually allowed himself to be drawn back to using.

It is important to reach out to others. You have something so good it needs to be shared with those who need it the most. But there is danger there, too. When you hang around the wrong people too long, you don't change, they change you.

Be careful about reaching out to others. Don't kid yourself that because you are doing better, you can handle the people you should be avoiding. Make sure that you spend more time with positive influences than you do reaching out to those who could drag you down.

■ *Make sure that you spend time with people who encourage you to work your recovery program.*

K.B.

WHAT DO YOU WANT IN A FRIEND?

As iron sharpens iron,
So a man sharpens the countenance of his friend.
—PROV. 27:17

In your recovery, you will be confronted with decisions about who to choose as friends. You probably haven't thought much about how you choose friends. More than likely you chose people who liked you and you liked to hang around. You shared mutual activities, and of course, using drugs and alcohol was the glue in your friendships. You didn't realize these friends were harmful to you and that you needed to change friends. By now, however, you realize that friends are an important factor in the success of your recovery.

What kind of friend are you looking for? Do you want one who is nice and makes you feel good? Do you want a "yes man" who agrees with whatever you say, who makes you feel important? Maybe you're the kind of person who wants someone you can trust, who is loyal and willing to question your decisions when you're on thin ice.

Without friends who "sharpen" us, we won't grow. Find a friend who is willing to challenge your usual way of operating and is willing to push you to change what needs to be changed, and you will have found a most valuable friend. If he is willing to do these things, then he is willing to show you how much you really matter to him.

■ *Father, help me to not be afraid of friends who push me to grow throughout my recovery.*

R.M.

Be Spicy!

"Salt is good, but if it no longer tastes like salt, how can it be made to taste salty again?" —LUKE 14:34 CEV

For so long Todd had thought everyone but his friends, the stoners, was dull and boring. Because of his focus on getting high, partying, and enjoying the wild life, this was the only group he considered exciting.

In order to recover, he knew he would have to totally give up this life. He was afraid that he would become dull too. From what he had heard about God, church, and stuff like that, he believed God would make him into a completely boring person, just like the preps, jocks, nerds and all those he never wanted to be like.

What Todd hadn't considered was that maybe the things he thought were boring might be interesting to someone else with a different focus. If drugs became less important, his outlook on life would also change, and the things he used to think were dull could then become more interesting. God doesn't intend for your life to be lifeless. If you allow God to change you, He will spice up the things you used to find boring, and things you previously thought you couldn't stand will be much more interesting.

■ *God, sometimes I'm afraid that I'll be depressed without drugs and alcohol. Make me spicy and interesting in newer, healthier ways.*

K.B.

THE REBEL

> *"Remember this, and show yourselves men;*
> *Recall to mind, O you transgressors."*
> —IS. 46:8

There is something romantic and mysterious about being a rebel. The image seems to give you the right to be different, unpredictable, and impulsive. The rebel is out to prove just how different he is by questioning others and living according to his own way and not everyone else's.

However, being a rebel impedes your progress in recovery because you once again define yourself according to others' expectations. The rebel determines his actions according to what will prove how independent and strong he is. In reality, he is proving just how dependent he is by looking to others to plot his behavior.

You don't need a role to help you make choices. Roles are only a way to hide from people and continue to be dishonest with yourself. Roles and images may give us the strength and purpose we don't have, but they get in the way of our ability to define who we are by our own values. Don't act the image of anything. Be yourself, and people will see your courage in being honest and up front with them. If you fix your sights on your goal for recovery, you will pursue a path that will take you away from just acting another image and will develop the strength needed to be yourself.

■ *Father, help me to be myself without trying to act an image.*

R.M.

Setting limits

Warn troublemakers once or twice. Then
don't have anything else to do with them.
—TITUS 3:10 CEV

Just out of rehab, Rob knew that his old friends would pressure him to return to his old self. But Rob wanted to recover.

Sure enough, during his second week back at school one of his old friends asked him to get high after class. Rob thought carefully about the things he had learned he should do in this kind of situation. He told his friend about rehab and that he was serious about recovery.

A few days later the same guy again asked Rob to get high with him. Now Rob was faced with a tough decision. He knew that if he hung around that kind of temptation he would relapse. So he told the friend to leave him alone and that he didn't want to hang around him anymore.

That made Rob pretty unpopular with his old buddies. He felt bad about it, and he also felt lonely. But he was serious about changing and knew he couldn't risk messing up.

If your friends don't take you seriously the first time you say no to them, you need to give up their friendship. It's a tough decision, but one you must make if you plan to finish what you've started. Don't kid yourself into thinking you can handle that kind of temptation.

■ *Have friends not believed you're serious about recovery? It's time to break off the relationship.*

K.B.

SPLIT DECISION

Jesus said to him, "No one, having put his hand to the plow, and looking back, is fit for the kingdom of God."   —LUKE 9:62

Have you ever disliked a job so much that you constantly looked at your watch? Time just creeps along at a snail's pace in spite of your prayers that just once God would speed up time. As a result of such behavior the quality of your work declines because your attention is on the amount of time that elapsed since the last time you looked. This behavior betrays a lack of commitment to your job. You just endure it for the money or for some other reason. It makes you miserable, and your employer probably isn't real excited either.

Do you notice such behavior in your recovery? Do you constantly wait for the time it will be over? If you do, you really aren't following through on your recovery. You are split in your decision. You want to recover, but you aren't really sure you can do the work. That is the kind of person Jesus was talking about, someone who puts his energy into work, but is looking over his shoulder for a better opportunity.

You need to decide once and for all whether to pursue your recovery or not. In the long run, you will accomplish the goal you have set out to attain if you make the decision to throw yourself fully into the task you have undertaken.

■ *Make your decision for recovery and throw yourself into it with all your might.*

R.M.

SPELUNKING

"The light keeps shining in the dark,
and darkness has never put it out."
—JOHN 1:5 CEV

Some brave sportsmen like to explore caves—it's called spelunking. Deep inside the earth where they crawl around, there is no light because the sun doesn't shine there. So they carry lights with them, usually attached to hats, in order to see where they are going. Without light they would become hopelessly lost and never find their way out.

Sometimes exploring your life might seem like a spelunking expedition. Deep in the darkest corners of your mind are things that need changing. At first they can be hard to see because for a long time they have been covered up and ignored. Without a powerful light, they might stay hidden forever.

Jesus has been called the Light of the world. That's because He goes into the darkest, most hidden parts of people's lives and shows them things they need to change. Because you've made God the chief of your life, you now have a light to show these dark areas and help you find things that need work. Don't run from God's light. Let Him shine in those areas that have been hidden and now are being brought out to be changed.

■ *Lord, shine Your light on areas that keep me from becoming the person You want me to be.*

K.B.

DON'T COMPARE

But if you have bitter envy and self-seeking in your hearts, do not boast and lie against the truth.
                                    —JAMES 3:14

Few things are more destructive for guys in recovery than comparing themselves to others. The reason is that we tend to compare ourselves to those we perceive as people to imitate or follow. Of course, we don't admire people who struggle and don't do well. Instead we choose people who have admirable qualities and, therefore, are doing well. So you are likely to compare yourself to someone you perceive as doing better than you—always. You will never "win."

This is a disastrous trend because you will always feel like a failure. What happens when you fail? You will lose your momentum in recovery or quit or, worse yet, relapse. It is better not to compare at all. Your recovery is yours alone, and the progress you make is yours alone. It is okay to feel good about that. You don't always need somebody to compare yourself to. You will succeed in your recovery if you don't compare yourself to someone who is always going to be better than you.

Finally, comparing leads to resentment and envy. You will get so focused on another and how he is doing that you will lose focus on your own recovery. When that happens, you will lose ground and wonder what happened to you.

■ *The best way to measure your progress in recovery is to remind yourself of how far you have come.*

                                                R.M.

BUT HE'S A COMPLETE IDIOT!

*Honor God by accepting each other, as Christ
has accepted you.* —ROM. 15:7 CEV

Even I had to admit that Keith could be a jerk at times.
The group simply refused to give him the time of day.
They had been working together for a while, and most
were much farther along than Keith. After all, it was
only his second day.

Everyone either totally ignored him or acted like he
was a moron. Keith did say some dumb things, but usually these came from his ignorance of what recovery was
all about. And he did try to make himself look better
than the others, but that was because he was new to
recovery and was still in deep denial. Still, the group
refused to accept him, making Keith feel lonely and isolated.

Throughout life you encounter people who are different from you. Sometimes they may bug you because of
the things they say or do, especially when they don't see
things your way. But once you decide you are better
than they are, you lose touch with the fact that you are
powerless, too, and are in no position to judge others.
Humility means you accept others, no matter how different, and take the attitude that they are just as important as you.

■ *God, don't let me lose touch with the fact that I am
powerless and no better than anyone else.*

K.B.

WHAT ARE YOU WAITING FOR?

And now why are you waiting? Arise and be baptized, and wash away your sins, calling on the name of the Lord. —ACTS 22:16

Sometimes it seems as if you are stuck in your tracks in recovery. It's frustrating because you feel that you are doing the work necessary to succeed, but you just can't seem to get beyond a certain point. You feel as if you are tied down.

When these times come, ask yourself if you are waiting for anyone to notice how you're doing. We seem to get to certain points in recovery where we secretly hope someone will give us the "pat on the back" we need, and that will give us permission to keep moving. That someone could be a parent whom you hope will notice that you're doing well, or a girlfriend, or a coach, or some other person of special significance to you.

It is certainly nice to be noticed and have someone commend us for how well we are doing, but you need to examine your motives for recovery. If you are waiting for your dad to notice your progress, and he doesn't know you are waiting, you may wait a long time. In the end, the only thing that suffers is your recovery. The longer you wait, the harder it is to get moving again. If you want someone to comment on your recovery, talk to him about it; tell him how much you would appreciate feedback once in a while.

■ *Don't wait for people to notice the change in you. Find out what they see so you can keep moving.*

R.M.

What is Love?

The second most important commandment says: "Love others as much as you love yourself." —MARK 12:31 CEV

Everyone is searching for love to fill an inner emptiness we all feel. The addict tries to fill it with alcohol and drugs, but it can really only be filled with love. Before we can find love, we need to know what it is.

The first and most important kind of love is *agape,* or God love. This is the love God has for us, the love we should have for Him and others. It is pure and wants the best for others.

Second is *phileos,* or brotherly love. We show this love to others when we care and try to make their lives better. *Phileos* is the love we feel for a friend. It always wants the best for others and is willing to be honest and tough when necessary.

Finally comes the most confusing and potentially dangerous: *eros,* or sexual love. This love is shared intimately between husband and wife and is meant to be shared only with that one person. When we show eros to too many people, it becomes empty and meaningless—a physical experience and not true love. Often people think this is the real meaning of love, but it is just one meaning. Be careful not to confuse the three, or love will lose meaning for you when you want it most.

■ *God, help me to practice love the way You intended it to be.*

K.B.

WATCH WHAT YOU GROW!

[Look] diligently lest anyone fall short of the grace of God; lest any root of bitterness . . . cause trouble.
—HEB. 12:15

Recovery is a lot like tending a garden. Sometimes it is a daily job to keep weeds from growing up and killing the good plants. Weeds never stay in one place. They seem to have an incredible capacity to spread and infect every part of the garden.

The Bible uses the metaphor of a garden to help us understand our own lives and the infecting power of bitterness. Bitterness is an extremely powerful force that has brought many recoveries to screeching halts. The reason is that bitterness lies beneath the surface. You never see it until it comes forth in other ways, such as sarcasm or biting jokes about a person. That is a sure sign that bitterness and resentment exist in your life.

You must be just like the gardener who scans the garden daily for evidence of weeds. You need to be on the watch for resentment and unresolved conflicts you have with others because that is what gives bitterness an opportunity to take root. Don't delay. Talk to the person you are angry with or whom you have some grudge against, and get the thing settled. That way you can be sure your garden of life is clear of weeds that will hurt not only you but others around you as well.

■ *Watch your life for evidence of bitterness and don't let it infect you and others around you.*

R.M.

THE POWER OF MUSIC

*Whenever the spirit from God was upon Saul
. . . David would take a harp and play it . . .
and the distressing spirit would depart from
him.*
                                    —1 SAM. 16:23

One day I borrowed a tape from one of the guys on the unit. He was burned out from too much dope smoking, and I was eager to find out what he was listening to. It was a tape of a popular heavy metal group. To be honest, it made me feel depressed and got me thinking about how music makes people feel, why certain people choose certain kinds of music.

King Saul got depressed at times. He would have David play tunes on his harp to cheer him up. After listening for a while, Saul would feel better. I imagine the kind of music he listened to was pretty upbeat and cheerful, because depressing music would have made him feel worse.

Since you are working on changing things in your life that keep you from staying clean and sober, why not think about the music you listen to. Does it glorify drinking, drugs, and immorality? Does it make you feel depressed and down? If so, that might be an area you should consider changing. It is in your best interest to avoid things that encourage a lifestyle you are trying to change. Your music could be holding back your recovery.

■   *Decide whether the music you listen to encourages
    you to do the things you've been trying to recover
    from.*

                                                    K.B.

RUNNING OUT OF GAS

Then Judah said, "The strength of the laborers is failing, and there is so much rubbish that we are not able to build the wall."
—NEH. 4:10

There is a time to go and a time to rest. If that is your recovery theme, you will master the basics of a good program. Most guys believe they must push in order to get anywhere, and before long they run out of gas. Like the workers at the wall, they are overwhelmed by the immense job before them. Fast-starters in recovery show their true stripes when they meet the first obstacle. They labor under the false assumption that the job won't take long. Therefore, they will just "blow it out," and it will be over. They are shoveling sand with a pitchfork. They haven't taken time to survey the work necessary to recovery.

Always keep an eye on how your recovery is going. Remind yourself that you are, indeed, making progress even if it doesn't look that way. Do you express your feelings more honestly and freely? Do you take feedback from your parents without defensiveness? Are you able to resist going out with friends who tempt you with alcohol or drugs? Do you encourage others to live a drug-free lifestyle? If you said yes to any of these questions, you are progressing. Keep asking questions like these. They will help you to keep from running out of gas and getting overwhelmed.

■ *Father, help me not become overwhelmed with the immensity of recovery.*

R.M.

QUENCHING THE THIRST

"No one who drinks the water I give will
ever be thirsty again. The water I give is like
a flowing fountain that gives eternal life."
—JOHN 4:14 CEV

Being an addict is like being thirsty in the desert. As he stumbles wearily over endless sand with the blistering sun beating down on his skin, he feels tremendous thirst. All he can think about is water. Nothing else matters. Sometimes he sees a vision of a lake ahead, but it is just his mind playing tricks on him.

An addict thirsts for the next high. He hopes that the next time will be fun, and wishes the deep thirst would finally be satisfied. But each time he gets high he realizes that it doesn't bring lasting happiness, and so he moves on to the next high, constantly wishing his thirst for happiness will finally be quenched.

There is something that can quench this deep thirst for happiness. But it's not drugs or alcohol. You have a deep spiritual thirst that no chemical can ever satisfy. As long as you look to substances, the thirst will get worse. Jesus said He was living water that could quench the spiritual thirst you've been trying to fill with other things. Instead of longing for things that don't quench your spiritual thirst, ask God to begin working in you to satisfy it. Once that thirst is gone, substances won't seem so important anymore.

■ *Quench my inner thirst with Your living water.*

K.B.

DETERMINED TO RELAPSE

"My people are bent on backsliding from Me.
Though they call to the Most High,
None at all exalt Him." —HOSEA 11:7

Gary was bent for destruction. He had worked hard in treatment and was on his way to a good program of recovery—at least that's how it seemed. Somewhere along the way, he got tired of being responsible and following his program. It was boring, and he longed for the excitement he once had. He came in to talk to me one day and wouldn't listen to any reason to stay on his program. He was determined to experience the fun times once more. He didn't realize that one "good time" leads to another and another. There is no end to that road once you begin your trek down it.

What will you do when you get tired of recovery? Will you become determined to just try it one more time, and get right back on track again? Think again. It rarely happens that way. I can just hear you say, "Yeah, but I won't do that. I can handle it." Those are famous last words that I have heard too many times. You don't have to experience the good times to know that you shouldn't go that route to spice up your life with excitement. Look elsewhere for excitement. Go out with some friends who are straight and do something fun. You may be surprised, and you may just avoid relapse!

■ *You don't need to relapse to have fun.*

R.M.

Eye Surgery

"You can see the speck in your friend's eye.
But you don't notice the log in your own
eye."
                                    —LUKE 6:41 CEV

Brett was sure he had his family's problem all sorted out. If his dad would give in once in a while, everyone could live happily together. Since Brett was working in recovery, he figured the problem couldn't be his and must be his father's.

In the next family session, he confronted his father and told him that he needed to learn how to compromise. Everyone in the family looked at Brett strangely. They all felt Brett was way off the mark, that *he* was the one who could never give in on anything, not Dad.

This made Brett mad. He kept pushing his view of the family, getting angrier and more defensive the more they refused to see things his way. As I watched him I noticed that he was just as uncompromising as he accused his dad of being.

Brett tried to take a speck of wood out of his father's eye, a small problem that bothered Brett. But what he didn't want to see was that he had the same problem to an even greater degree. Before you can perform eye surgery on anyone else, you need to first make sure there's no log sticking out of your own eye making it hard to see clearly. The reason he couldn't help his father was that he didn't want to see he did it too.

■   *God, help me to clear up big problems in my life*
    before I try to fix the same problems in others.

                                                K.B.

BEING WORSE OFF

If, after they have escaped the pollutions of the world through . . . Jesus Christ, they are again entangled in them and overcome.
—2 PET. 2:20

You need to decide early in recovery if you are going to put into it the effort necessary to make it work. Otherwise, you should quit now.

Peter made it clear to his audience that if they accepted Christ, and then got entangled in the world all over again, they would be worse off than if they never tried. That is true for recovery as well. You are worse off than before you started your recovery if you start, relapse, and give up. The person who attempts recovery and quits is sure to feel miserable and like a real failure. These feelings will push him even farther into his addiction because that is the way he knows how to medicate his pain. So he is in a deeper addictive condition than if he hadn't tried recovery at all.

This warning isn't to scare you. It is to help you understand that you need to keep your commitment level high even if you have difficulties and relapses along the way. Never give up working your program. If you do relapse, it doesn't mean the whole endeavor is doomed. If you get back up and get going again, you will regain whatever you have lost, and you will have learned from your relapse how to avoid it.

■ *Difficulties are to be expected, and they don't mean you should never have tried to recover.*

R.M.

THE DANGER OF NOT CONFESSING

*When I kept silent, my bones grew old
Through my groaning all the day
    long. . . .
My vitality was turned into the
    drought of summer.*

—PS. 32:3-4

Jamie rambled on about his week, what he had done, where he had gone, girls he was interested in—but something was wrong. He seemed depressed. Sometimes therapists must go on their hunches, and so I asked him what was going on inside.

At first he said nothing, just looked at me. Then he started to talk about how he felt like a failure. Then he dropped a bomb! He had relapsed during the week. He felt embarrassed and didn't want to say anything. But it was making him feel terrible, and it showed.

When you avoid problems too long without talking about them, you risk becoming depressed and unhappy. Guilt begins to build up inside, and the longer it is kept secret, the worse things get. That's why it's important to immediately ask for help when things start falling apart.

A good rule is to not even wait twenty-four hours before you tell someone when something is bothering you. When you try to handle things on your own, you may relapse, because you are trusting your own power too much. Recovery is all about being powerless, and that means sharing problems before they become too big that you turn to chemicals to help you deal with life.

■ *If you feel guilty or depressed, tell someone right away. Don't let problems build up.*

K.B.

RETURNING TO THE SCENE

*After you have known God, or rather are
known by God, how is it that you turn again
to the weak and beggarly elements?*
—GAL. 4:9

Do you know why you became addicted to alcohol or drugs? It may have been a way to escape from the painful feelings you had in your relationship with your parents. Maybe it was a way to medicate feelings of inferiority and inadequacy. It may have been just the fact that your friends were doing it, and you didn't want to look like a wimp.

It is important that you understand just what happened to make you an addict. If you don't, it will be mighty hard to see the same situations developing and avoid them in the future. If you fell into a hole and broke your leg, I am sure the next time you walked that way you would certainly watch for that hole! Recovery isn't much different. You fell into the hole of addiction, and you are now attempting to climb out. Once you are out of the hole, you need to know how you got in there or you'll end up in the hole again.

That is what Paul told the Galatians. They knew what it took to be free, but they refused to use this knowledge to prevent their relapse. Don't let that happen to you. You need to communicate how you became addicted and what led up to your addiction. Then you will be able to see it coming the next time, and you will avoid the hole.

■ *Use what you know to prevent relapse and see situations that are dangerous to your recovery.*

R.M.

DUMPING THE GARBAGE

He who covers his sins will not prosper,
But whoever confesses and forsakes
them will have mercy.

—PROV. 28:13

When Rick came out of a session with his therapist, something was different. He was smiling and looked almost like he wanted to dance, and when he saw me he said, "I did it!"

His biggest fear was sharing his personal moral inventory with someone else. He had done some things that he was ashamed of. As part of his recovery, he had to write down what he had done and share them with God and with another person. He felt certain his therapist would stop seeing him when he shared the list.

But he had not been rejected, and he felt free. By sharing his inventory, or dumping his garbage, he was able to start putting the past behind and begin living fresh and new.

If you're like most addicts, you are afraid of looking honestly at the wrongs you have done through your chemical use, and are nervous about sharing them with another person.

Until you reach this stage of recovery, you will be haunted by secrets that make you feel guilty and depressed. It is only after sharing them with God and another person that you can find freedom from the feelings that keep you from moving forward in your recovery.

■ *God, I've done a lot of things that I regret. Give me the courage to talk about them.*

K.B.

WEAKNESSES

For if they fall, one will lift up his companion.
But woe to him who is alone when he falls.
—ECC. 4:10

Are you afraid to show your weaknesses? If you are, you're not alone. People have various reasons for not showing their weaknesses. One of these is that if they show how weak they feel, they are sure others won't like them. Another reason is to make sure people think about you the way you want them to. Most guys want people to think they are tough and strong. To them, showing weakness is emotional suicide. Weakness is not compatible with the image of strength they are trying to forge. But is that image the "real" thing? If the "real" thing doesn't reside in you, what keeps you from showing what is really there?

True strength requires showing weakness. The strong person is willing to confront his weakness and deal with it. He doesn't cover it up by acting rough and tough. He doesn't cover his weakness by getting people to like him all the time. He is willing to be weak in order to become strong. If someone is not willing to be weak, it is unlikely he will ever grow strong in recovery because he must admit just how weak he really is. He hasn't established a place from which he must start—a position of weakness and need of help. If you can do that, you will avoid the trap of denial.

■ *Father, help me not to fear my weaknesses but to face them and find strength in my recovery.*

R.M.

A DIFFICULT CLIMB

The LORD God is my strength;
He will make my feet like deer's feet,
And He will make me walk on my high hills.
—HAB. 3:19

Sometimes recovery can be like climbing a mountain. You get exhausted and feel like you want to quit before you reach the top. The trails are narrow and rocky, the air is thin and hard to breathe, and the end seems a long way off.

You are also carrying a heavy load. There is so much in your past that keeps you from feeling light; it weighs you down and makes the climbing that much harder. You know that someday you will be glad that you stuck with it, but that day seems a long way off.

Don't give up. God is with you every difficult step. Just knowing that there is someone climbing alongside you can sometimes make the journey easier, but God also wants to help carry your heavy load and give you the strength to keep climbing until you reach the top. Today, when you feel you can't go any farther, ask God to give you strength, to make the way clear and smooth, and to help you remember that when you reach the top the view will be well worth the climb.

■ *God, sometimes recovery seems impossible. Help me remember You are with me.*

K.B.

WHY BOTHER?

"O my Lord, how can I save Israel? Indeed my clan is the weakest in Manasseh, and I am the least in my father's house."
—JUDGES 6:15

We hear a thousand excuses from guys who don't expend the effort necessary to overcome addiction. Imagine saying to a doctor, after he has named off all your problems, "I don't have all those problems; you're just exaggerating. I really don't want to get better anyway." Sounds crazy, doesn't it? But that is exactly what happens when you make excuses not to recover.

One of the more common excuses we hear is "Why bother? My dad is an alcoholic, and my mom doesn't think I can change anyway. I don't have a chance at recovery." That is the same tactic Gideon used to weasel out of saving Israel. He used the excuse of his family to claim his inability to do what God asked. He focused on the outward things that determine worth and strength, but God was only looking for someone to accomplish His purpose.

That is what happens in recovery, too. Guys look at external things and themselves. When you do that, you are sure to arrive at the same conclusion—it's hopeless, so why try? You need to keep your eyes on God, who has promised to heal you. His power will accomplish that, not your effort or your family. Your recovery depends on God and His infinite power to change your heart.

■ *Father, help me to depend on You rather than using my family as an excuse to not recover.*

R.M.

STUBBORN OR DETERMINED?

They did not obey or incline their ear, but
walked in the counsels and in the
imagination of their evil heart.

—JER. 7:24

James was one of the most stubborn people I had ever met. Every time I tried to point out something important to his recovery, he would argue. He had grown so used to denial that it was hard to break through to him. He simply wanted to do things his way, but both of us knew his way was the way that got him stuck in addiction. Unless James gave in and looked differently at himself, there was little hope he could change.

Stubbornness is a dangerous character trait. It puts your view over anyone else's, and that means you are not able to see yourself from anyone's perspective but your own. Until you are humble enough to seek others' help, you will be totally blind to things you need to change about yourself.

On the flip side of stubbornness is determination. While stubbornness is sticking to your own view no matter what, determination is sticking with the right view. When you are honest enough to admit that you need help to see things clearly, you will then be able to learn new ways. As you get help to discover healthy ways of seeing things, you can then stick to them. Be *determined* to do what is right.

■ *God, take away my stubbornness and put in its place*
determination to do the right thing.

K.B.

UP FOR THE JOB?

*"There we saw the giants . . . and we were
like grasshoppers in our own sight, and so we
were in their sight."* —NUM. 13:33

The Israelites looked at the people in the land of Canaan and said, "We're too little. We're not up for this job." They had to conquer the land of Canaan, but they looked at their weaknesses and were ready to quit before they began. They not only looked at themselves, they thought that they could speak for the other people in order to strengthen their case to not do what needed to be done. When we don't want do something, we find ways to get out of it. Two different ways are demonstrated by the Israelites: claiming weakness and that others see that weakness.

They didn't want to do the job, but they weren't willing to be courageous enough to say the truth. In recovery, there are things you have to do that you won't want to do. One thing that most guys don't want to do is to confront a friend about his drinking or use of drugs. It is terrifying as well as risking rejection. Don't cop out of your responsibility to your friend, or even to the progress of your own recovery. If you don't want to do something, say so, don't make up excuses not to do it. If you tell the truth you can talk about it and begin to gather the strength you need to face the hard job that faces you.

■ *Father, help me to see the strength You give me throughout my recovery.*

R.M.

DAVID AND GOLIATH

"I come to you in the name of the LORD of hosts, the God of the armies of Israel, whom you have defied."   —1 SAM. 17:45

David was just a kid. The Israelite army thought he was joking when he told them he would defeat the dreaded Philistine giant. But they let David give it a try, and he shocked them when he won.

Like David, you face a giant: your addiction. At times you may believe that recovery is impossible, a task that many people before you have tried and failed. You might think you're too young, don't have the right ammunition, and just can't defeat the giant you are facing.

David walked right up to the giant. Instead of sword, shield, or armor, he had a slingshot and five smooth stones. David might have been afraid, but with God on his side he knew he could do anything. Against the odds, David won.

With God on your side, there is nothing to fear. You have the most powerful weapon anyone could have, God's healing power. Fear will only make you nervous and will keep you from trusting God to do what He says He will do. Face your addiction and win! Even though you may be young and inexperienced at this kind of thing, God will give you what you need to beat the giant that has haunted you for so long.

■   *With You on my side, I can defeat my addiction. With Your help I have nothing to fear.*

K.B.

JUMPING SHIP

I am astonished that you are so quickly deserting the one who called you by the grace of Christ and are turning to a different gospel.
—GAL. 1:6 NIV

What will you do when the girl you fall passionately in love with parties a lot and doesn't think a thing about getting drunk after a social function at school? Will you choose the girl or your recovery?

You will eventually have to choose between living life as other people live it and living a life of recovery. If you don't plan how you will live when you are around people who are living a life of addiction or dysfunction, you will probably relapse. That is the place where most guys go wrong. They live in the land of "It will never happen to me!" You will make better choices if you plan for the tough situations you *could* face.

If you think this perspective is too severe, just ask a few friends who are also in recovery what led to their most recent relapse. You will find that people who relapse have chosen to please people. They are now paying a heavy price for their decision.

Is it worth it to relapse when you could choose, instead, to be around people who appreciate and admire the courage it took to overcome your addiction?

■ *Father, help me to make my choices in terms of recovery and not to live life for short-term gratification.*

R.M.

HE'S ALWAYS THERE

The Lord has promised that he will not leave us or desert us. —HEB. 13:5b CEV

All his life Andy never seemed to fit in—until he started hanging around with the burnouts. They accepted him, so he started to lead their lifestyle. He began smoking, getting high, dressing differently, and listening to different music. He soon realized he needed to stop using drugs, but was afraid he would lose his friends.

Before he met his new friends, he spent a lot of time alone. He would watch people having fun and hanging out, but he didn't know how to be part of the action. He wanted relationships so badly that he was willing to do things he had sworn to himself he would never do. Now he believed he would again be alone and miserable.

Some people might reject you as you start changing your lifestyle. You must decide whether keeping your friends is worth risking your health and your future. You also need to realize there is someone who will never reject or abandon you, God. The last thing God wants is for you to be lonely and unhappy. Furthermore, as God begins to help you change, you will find yourself a much better person inside, one who likes himself more, and who others will like more, too.

■   *Thanks for caring so much about me. Even though I've messed up, You will never leave or reject me.*

K.B.

NEW, IMPROVED TESTS

Your faith . . . though it is tested by fire, may
be found to praise, honor, and glory at the
revelation of Jesus Christ.   —1 PET. 1:7

Most people complain about the obstacles they face in recovery, but it is these same obstacles from which they learn the most. It is usually true that we are much too quick to pass judgment on the tests that God brings along to refine our focus and help us grow strong in recovery. Without the tests, we wouldn't know where we were and what we need to work on. But, you say, "I could do without such hassles!" How good would any basketball or football team be if they only scrimmaged against themselves? They would never find out just how good (or bad) they were without some kind of test—the game itself. You need tests and obstacles to grow.

Don't be quick to complain when you bump up against some difficulty in your recovery. No one enjoys the pain and discomfort of coming face to face with weakness, but keep in mind that after it is over you need to spend some time asking yourself what you can learn from what happened. I'm not asking you to be superhuman. I'm just asking you to remember that after you have expressed how you feel about the difficulty you face, God is orchestrating things so that you will recover fully from your addiction.

■   *Father, help me to remember that You bring tests*
along to help me grow stronger in my recovery.

R.M.

BEING GRATEFUL

Let the peace that comes from Christ control your thoughts. And be grateful.
—COL. 3:15 CEV

When he was using, nothing anyone did for Bruce was ever enough. He felt he deserved more than he got; life had cheated him, so others owed him. He was hard to get along with, especially in his family. He constantly picked on his brothers and sisters, and criticized his parents' faults.

Now that he was changing, he began to realize that this attitude was dangerous. It was the same way he thought when he got high and didn't care about how it affected others. He knew he needed to change, but wasn't certain where to start.

The me-first attitude is common among persons addicted to chemicals. Bruce was right, it is dangerous. And there is a definite way to begin acting differently. In order to live peacefully with others, you must first be grateful. You need to stop looking at others' faults and be thankful for the good things about them. It means changing the way you look at things, from negative to looking at the positive.

When you tell others that you appreciate them, they feel better. When you put them down, they become resentful, and it makes both your life and theirs miserable. The first step to changing a self-centered attitude is being grateful to those around you and telling them so.

■ *God, teach me how to be grateful to others and thank them for caring, rather than put them down.*
K.B.

TAKE A REST

He makes me to lie down in green pastures;
He leads me beside the still waters.

—PS. 23:2

Recovery is tiring work that consumes a great deal of emotional energy to be successful. Because of that, it is important to give yourself an opportunity to rest. I have met guys who get so compulsive about recovery that they are "sick" in their recovery. They have turned from one addiction to another. The new one is recovery. No matter what you undertake in your life it has to be done with balance and good timing. There is a time for work and a time to rest.

Have you developed healthy ways to rest from the work of recovery? Remember this doesn't mean putting your recovery aside. You rest in your recovery. A soldier on furlough leaves his military base and goes home, but he doesn't quit being a soldier. He still has an obligation to conduct himself in a way that is representative of his branch of the armed forces.

Take a rest from recovery, but don't stop trying to recover. Sit down and read a book about something other than recovery. Ask a friend to go out for a Coke, and talk about girls or sports or anything else that strikes your interest. It's healthy to pace yourself. If you don't you will burn out in your desire to overcome addiction.

■ *Father, help me to pace myself in my quest for recovery.*

R.M.

FREEDOM!

The LORD is my strength and my shield;
My heart trusted in Him, and I am
helped;
Therefore my heart greatly rejoices.
—PS. 28:7

A heavy weight had been lifted from Rick's back. For two years he had carried a ton of regrets and guilt over his addiction. At times he felt so depressed that he didn't want to live. Every time he tried to make himself feel better, it only got worse, and he lost all hope. Then he discovered freedom.

He decided to give God all the guilt and misery he was carrying. He realized the burden had become too heavy for him, and he needed something more. So he asked God to take over the load.

When I saw him next, it was clear something was greatly different. His eyes had a twinkle that wasn't there before. His face seemed more relaxed. He felt an excitement that was easy to observe. It was as if he had found the happiness that for so long he couldn't find in chemical substances.

Not all people have dramatic changes like Rick's. In fact, some struggle a while, trying to give their burden to God. Often people in recovery give their burdens to God, only to take them back and try on their own power. But one thing is true—there is a higher power who wants to help you deal with the negative feelings you are carrying. All you have to do is trust.

■   *God, help me to find the freedom that comes from*
    trusting Your strength and protection.

K.B.

THE FAMILY EXCUSE

*He said to another, "Follow Me." But he
said, "Lord, let me first go and bury my
father."*
                              —LUKE 9:59

You have probably realized by now that you are not
the only one who has had to adjust to your new attitude
and lifestyle. Even though your family doesn't mean to,
they can often get in the way of your recovery. It is
important that you remember that they have some
pretty big adjustments to make as well.

If you think back to how it was before you decided to
seek recovery, you will recall conflict and tension. People get used to such tension and conflict, and when it is
gone they don't know how to behave toward one another. Don't expect your family to openly and uncritically accept the changes you have made. They have
probably been burned before by the false hope of your
recovery.

Don't make the success or failure of your recovery
depend on their assessment of you. If you do, you will
make them responsible for your recovery and once
again enter into an unhealthy dependency. Be sure to
get more than just their feedback about your progress.
Everyone will see it differently, but you should hear a
consensus of opinion that you are improving. Let your
family see your change in their own time, and then they
may be your best cheerleading section.

■   *Give your family time to adjust to the changes you
    have made through your recovery.*

                                                    R.M.

A NEW LIFE

Jesus replied, "I tell you for certain that you must be born from above before you can see God's kingdom!" —JOHN 3:3 CEV

It's like my life has started over!" exclaimed Chuck. And he was right. Since he began recovery, he was a different person. A lot of built-up resentment and anger that used to keep him from being happy had started to fade. In their place was now contentment and a new sense of excitement for the things he was finding out about himself.

When you begin recovery and turn your life over to God, it is like being born all over again. You have a chance to start making things better, and you are wiser, learning from the mistakes of your past and avoiding problems that kept you bogged down in negative feelings and behaviors. God has given you a new life.

It comes with some responsibility too. Now that you have another chance to make things different, you must decide to handle your new life with care. If you are reckless and don't pay attention, this chance might end up being like the old life. Take care of the new person you have become. Treat your new self with respect and love, avoiding the old ways that messed up the first life you were given.

■ *Thanks, God, for my new life. Teach me to handle the new me with care and respect.*

K.B.

USE YOUR OWN TOOLS

*David fastened his sword to his armor, and
he tried to walk. . . . And David said to
Saul, "I cannot walk with these, for I have
not tested them." So David took them off.*
— 1 SAM. 17:39

When the going gets difficult, we are tempted to try
someone else's ways of doing things. Sometimes people
even insist that we try their way because they are convinced their way is the right way. That's what Saul did to
David in this passage. Saul was a warrior and had his
own ideas about going to battle and being successful.
David, on the other hand, was a boy who had spent
most of his days as a shepherd. He knew nothing of war
or armor. So when Saul insisted that David wear his
armor, David realized this set of tools wasn't what he
needed. He had the guts to say to the king, "Thanks,
but no thanks."

That happens in recovery, too. People around you
will have been in recovery longer than you, and you
might assume they know the best way to work a program. So you'll watch them and might consider imitating them. Don't be surprised if their tools don't fit you.
Recovery is a process of developing skills to cope with
the challenges of overcoming addiction. Through what
you have learned in your counseling or in a treatment
center, your tools will come to fit you and no one else.
Develop your own tools to fit your needs rather than
using what someone else has done.

■ *Father, give me the courage to develop my own tools
for recovery.*

R.M.

A CHRISTMAS TRAGEDY

A prudent man foresees evil and hides himself,
But the simple pass on and are punished.
—PROV. 22:3

On a television "rescue" show, I saw the story of a man who climbed up a tall Christmas tree in the middle of New York. He had been drinking and was not thinking clearly. Someone videotaped his climb and caught the whole scene as he fell thirty feet to the ground. Because the area around the tree was so crowded with people, riot police had to make a way for the rescue squad to get to him.

The doctor at the hospital said the guy should have broken his back and been paralyzed from the neck down. Fortunately for him he lived through it and was not paralyzed, but he had to stay in the hospital for several weeks and needed major surgery. His message to others was: don't drink; it makes you do stupid things.

Many people do not learn from experiences like his. If they escape harm, they continue abusing chemicals. In fact, I wondered if this guy would really change. One of the important things you need to understand in recovery is now to start learning from your mistakes, and from the mistakes of others. You probably did some stupid things when you were drunk or high, and now is the time to start looking back and learning from those mistakes. If you don't, you might not be as lucky as the guy who fell from the Christmas tree.

■ *Help me, Lord, to start thinking realistically about the danger I caused by abusing substances.*

K.B.

IS THERE ENOUGH?

"If you can find a man . . .
Who seeks the truth,
. . . I will pardon [Jerusalem]."
—JER. 5:1

If you were in court, accused of being a Christian, would there be evidence enough to convict you? That's a thought-provoking question. That same question was on Jeremiah's mind: "Is anyone in Jerusalem seeking truth and dealing honestly with anyone?" This same question can be applied to your recovery. If someone were to ask one of your friends, "I hear Joe is in recovery from his addiction. Do you see anything?" and your friend said, "Yeah, I see plenty. Let me give you an example," that would be the sure test of progress—evidence to back it up.

It is important throughout your recovery to remember that it doesn't count for much if you're not practicing it in a way that people can see. If you don't experience some discomfort from your struggle to overcome addiction, you probably aren't moving very fast and accomplishing much. Discomfort with friends or the pain of growth is a good sign that you are indeed making progress in recovery. Remember that pain in recovery isn't all that bad. It is a sure sign that you are pushing the limits of your old behaviors. If that kind of pain isn't there, you need to take a hard look at how well you are doing at living out your recovery among your friends and family.

■ *Be living proof for everyone that you are working your program of recovery.*

R.M.

KEEP ASKING

*"Ask, and you will receive. . . . Everyone
who asks will receive. . . . And the door will
be opened for everyone who knocks."*
—MATT. 7:7–8 CEV

How can I be sure God will hear and answer me if I talk to Him about things in my life?" Many people ask that question. You've probably wondered the same thing at times. You want to be certain that if you trust your recovery to God, He will hear and answer your prayers.

Jesus said that if you ask for things you will get them. Maybe not all at once, and maybe not exactly in the way you planned, but God will take care of you. Sometimes we need to keep asking, searching, and knocking; once or twice may not be enough. As God mends your heart and makes you a better person, He does it slowly to be sure the changes will last.

Be assertive with God. Because He wants the best for you, when you ask Him for good things, He will deliver. Don't get discouraged because things don't happen as quickly as you might like. After all, when you trust God, you also need to trust His timing and not demand things when *you* want them. If you ask, search, and knock long enough, and if God thinks it will be helpful to your recovery, He *will* answer.

■ *Lord, help me to keep searching for answers to my problems. Open doors that lead to health and growth.*

K.B.

"Penny wise . . ."

"Now you Pharisees make the outside of the cup and dish clean, but your inward part is full of greed and wickedness."
—LUKE 11:39

Penny wise and pound foolish" is a phrase used to describe a person who is wise about small, insignificant things, and foolish about big things. For example, a man spends all afternoon looking for the best bargain on a can opener. Later he decides to buy a new car. Instead of looking for the best bargain, as he did for his can opener, he goes to a car dealer, picks out a car, and pays the sticker price. Do you see the problem? His focus is all wrong. He pays attention to the things that really don't matter in life and overlooks the things that really do matter.

Don't let this be the case for your recovery. It is important to focus on the interior of your recovery process. As a therapist, it doesn't matter to me how someone looks during recovery as much as the changes I see inside him. Anyone can look good in recovery and have no growth at all. It's all show and no action.

On the other hand, someone may not "look" very good during recovery, but on the inside change is happening. That is what counts. That is what will produce a person who will overcome his addiction. Don't worry; the looks will catch up when the changes are made from the inside out.

■ *You will need to focus on change from the inside out, and not worry about how "good" it looks.*

R.M.

BRAVELY APPROACHING GOD

*Whenever we are in need, we should come
bravely before the throne of our merciful
God. There we will . . . find help.*
—HEB. 4:16 CEV

In ancient times, one could only come near the king's throne with permission. If the king did not hold out his scepter, the guards would take the seeker out and possibly put him to death. Needless to say, many were quite afraid to go anywhere near the throne. Besides that, often the king did not understand, or even care about, the needs of his subjects. Because he was royal, he never lived like a regular person. Sometimes they were a bother to him.

The King in charge of your recovery, God, is not like that at all. Because Jesus lived on earth and experienced the same feelings and temptations you face, God completely understands your needs. Whenever someone goes through an extremely difficult time, he understands and is able to care more than someone who never went through it.

Sometimes, though, we get a little nervous about asking God for help. We ask, "Can God understand this?" "Isn't God sick of my always asking for help?" or "Will God get really mad and zap me?" This leads to fear or nervousness about approaching God with our needs. Instead we need to bravely tell Him what we need. God will be kind and will show mercy, and you will find help.

■ *Bravely share with God your list of needs. Expect
Him to help because He does* understand.

K.B.

Facing Adversity with Hope

Happy is the man whom God corrects;
Therefore do not despise the chastening
of the Almighty. —JOB 5:17

We groan when we face frustration and adversity. We have an irrational belief that life should be good and fair and easy—especially to us! This attitude is short-sighted and robs life of much meaning. We couldn't even survive very well without adversity or tension; they are often what motivate us to change. What prompted you to overcome your addiction? Getting into trouble with the law? Your parents' getting fed up with your deceit and abuse of yourself? Whatever the reason, frustration and adversity are often the prods God uses to get us to change. Anything short of this adversity isn't enough to get your attention.

We also need adversity and pain in order to grow. Why do body-builders put themselves through such agony? Every muscle in their bodies screams for mercy. But in response to the adversity they face, their muscles grow strong in response to the demand. That is how we are when it comes to growing emotionally and spiritually. We must have adversity to demand that we change in order to prompt us to meet that demand. The next time you face adversity (maybe even today?), think of how you might be able to use it to your advantage instead of moaning about it.

■ *Look at adversity as a crucial part of your recovery.*
Don't try to avoid it, but use it.

R.M.

ASK FOR WISDOM

"Give to Your servant an understanding
heart to judge Your people, that I may
discern between good and evil."
—1 KINGS 3:9a

At one point in his life, Solomon was given a choice. God told him to ask for anything and it would be given to him. Faced with this decision, what would you ask God to give you? Would it be money, popularity, better clothes, a nice car? How would you choose?

Solomon chose wisely. He simply asked God to give him wisdom. Now at first that might seem like a dumb choice. With all the things he could have asked, he asked only to be wise. God, however, did not think he was stupid; in fact God told Solomon that it was a great choice and made Solomon the wisest man of his time. In fact, he was so sharp that all the other things he could have asked for came to him anyway, because people were so impressed with his wisdom.

It would be incredibly selfish to ask God for wisdom so that you could have money, clothes, or fame. On the other hand, wisdom is extremely important as you work toward recovery. You need wisdom to make decisions about life and to keep yourself clean and on the right path. I suggest that you be like Solomon and ask God for wisdom. Because you need it right now, God will give it to you.

■ *God, give me the wisdom to make the right decisions*
   about how to do the work of recovery.

K.B.

About the Authors

Kevin Brown is a psychotherapist and program director of the adolescent inpatient hospital program at the Minirth-Meier Clinic in Wheaton, Illinois. He specializes in the treatment of abusive families and those recovering from traumatic relationships. He received his M.S.W. from the University of Illinois at Chicago and his B.A. from Wheaton College. Brown and his wife, Sandy, and son, Seth, live in the Chicago area.

Raymond Mitsch, Ph.D., is a clinical psychologist and the director of the child and adolescent division of the Minirth-Meier Clinic in Wheaton. Dr. Mitsch received his M.A. and Ph.D. in counseling psychology from Indiana State University, and his B.A. from Wabash College in Crawfordsville, Indiana. He served as staff psychologist for Michigan Technological University Counseling Services for two years before moving to the Minirth-Meier Clinic in Wheaton. Dr. Mitsch, his wife, Linda, and their three children, Corrie, Anne, and Abigail, live in Wheaton.

For general information about the Minirth-Meier Clinic branch offices, counseling services, educational resources, and hospital programs, call toll-free 1–800–545-1819.

Library of Congress Cataloging-in-Publication Data

Brown, Kevin (Kevin J.)
     You take over, God, I can't handle it : daily devotions for
guys / Kevin J. Brown and Ray Mitsch.
          p.   cm.
     "A Janet Thoma book."
     ISBN 0-8407-3425-5 : $7.99
     1. Young men—Prayer-books and devotions—English.
2. Alcoholics—Prayer-books and devotions—English.
3. Narcotic addicts—Prayer-books and devotions—English.
4. Devotional calendars. I. Mitsch, Ray. II. Title.
BV4855.B76   1992
248.8′6′08351—dc20   92–20916
                                                            CIP